Educating Women for a Changing World

Educating Women

FOR A CHANGING WORLD

by Kate Hevner Mueller

44663

UNIVERSITY OF MINNESOTA PRESS
Minneapolis

Library of Congress Catalog Card Number: 54-10290

PUBLISHED IN GREAT BRITAIN, INDIA, AND PAKISTAN BY
GEOFFREY CUMBERLEGE: OXFORD UNIVERSITY PRESS, LONDON, BOMBAY, AND KARACHI

Preface

THIS book records a ten-year struggle with some of the unwieldy and treacherous problems in women's education. It reflects the dreams of the mothers and fathers for their daughters, and the bewilderment which creeps over them when their dreams encounter the grim or alluring complexities of modern society. It reflects also the frustrations and compromises of the daughters themselves, and of their teachers and counselors, as all of them work together to enlarge the opportunities and increase the happiness of modern women. It takes a brief backward look over the history of women to find the sources of their present strengths and weaknesses as well as the parallel excellences and deficiencies of men. It looks at the colleges and their curriculums for women, and offers some methods for evaluating them.

In fact this book is addressed to the many thoughtful laymen of both generations, the younger and the older, who have studied the catalogues, listened to the specialists, and hammered out their own arguments and directives for the needed education. It is addressed also to those very specialists, the conscientious teachers and counselors, who have done most of the worrying along with the parents about courses of study and careers for their daughters.

In order to achieve a better perspective for dealing with their education, it endeavors to arrange in orderly fashion the data and arguments about women and their problems. Often, however, what the layman perceives as a clarification of the issues, the specialist denounces as a dangerous oversimplification. Pages which seem burdensomely quantitative to the one may seem tantalizingly inadequate to the other. Yet the thinking of those who are shaping the trends in the education of women must find common ground with the thinking of the individuals who will search among all the various patterns for that one most feasible plan to meet their own special needs. The profit for each lies always in the quality of the thinking engendered by the reading, before it finally emerges in decisive action.

For any reader, amateur or professional, man or woman, this book can be only a preparation, an assessment of the resources, an appraisal of the obstacles, a sighting of the goals. Moreover this preparation will be directed toward a solution which it is destined never to reach, for in the problems and education of women there are *no* solutions — plenty of decisions, directives, and achievements; many satisfactions, disappointments, and appeasements; but no arriving at the actual goals. In education, solution is a concept with an exaggerated past, a nebulous and irritating present, and no conceivable future.

I am much indebted to the intelligence and good humor of several generations of graduate students, both men and women, in my seminar on women's education, who have helped trace the flow of facts and ideas along the older and the newer trails. I also acknowledge with as much pride as gratitude the help of three colleagues who read the entire manuscript in its early stages and gave it the benefit of their wisdom and sophistication: Professor Esther Crane of Goucher College, Dean Margaret Criswell Disert of Wilson College, and Dean M. Emily Taylor of Miami University. Faculty and staff members from many a campus served as inexorable critics in all the immediately practical problems of women students and women's curriculums, especially the eleven women who served with me on Indiana University's Committee on Women's Education, and Dean Helen B. Schleman and her staff at Purdue University. Increasing dividends of educational philosophy and insight have also come to me through twenty years of association with Dr. Wendell W. Wright, first when he was Dean of the Junior Division during the period when I was serving as Dean of Women, and later in his capacity as Dean of the School of Education and Vice President of Indiana University. From the University of Minnesota Press, the editors' skill in giving form to the manuscript has been more than any author has a right to expect.

The continuing judicious objectivity of the social scientist which is apparent in many of these paragraphs is the contribution of my husband, John H. Mueller, Professor of Sociology at Indiana University, a collaborator of long standing who fenced with equal adroitness and conviction in the defense of the gentlemen or the support of the ladies, attacked with unflagging vigor any weakness in logic, facts, or semantics, and bought every compromise at the highest possible price.

K. H. M.

Bloomington, Indiana
July 15, 1954

Contents

ix

Educating Women for a Changing World

The Need for Perspective

Men, in the four thousand odd years that they have assumed the major responsibility for the world, have preferred to solve women's problems by cliché and proverb. Women, the other, the weaker, the fair, the lost, the second sex, fit better into sonnets than into politics, look better in halos and furbelows than in togas or mortarboards or epaulets. Crowned as "earth's noblest thing," "her beauty is like music," "she moves a goddess and she looks a queen." No room for human problems among the classic attributes of such celestial bodies.

Women do have one thing in common with the starry heavens above: only a few decades ago the two were equally mysterious; today both have lost much of their mystery, but they have proved to be vastly more complicated than the early philosophers and cosmographers could have imagined. As more powerful telescopes have revealed new galaxies beyond the old, so has exploration of every phase of women's life yielded more and more complexities.

It is these bewildering complexities which make her problems so baffling. Pull her out of her romantic bog and she will flounder in a financial quicksand; find her employment and she suffers multiple frustrations. If her husband adores her, their children may revile her. She can be ecstatic at twenty, disillusioned at thirty, militant at forty, and mellow at fifty.

If freeing her from one dilemma must always create a dozen new ones, shall her education prod her into more of these upsetting compromises or ease her graciously toward a valorous acceptance of the status quo? The answer will undoubtedly determine not only her own destiny but that of the society on which she may have so benign or so disastrous an influence. Women are not only here to stay but there are more of them than men, 53 to 47 in every hundred persons fourteen years or older. This is of course largely because women live longer than men, being destined from birth to outlast their husbands by five years, seven months, and seventeen days.

Quips and cartoons would have us persuaded that women live longer because they are more stupid than men and have so much more fun and trouble. They are more modest and shy, but also more intrepid, more quixotic, fickle, and persistent, more cunning and clever. They are more sentimental and naïve, but also more bad-tempered and of course more charming; more hard-working but more outrageously lazy and obviously more loquacious. What every woman knows she tells abroad, which does little to explain why as a "lost sex" she is so frustrated.

Woman has been denounced for her hovering "momism," her explosive or "gunpowder" qualities, her fantastic hold on the nation's purse strings, her threat to our economy as a wage earner, the earnest nonsense of her club programs. Her idle and empty life, it is said, sends juvenile delinquency and divorce rates soaring and keeps the psychoanalysts' couches perennially filled. But women are also called the backbone of the church, the hope of the world, of the arts, and of politics. It has been said that they can elect presidents and perhaps they have.

The suggestion has frequently been made that all these complex faults and insignificant virtues stem from the inadequate education of women, and on this subject thousands of pages, professional and popular, have been written to arouse and inform them. Perhaps women should be flattered and not a little grateful that their welfare has been so widely debated. Many of the pronouncements have come from distressed hus-

bands and disgruntled alumnae, and as many more from thoughtful professional educators—the greater volume perhaps from
men, but the more searching and pertinent comments from
women. From this barrage of speculation and recommendation
by a host of critics and countercritics, the more sober and systematic discussions of women's education emerge as both pedantic
and unrewarding.

The really important problems in planning education for
women have been obscured by the centering of attention around
the one logically and psychologically absurd question: Should
the education of women be different from that of men?

This question has achieved its phenomenal popularity for two
reasons: It has reduced the whole complex field to an irresistibly
simple alternative, and it forces the matter into a kind of challenge which everyone feels impelled to accept. There is no middle
ground. The answer is either a loud yes or a sharp no, and
arguments can be picked up on the run. Logic is as infallible
and rhetoric as convincing on one side as on the other. The
game is open to everybody, and there seem to be no rules.

How did this lively problem ever come to be stated in such
static and oversimplified terms? Why can it not be solved on
this clearly formulated basis? History and tradition furnish the
answer to the first question, and twentieth-century science, plus
the complexity of modern life, brushes aside the second.

In our first colleges, before 1860, higher education was of
course restricted to men. When women first sought to break that
monopoly, it was scarcely conceivable that young girls should
leave the shelter of the home to live in close proximity to young
men and to associate with them in the loosely supervised situation of the classroom. Providing advanced education for women
therefore meant establishing separate colleges for women, and
once that pattern was set, there were many reasons why it should
tend to continue.

As the movement for women's education expanded, it encountered resistance in many quarters and was forced to justify
itself by demonstrating that women were intellectually equal to

5

men. Women's colleges found it necessary to offer the same curriculums as men's colleges in order to prove that women could acquire the same mental skills and meet all the standards for a duly accredited college. The new movement was predicated on the assumption that women were equally deserving of all the opportunities then open exclusively to men, and therefore the women's colleges undertook to meet all the requirements of the previously denied professional careers which they sought to gain for women. Thoroughly aroused to the civil and economic discrimination against women, the leaders of the movement could be satisfied with nothing less. Likewise when the state universities began to open their doors to women, no concessions were made or wanted. The only way to be exactly equal was to be exactly the same.

For the first few decades, the relatively small numbers of women who attended college accepted the challenge to prove themselves and seemed satisfied with the courses offered. Naturally, subtle changes in emphasis crept into the subject matter, and electives catered to some of the special interests of women. Finishing schools still continued to flourish, and at a later period junior colleges met the needs of the more tender-minded young women. But on the whole, the pattern of higher education was the same for women as for men.

Then, with the first quarter of the new century, the college population of both men and women began to expand phenomenally, and as the curriculums were adapted to the changing interests of this larger and more heterogeneous student group, they came to include more and more vocational and semiprofessional training. Here of course the predominance of men determined the direction of curricular modification. All men planned to be gainful workers, and they therefore demanded above everything else that higher education prepare them for better jobs and higher salaries.

It was at this point that women began to feel the pinch of inadequacy. They too had need for vocational training, but not nearly so unanimous a need as men, since the earning career of women is frequently interrupted or delayed and sometimes terminated by marriage.

And yet many women, as well as many men, at the time they are in college, feel little urgency to cultivate nonvocational areas to prepare themselves for good citizenship, the wise use of leisure time, or the development of spiritual values. Especially in the large modern university, with its more heterogeneous groups and its wider range of choice in curriculum, too many students are convinced that they can acquire their liberal arts education outside the classroom. Usually their parents too feel that money must not be squandered on courses which do not directly further the achievement of profitable professional goals.

In current higher education, therefore, the ills and deficiencies have accumulated and been aggravated—especially so, it seems, for women. Parents and educators disagree on objectives; students claim the right to choose their own goals, which includes the right to choose unwisely and to repent later; liberal arts curriculums refuse to be compromised; tradition outweighs current needs; improvements are twisted out of shape by economics; and good intentions get lost in red tape.

How imprudent to sweep these unmanageable intricacies into two mutually exclusive categories! To set up different curriculums for men and women is no more feasible than to plan separate programs for the rich and the poor, the good and the bad, the introvert and the extrovert, the bright and the dull. The individual differences among the members of any one such group, in abilities, talents, opportunities, will immediately nullify the very concept of one educational program for that group. Such unthinking short cuts serve only as dangerous diversions from more effective methods.

When the professional leaders, men and women, convene year after year to study the needs of women in education, invariably they tend toward one conclusion: The needs of women and men students are the same; both have the same intellectual hunger, the same citizenship and family responsibilities, and the same need for inspired and scholarly teaching, for faculty leadership,

7

and for wise counseling. Whatever men need, women need, and vice versa.

But is it wise to maximize these likenesses at the expense of minimizing the differences? If all their needs are the same, are we to say that men's education should be the same as women's? This would mean some fairly radical changes, especially in the colleges exclusively for men. For example, Yale, Amherst, Bowdoin, and the others would have to employ their proper quota of women professors—up to 30 per cent of the teaching staff. And 80 per cent of the presidents of these colleges would have to be women, and women would occupy 70 per cent of the seats on the governing boards. Women, in other words, would immediately assume their full share of administering the education of men, even as men have been directing the education of women.

Intercollegiate sports would be practically eliminated, except for a few cooperative play days in the spring and fall, given over to friendly demonstrations of swimming and other individual sports. The men students would organize themselves into strong governing groups for building morale and supporting campus regulations, would sign *Out* slips for week ends, would return to their residences no later than 11:00 p.m., and so on.

The men's colleges would set up strong departments of homemaking, with courses in nutrition, child care, clothing, interior decorating, gardening. They would organize biweekly forums on the joys of household management and child care, bringing in speakers of national renown to persuade the young men of the greater importance of happy family life over business success. They would form student and faculty committees to study the ways and means of combining homemaking and careers, and offer symposiums on how to choose and win a wife, promote her professional career, and keep her happy. There would also be clinics on dress, grooming, manners, general ethical and social responsibilities, and such problems as the equitable sharing of household chores and expenses.

The "same as" position, phrased in these terms, may seem less than practical to most readers, and they will turn to the opposite

8

point of view for a better solution to the educational dilemma. It becomes obvious that there must be curriculum changes which will make allowance for the many differences in the life patterns and social roles of men and women.

Those, however, who argue that education for women should be different have as yet only one plank in their platform. For them, the one significant difference between men and women lies in the homemaking function of women, and therefore they would place the emphasis in women's education on training for this one role. They would include, obviously, all the usual courses in nutrition, clothing, household management, child guidance, and family relationships. These would be enriched and properly intellectualized, partly by the study of the scientific foundations of their subject matter and partly by tracing its origins and history. But more especially these courses are to be enhanced by the study of the social significance of their content.

The problems of our times are all to be solved, it would seem, by proper attention in our colleges to the science of homemaking, which is to be taught to women exclusively. Homemaking would thus acquire in our society a high prestige, a truly appropriate value. The college woman would be, must be, made to see home-making as a difficult, remunerative, glamorous, satisfying, enviable career, far more significant than such sordid work as accounting, nursing, research, teaching, or such drudgery as social work, public service, or fashion designing.

But today's housewife lives in a world where press, pulpit, radio, stage, fiction, and her own intimate experience tell her: "Talents must never be wasted and it is the constant use of the intellectual powers which sharpens them." "Each must live up to the best that is within him; each has the right to the best job he is capable of." "In our democratic and mobile society, status is measured by the kind of job one holds." "It's the professions that get the best incomes and the greatest prestige." "It takes travel, smart clothes, theater, business experience to achieve real sophistication."

Once upon a time such values belonged exclusively to men;

women had their own world and their own feminine values. But in today's world, men and women intermingle their lives and their values. Even the most rigorous indoctrination of the college woman cannot avail against the rising tide of social change.

The times and the colleges are out of joint for both men and women, but more obviously for women than for men. It is a herculean task to bring all phases of the situation into proper perspective, plan for progress in all of them simultaneously, and sell the plans to those concerned with the problem. On the other hand, it is easy and tempting to focus on one conspicuous discrepancy, analyze it minutely, draw up a plan to correct it, and then convince oneself or some docile audience of the merit of this specific solution.

Confidence born of a successful academic career and insights sharpened by a couple of daughters may impel any pedagogue, be he administrator or professor, to use the lore and logic of his own particular scholarly discipline for "a solution" to "the problem"—and then to present it with such force and charm that its limitations go unnoticed by all but a few of his hearers and his readers. Unhappily, perhaps, no one method of education can be generalized into a single program that will fit all comers. There are too many different kinds of girls, too many individual needs, and a corresponding proliferation of problems. There must be an equal variety of solutions.

True, many a college administrator has been pushed by his own job into dealing with one kind of women's education and into building a very satisfactory design for a selected group of students. These shining experiments in method and curriculum not only fill many needs of the present generation but are the frontiers of new life and thought for women. The women's colleges serve especially well as laboratories where fresh ideas are tested and still more novel theories are generated. Some of these ventures have been better publicized than others but every one of them has been suggestive and useful.

At Vassar, Scripps, Wilson, Keuka, Sarah Lawrence, Stephens, Mills, Simmons, and others, problems not only of curriculum but of admission, recruitment, counseling, financial organization, interaction with social institutions, employment and placement, even of national defense, housing, and sex, have been explored and methods of dealing with them improved. Likewise some of the larger public institutions, though inevitably committed to their male majorities, have nevertheless probed and prodded their unwieldy curriculums into surprisingly better adjustments for women.

In spite of their excellent pioneering, women's colleges have been the special target for those critics who fail to keep in view the many varieties of educational objectives and the weight and worth of different educational traditions. Under continuous and often misdirected fire, these colleges have conscientiously searched their souls, remolded their programs, and kept both their tempers and their students. Their alumnae seem unable to qualify for any special deficiency, either lower marriage rates, poor homemaking, or lack of civic responsibility. They are apparently pursuing their legitimate functions with satisfying success.

It is especially in the younger colleges, those that can operate in the new century without a burden of accumulated traditions, that some of the boldest steps have been taken in refashioning higher education; they have added significantly to the variety of educational structures which are now available. Since there is not space to describe them all, even briefly, it would be unfair to single out any one campus as an example of special excellence.

But even those admirable schools which tailor a curriculum to the needs of the individual student cannot be successful with any and every freshman who knocks at the door. She must bring some measure of ability and discipline, some store of knowledge, some special curiosity or independence. And for more material reasons the tailor-made curriculum is not within the grasp of more than a few. It might serve the purposes of many others, but so too might a year in Europe, a new water color by Marin, or a mink coat meet the needs of any woman, young or old, for a healthier mental outlook and the development of latent powers.

The specialized curriculum may be the most completely admirable education of the century, may lead to the best job, may prove in the long run to be the best possible investment. But it still may be too expensive for the average pocketbook. At least, too expensive today. In education as in economic production, the vital problem is one of mass distribution, and American ingenuity may someday be able to bring within everyone's reach what is now a luxury college program.

Other kinds of educational experiences have evolved usually from the combination of a good idea, a forceful personality to mobilize others for its support, and at least a few hundred of the youthful thousands whose needs it explicitly serves. In these mid-century decades the varieties and excellences of college offerings for women probably outstrip the public's capacity to understand and choose among them. Mothers and daughters are called upon to make too many difficult decisions in too little time and with too little information. Colleges engage in propaganda and artistic photography rather than clear explanations of the simple facts.

As a result, our daughters continue to drift with the traditional, geographical, and financial currents into colleges where their presence puts the greatest strain on the academic moorings. Better public relations programs and better counseling may temporarily assist the new generations of students, but they do not reach the basic problem. The challenge the students offer, once they are in the college, is still largely met by the enterprise and intelligence of the classroom teacher rather than by flexible and efficient curriculums. The most hopeful prospect is that the moorings will eventually loosen and the pressures from inside and outside will carry the colleges in the direction of the needed developments.

Too often it has been assumed that the education of women is only a special and simpler case in the whole field of education. But women do not constitute a corollary to the main proposition. Their problems, never quite so simple as those of men because of the diversity of women's functions and the more widely varied patterns of their lives, are not side issues; they are related to every other educational problem and should be a part of every theory, every program, every experiment in the field.

Modern education, like modern business and government, is a leviathan of interlocking ideas and people and functions. No one citizen, suffering vividly from one of its minor maladjustments, can hope to have a clear view of all its major symptoms. Every decade adds to the information and skills which must be imparted to the child and makes it more difficult for him to connect his daily lesson with his future needs. In our mobile society who can predict whether he will become a carpenter or a clergyman, a plumber or a senator, a housewife or an accountant? What will be his major problem as an adult: the mere cost of living, or strikes and race riots? the protective tariff or potato blight? melancholia or arthritis?

The disparities in the programs offered for the proper education of women arise from the diverse viewpoints of those who advocate them and the different habits of mind of those who receive them. Those who argue for a curriculum for women identical with that for men, or for this or that proportion of liberal or vocational subjects, for a rigidly classical education or for a loosely functional and progressive education, are alike in viewing too large a field from too limited a corner. What they want may be exactly right for their own daughters, or for the small group of women who are included in their view, but who could be sure that it would be good for the majority of women? Or whether most modern young women would like it? Would find it useful? Could afford it? Have the ability to absorb it? Could build a better world with it?

Knowledge of all the educational goals and values, of the many kinds of curriculums, of the myriad varieties of young women—in a word, *perspective*—is the essential ingredient for progress in the education of women. The lack of it constitutes the most formidable deterrent.

The first task of any mother or teacher is to repudiate the urge to define, even to understand, and certainly to reconstruct women's world. She must expect rather to feel restless, uncertain,

13

sometimes bewildered. Her task is to learn how to think about women more objectively and constructively. Then although she may never be able to choose sides in the general hullabaloo on "same as" or "different from" men's education, she will be able to apply her thinking more profitably to her own daughter's educational future.

Her own daughter's education is for her the one focal point for all other related problems in women's education. What shall this one female child learn? That is the question of greatest importance for each mother and each daughter. It is also the only significant question for all counselors and educators of women. It grows out of the infinite variety of modern young women, and it can be answered only in terms of the engaging variety of schools where they may study. The thoughtful woman's first duty is to survey all these colleges and the programs they offer and to learn how to appraise these in relation to the individual personality of her own daughter.

This assessment will not be easy, because our own experience with education has given each of us a very limited viewpoint from which inevitably we survey the whole field. Each of us stands on the warm and vital facts of her own textbooks and teachers and her own peculiar satisfactions and frustrations, rather than on such cold and impersonal facts as the numbers and salaries of women in the labor force and the social and economic realities which these data imply. Each one of us tends to project his or her own feeling of educational success or failure into the immediate and the distant future for all others. To obtain the latitude and longitude of our individual viewpoint is as important as our knowledge of the larger map of the whole area.

The atmosphere over most of the area is highly charged with conflicting ideas, opinions, and attitudes. But like our own hesitant utterances, the thunder of more dominant voices comes always from one specific and describable vantage point. The proposals and the criticisms launched by the economist, the southerner, the artist, the social worker, the linguist, the thirty-year-old, the businesswoman, will reflect the social faith which each has developed. Some of the leaders speak from a broad background of relevant facts and substantial experience, and some from a very narrow platform of their own construction. But no matter whose the voice, whether grandmother's or Hollywood's or the grocer's or the minister's or the college president's, before we can evaluate its pronouncements or incorporate them into our own thinking, we must discern as well as we can at least the general social source from which it comes.

To identify a point of view is not necessarily to distrust it. Any opinion, including our own, gains stature as we realize what experience has nourished it. Our intellectual maturity requires that we understand why some particular doctrine of education urged upon us by the president of a women's college dedicated to the nurture of a highly selected group of young women should differ from another philosophy sponsored by an administrator on a more diversified coeducational campus. To identify the origin of each pronouncement will highlight our facts and stabilize our attitudes. Let no mother or teacher embrace any educational idea until she knows its ancestry, what company it keeps, and the financial circles in which it moves. It may prove disappointing, or surprisingly good; but she won't know which until she has dispassionately examined it.

Why is it important for thoughtful women, both as individuals and in their organized groups, to question their own convictions and seek new kinds of education for the younger generation? Simply because it *is* a younger generation, living in a world which is a few decades and at least one depression and one war older. Today's mothers and teachers and counselors developed their attitudes under a psychology which emphasized the individual, and for them this is still the preferred psychology. It taught the importance of the individual, sought always to measure and describe individual differences, and tried to devise ingenious new methods for meeting individual needs.

Long before the psychologist developed this scientific interest in the individual, our thinking was shaped by the great tradition of individualism in the arts and humanities. Wherever the romantic movement invaded and lingered, with Rousseau, Wordsworth, Goethe, and countless others, the personal importance of the individual gave life and colorful variety to every human product—to music, poetry, art, philosophy, religion, and also to education, politics, and business. The inward look in religion and the arts, personal initiative and aggression in business, confidence in one's own dream, and the sacredness of every individual destiny have been in our psychological atmosphere, especially in the feminine atmosphere, for generations.

But for the coming generation, a social psychology as well as an individual psychology is claiming attention. The outward look is now to be emphasized. "Social self," "group techniques," "communications," and "sociometry" are the new watchwords. Sociology, history, anthropology, as well as psychology itself, have originated new methods and attitudes and developed a social ideology which education must inevitably reflect. The layman naturally lags behind the scholar and scientist in his sensitivity to this change, but he must conquer his reluctance to take the daring step that will bring him abreast of the best professional leaders.

A second reason for urging all women, and especially teachers, counselors, and mothers, to re-examine their convictions is that psychology and sociology and other social disciplines now offer us much better methods for probing into our individual attitudes and consequently more confidence in discarding those which are not truly constructive. Previous generations required a lifetime of experience for understanding social and cultural and political pressures, and such sophistication was guaranteed only to the privileged few who traveled widely and who assumed leadership in government and business.

Today the conscientious college student, if he chooses to study the accumulated learning in the social sciences, can be as sophisticated as the most widely traveled man of the nineteenth century, for he may know intimately, through books and films and broadcasts, the inhabitants and cultures of the most remote

and varied lands. He understands the working of propaganda and
advertising, may penetrate the origin of prejudices and the
growth of attitudes. He may analyze society either vertically, to
expose all its different strata, or horizontally, to trace the waxing
and waning of any of its groups or institutions.

The individual woman, then, may have lost none of her importance, but a social psychology has taught us to see her as a
person constantly interacting with the forces of society. Each
individual sees herself, and her teachers and counselors see her
in turn, as the center of her family, her school, her church, her
neighborhood, and her clubs, the magazine and newspaper stories
she reads, the stores at which she buys, the radio programs and
movies she chooses. She is constantly in interaction with all of
them, adapting her behavior to them or rejecting them and seeking replacements. Now they press inward upon her and mold
her, and again they reach out to her and invite her to manipulate them. But the immediate framework which they form about
her can never be relaxed, for it is in turn held in place in a still
larger constellation by the extensive forces that constantly mold
and manipulate the institutions—family, movies, church, club,
school—which surround the individual.

To the growing child, the high school senior, the young career
woman, these spheres of influences pressing in and pulling out
do not seem to be the "blooming, buzzing confusion" of James'
infant's-eye view. In mid-century and in these United States,
they appear as an inexorable but well-ordered complexity, with
a few dangerous or frightening or undeveloped areas which fall
into relative obscurity in the press of more immediate and necessary contacts. She rails at them, struggles with them, and tries
to keep control of them, but she is vaguely aware that it is their
constant irritating and provocative effects which give to each
individual, if not growth, at least life.

The educational engineer must disentangle the strands that
interconnect the student and each of the institutions that surround her, to determine the relative stress of the social, economic,
and political forces in which she is enmeshed. He must be able to

17

estimate from which items in her environment the infant or the school girl is deriving her education, formal or informal, at any one time; which of them are of most importance and significance *to her*; which can be manipulated to her advantage; which satisfy or fail to satisfy her various needs. Which of the institutions and pressures that surround her can be changed, and how may these changes affect thousands of other individuals each in the center of a different but interlocking universe of her own? It is the immensity and complexity of these problems which makes the idea of a simple, single solution so ridiculous.

To think in terms of one total program of education "for women" is to indulge in unforgivable oversimplification. Educators must devise many curriculums, in an appropriate variety of length, depth, and scope. And the first step toward this is to differentiate the sociological layers and the psychological diversities of the women for whom these curriculums will be needed.

We must first of all consider the individual differences which have been so thoroughly explored by the psychologists. We mean the significant differences—not the small, entertaining whimsicalities which we notice among our friends or in our reading, but the much more fundamental physiological, intellectual, emotional, and environmental differences. In view of the colossal variations among women in age, ambition, religion, opportunity, native endowment, and socioeconomic status, mere sex differences will assume a much less significant role than history and tradition have assigned to them. The obvious differences in biological functions must of course be taken into account, but it is the more nebulous differences in life patterns and opportunities that will be accorded the greater importance in future educational programs.

Consider, for example, the differences among high school seniors in their capacity for college work. Some of them have acquired remarkable facility in verbal skills. They read rapidly, comprehend readily, speak fluently, and enjoy the play of words. Others are slow readers with scant practice and fleeting interest in verbal expression. Some have been oriented since childhood toward the college campus. Their parents, their cousins, and their friends have preceded them in college, and the conversation and interests of professional people constantly surround them. Others lack motivation and interest and do not have even a general knowledge of college curriculums and activities. Some respond sensitively to competition and have developed good habits of work and study. Others are relaxed and easygoing, content with average or low accomplishment.

How infinitely great is the distance between the valedictorian and the pupil who stands 870th in a class of 892. How little the average senior in a class of twenty in a consolidated rural school has in common with the average senior in the college preparatory course of one of the excellent suburban high schools or private schools in prosperous geographic areas.

We too easily lose sight of such individual variations among all the thousands of high school seniors, and also of the differences in the numbers of children to be found in the various socioeconomic strata. How many are in the group which must seek the nearest and the cheapest campus to get the quickest preparation for earning power?

There is a kind of basic formula which is as essential for any woman who is thinking in this field as the multiplication table is for her budgeting. Although it has not the eternal verity of the multiplication table, and undergoes some change from one decade to another, at present it runs in general about as follows:

The upper socioeconomic levels (professional people, owners, managers) produce about 8 per cent of all the children of this country, of whom about 90 per cent complete high school and go on to college.

The middle classes (small businessmen, clerical and office workers, minor professional people, farmers, foremen, a few skilled workers) produce a little more than 30 per cent of all the children, of whom 60 per cent finish high school and 15 per cent enter college.

The lower classes (skilled, semiskilled, unskilled laborers, etc.) produce about 60 per cent of the children, of whom 30 per cent go through high school and only 5 per cent enter college.

19

These figures determine the planning of every detail of the educational programs of our high schools and colleges, and tables of such data will be needed for each successive decade.

These facts achieve their greatest significance when contrasted with the more rigidly stratified society of any of the countries of Europe and the parallel structure of their educational systems. As we visit their colleges and their secondary schools we can only admire the well-rounded education they provide, with its emphasis on the liberal arts, languages, and philosophy, its meaningful cultivation of the classics.

We cannot forget, however, about the 80 or 90 per cent of the children who were separated forever from these learning opportunities when at the end of the fourth grade they were earmarked by their parents or teachers for the trade schools or for apprenticeship learning on the job. Only about 5 to 10 per cent of the children in some of these systems reach the *secondary school level*, in comparison with the 75 per cent who attain that level in the United States. In England or anywhere on the Continent less than 2 per cent of college-age students (and these are principally men) are in the universities, compared with the 18 to 20 per cent in the United States.

Do we endorse the kind of liberal education which is bought for the fortunate few but paid for by the unfortunate many? Especially when the price is extracted from fourth- or eighth-grade children who have had no chance to learn about the advantages which they are required to renounce?

If our answer is no, we must be prepared to accept, in our educational planning, the implications and demands of a college population that is as heterogeneous in every respect as is our entire citizenry.

Even among students coming from a common cultural and geographical background there are differences in emotional maturity, in temperament and outlook. Some are self-reliant, almost irritating in their individuality, while others have personalities that are colorless and ill-defined. Some are immature, some astonishing in their stature and poise. Some look forward to easy financial gain, others prefer to seek professional gratification, and still others can never hope to escape their economic burdens. There are wide variations in their social and moral values and therefore in the goals which they hope to achieve in their educational programs.

In view of these facts, what do we mean when we use the phrase *the education of women?* What women are we talking about?

Some colleges attract almost entirely the upper socioeconomic classes, and some almost entirely the middle classes; some attract only the upper and middle classes, while the larger tax-supported universities of course educate students from all classes. Have we been talking about a total program for all women? Or have we meant the *higher* education of a *small* percentage of women? Could we possibly mean to imply that there is one kind of education which would fit all women? Could we hope to find one omnicompetent educational formula which would fit even the 15 per cent of all women who reach the college campus?

As a basic factor in our thinking about the education problem the differences between women and men must be precisely delineated, the better to understand how and why modern society behaves in relation to them. An individual woman may manage very well in her safe adult world on some quaintly distorted convictions about woman's nature and her place in society, but effective education for the new generations cannot be established on unrealistic assumptions.

In the society of the future, women will probably function more and more "like men" as earners and citizens, and less and less "like women" in their homemaking and their cultural activities. But as they encroach on the men's prerogatives, and withdraw from some of their own, some alteration will occur in the functioning of men, and for this change the men also need careful education in attitudes and skills. Parallel changes may be necessary too in the activities of the children, especially the older and adolescent children whose functions in society have deteriorated along with the housewife's, with deplorable consequences. The mother will no longer be a self-effacing and stationary pivot around which the family life revolves, but a much more dynamic and sophisticated personality, more securely integrated with the life of her times.

This role will be no more exacting for her than the earlier one, but obviously it will call for different kinds of skill, less patience and more aggressiveness, no less wisdom but much more economic and scientific information than she has previously needed. Society has forced the new role upon her, and with it the need to make decisions which will be critical not only for her but for society itself. If she is passive and uninformed she will inevitably be victimized, but if she can gather her forces and take the lead, she may turn the situation to her own and everyone's advantage.

This is her present choice. The dilemma is not of her own making, but it is hers to resolve nevertheless. Men can and will help her, but they will not assume the leadership in dealing with what is so patently (to them) a "woman's problem." Women must study for themselves their precise status in each of their present roles, as wives, mothers, citizens, earners, and as individual, integrated personalities in their own right. They must then make the best possible forecast about their future status in each of these roles. Only such facts and forecasts, honestly faced, can provide a serviceable foundation for future educational planning.

. . . 2

The Question of Sex Differences

ALL the problems peculiar to women's education arise out of the differences between the sexes, whether these be imagined or real, and no effective compromises or lasting progress can be achieved without a sound knowledge of them. But how many parents or educators have an adequate working knowledge of the fundamental facts about physical (fairly easy to learn), psychological (difficult), and sociological (extremely difficult) differences between men and women? The hard-won data from the laboratory are too often embalmed in a monograph or impaled on a footnote for storage in the library vaults. There is occasional lively discussion of their implications in the yearbooks and seminars, but they seldom reach the practicing educator or the still more remote but solicitous parent with either promptitude or convincing impact.

The myths about mankind and especially about its feminine branch are more colorful, more fun. For centuries men and women were obliged to rely on the evidence of their senses and their immediate experiences to solve the riddle of masculinity and femininity. From these sources society gradually evolved its own "man" and its own "woman," and these stereotypes have been re-created with every succeeding generation, each truly in its own image.

As a part of the process, certain feminine qualities have been painted by the artist, sung by the poet, worshiped by the church, and glamorized by Hollywood. The spell thus cast over everyone's thinking has been both pleasant and serviceable, and the "woman" thus kept alive has been a real and useful personality.

It is asking a good deal of everybody to suggest they turn their backs on art, poetry, religion, history, tradition, and the scholars of former centuries—just because the academic laboratory has classified their cherished convictions as illusions. It is a wrench to the ego, endurable only by the tough-minded, to move from the soft warmth of tradition and feeling about men and women into the chilly impersonality of scientific evidence. What Aristotle, Dante, Shakespeare, or Tolstoi pontificated about women is as fascinating as ever, and we continue to read it as a great educational and a very great esthetic experience. But even as we have profited by abandoning Dante's cosmography as a basis for present-day navigation and space calculations, so we may gain, for the purposes of twentieth-century education, by replacing the old literary "woman" with the more valid conceptions provided by modern science.

The specific direction into which research is channeled is a reflection of the intellectual climate in which it develops. The early twentieth century saw the rising strength and final triumph of the suffrage movement, the great increase in educational and employment opportunities for women, together with the development of the first quantitative methods for exploring human intelligence. In such a climate it became increasingly necessary to find an incontrovertible answer to the specific question: Are there intellectual, emotional, personality differences between men and women, and *in whose favor?*

In 1910 there were 25 published studies on this topic; in 1935, 327 were undertaken, and the drive gathered momentum for still another decade. But modern techniques only confirm the early conclusions: Inherent psychological differences, if any, are infinitesimally small, and most of them can be accounted for sociologically rather than psychologically.

So much for the suspicion, prevalent even as late as the nineteenth century, that women are not as intelligent as men, that their mental processes are somehow different in quality as well as in quantity, that woman's mind is possibly in a state of arrested evolution.

A later popular thesis was that, although the sexes might show no difference in average intelligence, men possessed greater range and greater variability in mental power. More men scored the very highest ratings on measured intelligence, but also more of them had the very lowest intelligence ratings, gathered from the inmates of institutions for subnormals. But this was a social circumstance rather than a "natural" event, and the tightening of the loose ends of statistical methods easily proved the hypothesis untenable.

Today when the parent-teachers association and the school board share interest and action with the professional educator, parents need to be as sophisticated as teachers in their evaluation of psychological data. It will always be easy to "demonstrate" the superior ability of girls or of boys because of what the statistician calls "selected sampling." For example, if high school boys show a slight superiority over girls of the same age group, it may be due to the fact that boys who do not have the native ability for academic success in high school find it much easier than girls to obtain work certificates and drop out of school. The average intelligence for the boys who remain in school is, therefore, artificially raised.

Likewise in test-measured intelligence, the socioeconomic background of one or another group may push its members up or down a little on the scale, depending on the previous familiarity with the language used in the phrasing of the questions or on the interest and effort to which the test may arouse them. Every high school population is a "selected" group from which broad generalizations are hazardous.

Study of the subject matter used for testing sex differences is sometimes more profitable than the study of any actual differences in test results. Tests may be made from materials which have more appeal for men than for women. A question of simple logic, if it happens to be phrased in words, may be easier for girls, because they consistently excel in their use of words. An exactly comparable question in logic, if it makes use of numbers instead of words, or uses spatial relationships or geometric figures, may be easier for boys to answer.

Psychologists have become very skillful in analyzing their test items and in tracing apparent and even seemingly significant differences to the form of the question or the material used in it. Today more than ever they hold to their oft-stated premise: Psychological tests measure the ability of the subject to pass the test. This keeps them properly skeptical and should also make the layman wary of unqualified categorical statements of differences. Too often it is the child's experience and opportunity that are being measured rather than his capacity; in fact, the inherited and the acquired are invariably intricately compounded.

When there is a wide variety of content in the test materials, when groups tested are carefully equated for errors which might have crept into the results by way of special selection, and when all factors are held constant, inherent sex differences in intelligence are shown to be nonexistent.

In other words, as of autumn 1954, men are just as intelligent as women, but no more so.

Sex differences in achievement constitute a much more baffling question. It is an obvious and socially significant fact that far more men than women have achieved the pinnacles of success in recorded history. Why, if there is no sex difference in intelligence?

Attacks on this problem are commonly made by analyzing the compilations from *Who's Who* and other biographical catalogues of eminent personages, and such analyses have given us an eminence ratio of about 92 per cent men to 8 per cent women. These statistical summaries must be separated according to the various fields—politics, arts, sciences, education—because of variations among these fields in the opportunities open to women and the resistance they encounter. For example, more than a third of the eminent women achieve fame through literary pursuits, where opportunities are more nearly equalized, and it is about ten times as easy for a woman to achieve eminence in psychology as in physics.

In interpreting studies of eminence, it is also well to keep in mind the similarly limited numbers of women in activities of questionable respectability. The count in the 1950 census shows that of the 264,557 persons over fourteen years of age who were confined in prisons or reformatories, jails, and workhouses, 12,995, or 5 per cent, were females and 251,562, or 95 per cent, were males. In both cases the data may reflect the wider social scope of man's activities. Criminality and eminence may both be a matter of opportunity.

In any event, it is not easy to reconcile school achievements or measured intelligence with so large a discrepancy in these eminence ratios from biographical dictionaries. Every teacher knows, as the record invariably shows, that girls consistently reach higher achievement levels than boys in terms of grades recorded in the principal's office. When standardized tests are made, girls reveal themselves as different from boys, but on the whole about equal to them. Girls are better in English, spelling, writing, art; boys are better in arithmetic, history, geography, and science. Such findings point merely to differential rates of maturing, to special aptitudes and interests, or perhaps to attitudes and personality traits.

Psychologists find that girls consistently demonstrate their superiority in verbal abilities; they talk earlier, have larger vocabularies, and excel in any tests involving language. They also have better memories, quicker perception of the details for clerical work, and much greater finger dexterity. But the boys have a greater amount and range of general information and better ability in mathematics and spatial relations and in mechanical manipulations.

One searches in vain for differences substantial enough to explain or justify an eminence ratio of 92 per cent to 8 per cent, and is forced to agree with the scholar who commented: "The nondefinitive results with respect to differences between the sexes suggest that perhaps differences *in life performances* should be construed in terms of observable environmental differences *in the training* of the two sexes."[1]

In other words, the most likely explanation for the eminence ratings is the difference in sex roles in our culture, for which the individual is prepared, from infancy onward, in a thousand ways, some of them planned and direct and even more of them just breathed in with the air around him.

More than a century ago Stendahl said that all the geniuses who are born women are lost to the public good. And "to tell the truth," Simone de Beauvoir adds, "one is not born a genius; one becomes a genius; and the feminine situation has up to the present rendered this becoming practically impossible." She also points out, "It is only since women have begun to feel themselves at home on earth that we have seen a Rosa Luxemburg or a Madame Curie appear. They brilliantly demonstrate that it is not the inferiority of women that has caused their historical insignificance; it is rather their historical insignificance that has doomed them to inferiority."[2]

The present eminence ratio was, of course, based on social conditions of the earlier half century, and as present generations, with more nearly similar opportunities for boys and girls, reach maturity the ratio may be appreciably altered. If so, one wonders what traumas may be in store for the men as their expectations of superiority come to be denied with increasing effectiveness. The clever and well-situated men will suffer least and be most charitable; the average middle-class worker and husband will be most affected, and perhaps all too soon educators and psychiatrists will find themselves beginning to worry about a new "lost sex."

Or, perhaps just as likely, some men will be able for the first time to follow their natural bent without a sense that they are somehow betraying the "natural" role of their sex. If the psychiatrists can argue that the more restricted role of women in courtship and sex relationships is one of the sources of their frustration and maladjustment, why cannot an equally good case be made for the parallel frustration of men in the esthetic role. With the dominance of men among the successful practicing artists in all fields, no case could be made for a less strong creative or artistic talent and motivation in the male personality. Undoubtedly many men who fall short of the drive or the talent necessary for a full-time career in these fields suffer a great deal, even if unconsciously, from the pressures of society which make it unrespectable for them to belong to the dilettante class.

Women should quietly undermine these pressures, for the sake of the larger community of interests which their elimination would permit in family life. Cultivation of more comparable standards for the sexes in behavior and personality also holds possibilities for more enjoyable family and marriage relations. Voice and bearing, figure and grooming, music appreciation, "Sunday" painting, even needlework, may in time become as important for men as for women, and charm of personality may eventually carry as much weight in masculine social success as does financial or political power.

Some of the culturally dictated sex differences that are most important in affecting achievement seem at first glance to be trivial. Marjorie Nicholson once lectured on the text that professional women are handicapped in their march to the heights because they do not have wives! Ridiculous? Not at all. Consider the young male artist or scholar or business executive whose wife cooks his meals, looks after his clothes and his home, types his papers, acts as his chauffeur, entertains his colleagues and their wives—in general arranges for him all the myriad essential details of living. Why should he not get ahead faster and go farther than his female counterpart who must take time and energy from the job to keep her own home in order, do her own shopping, cook and serve her own dinner for the boss or the visiting celebrity?

Another "superficial" matter is the enormous difference in the importance of clothes. Woman's dress is her autograph, her price tag, her ammunition, her chaperone. Woman's personality is not only revealed, it is frankly nourished, by her clothes. She is happy, aggressive, witty, in proportion as her garb is new and becoming, not to say costly and distinctive; or she is irritable, uncertain, dull, if for any reason her clothes are embarrassing to her. But since the Baroque days of Louis XIV, men's clothes have required a minimum of their attention because they are more standardized and practical and because they are evaluated in terms of comfort and convenience rather than elegance and fashion. Neither self-consciousness nor self-expression is characteristic of men in their dress.

The hours of time and the amount of energy required of a woman for the interminable details of personal appearance affect her working efficiency, her interests, her attitudes, her grasp of world affairs. A girl's life for a whole year may be oriented around the purchase of a fur coat, with its personal, social, and financial implications. She lets herself be preoccupied with these interests and she budgets too much of her income for them, but there is no escape. Custom dictates that the successful woman declare herself by her fashionable, elegant, and fragile clothes. Even a few subtle compromises may jeopardize her social or employment status. Any major denial of the preeminence of appearance would be gambling with her feminine destiny. To be attractive to men, to be partnered, wooed, and blandished, she must approximate as closely as possible the current models in the world of fashion.

It is obvious that fashions for both men and women are more than merely capricious, and that they are slowly evolving in the direction of stability, efficiency, and comfort. Women are showing less and men more of diversity and individuality. Gradually the present sex differences may be almost equated. Gradually too the standards in grooming and personal habits for men and women may reveal a similar interweaving: tousled hair and dirty fingernails, harsh speech, gauche manners and movements, may become as intolerable for men as for women, and such virtues as modesty, neatness, finesse, and gentility may be looked upon as a credit in the masculine as well as the feminine ledger before too many more years go by.

In the meantime the women's magazines revolve relentlessly around their twin axes of fashion and romance and continue to lure the fascinated women farther and farther out of the men's orbit. Women under the weight of tradition have both compulsion and needs for this monthly magazine fare, but until they can rid themselves both of these reading habits and the societal pressures which lie behind them, the mark of their enslavement is clear for all to see. The one best measure of wholesome maturity and independence for the female of the species is range in current reading and freedom from the women's magazines.

Biological functions have of course been brought forward as an explanation for the unfavorable eminence rating of women, but even here the effects come more from sociological than from physical factors.

It is undoubtedly true that the time and energy drained off into the bearing and rearing of children has had an incalculable deterring effect on professional achievement, especially before these functions were technologically streamlined. It might be argued that a less well advertised function of women, the menopause, often coming as a disrupting and little understood experience at a time when many women are at the peak of their professional or business services, is even more significant for explaining women's lesser accomplishments.

Women have the consciousness of sex forced on them more poignantly than men, not only because of the regularity of menstruation and the physical symptoms accompanying it, but also because of pregnancies and the menopause. The interrelation of the endocrine glands are still relatively obscure in both men and women. It is easier, however, to relate subjective feelings to the sex functions in women than in men because of the inescapably observable monthly phenomena. It is unfortunate that data for tracing fluctuations of feelings in men to comparable sources are not so readily available.

Compared to men, "women are much more often ailing," asserts Simone de Beauvoir, "and there are times when they are not in command of themselves." [3] But this probably is not equally true at all socioeconomic levels and not true at all in some societies. Education and good standards for physical and mental health can and do eliminate most of the "female ailments."

These physical factors, especially the child-bearing function, have never assumed their proper importance in the education of women, and the clearly indicated courses in biology, physiology, marriage hygiene, and child rearing have been widely neglected.

But it is the social rather than the physiological aspects of childbearing that actually make the serious demand on higher education for women. If at the birth of the child the father assumed comparable responsibility with the mother for the details of its care, feeding, sleeping, cleanliness, health, and personal, intellectual, and social training, the whole pattern of women's life and education would be greatly simplified. The fact is that a complicated cultural pattern has become attached to a biological difference. There is no logical reason and certainly no biological reason for the child's welfare to be fixed on the mother rather than on the father. Nevertheless, as long as tradition has it so, education must treat it as a true sex difference.

That it is not inevitably so, however, is made fairly clear by anthropological studies of primitive societies. If in these simpler cultures, where the biological sex function would be even more compulsive than in our own technically controlled society, one may find either man-dominated or woman-dominated societies, there is no reason to assume that the culture pattern must be entirely determined by human biological functions.

For example, among the Tchambuli, as described by Margaret Mead, our own Western sex roles are reversed. Men are the artists, the dancers; they are coquettish and leave the sexual initiative to women. Women are efficient, comradely, jolly. The men, who are usually found at home, depend upon them for food, support, affection. It has been observed that though the Tchambuli are a small tribe, they are enough to upset a world-wide fallacy. So long as they flourish, there can be no argument that cultural patterns are necessarily set by biological functions. Would that Hollywood would tell Americans about the Tchambuli in a grade-A, full-length, three-dimension movie in technicolor!

Personality characteristics, too, come largely from the environment. These are elusive and difficult to measure, but some data about them are available. Boys are twice as frequent offenders in tardiness and are outstanding trouble-makers in our schools, while girls are more cooperative, more inhibited, more persevering, more docile. There are no sex differences on the introversion-extroversion scales, except in the kinds of items by which each sex achieves its high or low ratings. On one of the widely used personality scales, women students show themselves to be more neurotic and unstable, less self-sufficient, less dominant, less self-confident, perhaps more dependent socially. But the differences are not large and the investigators are quick to say that perhaps girls are a little more willing to admit to such traits. Measured differences are not always real differences.

The surprising thing is that psychologists can find only these minute differences in personalities in view of all we know of the effects of environment and accumulated individual experience on the total personality. In the American culture the environment for male and female children, especially in the upper middle classes, has been carefully controlled from early childhood. Their play, their toys, their privileges, entertainment, reading matter, and freedom of mobility are prescribed by the folkways. Their treatment by parents, teachers, and other adults is sex conscious. Some of the more conspicuous differences in toys and treatment have dwindled a little since grandmother's day, but today's attitudes, if more subtle, are no less pervasive.

Intelligence and personality tests, then, tend to emphasize, not the differences, but the human likenesses in men and women.

But measurements of activities and values very nicely confirm the common sense observation that the interests which men and women cultivate are different. One of the more novel research techniques, systematic eavesdropping on conversations, utilizes the very method by which the layman has reached his more casual but similar conclusions. It is now documented that women are more interested in clothes, males, and decoration; and men in business, money, sports, and amusements. At the high school level, the major areas for discussion and reading among girls are personal attractiveness, etiquette, and getting along with people; and for boys, money, health, safety, recreation, and civic affairs.

College men place higher values on theoretical problems, especially political and economic, show more interest in abstract ideas, more emphasis on success, and more desire for influence and power over others as their life objectives. College women place more value on esthetic, social, and religious aspects of life, and show more interest in art and music and more concern for the welfare of others as a life goal.

The laborious collection of data about these interests and the elaborate statistical computations for their interpretation may seem to be so much boondoggling; but occasionally they cut to the heart of a problem and provide the social scientist with a useful working hypothesis. The factor analysis technique, applied to the Strong Interest tests for example, organized the widely varied interests of high school seniors into a few constellations of controlling concepts around which their more specific preferences tend to cluster. For men there are a large number of these constellations, but for women there are only four main types and one of these four predominates so strongly that 90 per cent of high school seniors exhibit it as their controlling interest. It has been designated "interest in male association," and it represents no doubt the general attitude of the woman who does not anticipate a career for its own sake, but who, pending marriage, is satisfied to pursue any congenial activity that offers itself.

This one-interest complex covers housewives, office workers, stenographers, and nurses—all members of occupations that involve working for, or with, men. In contrast, the other three constellations, comprising the remaining 10 per cent of the activities that appeal to girls, are languages (librarians, teachers, writers, etc.), science (physicians, mathematics teachers, etc.), and of course the social service occupations.

This is a quantitative and erudite manner of saying that girls will be girls, or at least that 90 per cent of them will be girls, and the other 10 per cent may find themselves in *Who's Who*!

The significant thing is the far more uniform and standardized pattern of feminine interests than of masculine. John may want to be a lawyer, physician, engineer, farmer, statistician, radio announcer, but Mary, nine times out of ten, can see no farther than her marriage. She wants a little job that will put her immediately into the company of men. She will also admit that this desire, which factor analysis has wrung from her, is not fleeting or changeable. She has nurtured it since her eighth-grade days, and won't give it up even though she goes on to college. The researcher will tell you that any helpful career-planning for Mary must reckon with these romantic propensities.

This concentration of feminine interests may come as a surprise to some parents, because most of them have not been thinking about sending Mary to college merely because she wants companionship with men. Whenever parents have been given a chance to declare their own projects for Mary's education, they have stressed vocational needs. Above all, they want her to be able to earn her own living. And Mary herself will be quick to shift her interests as soon as her major objective, marriage, has been achieved.

Teachers, counselors, and school administrators have always known that "interest in male association" is dominant in the high school and college ages, but now that the fact is quantified so ceremoniously, it seems all the greater folly to ignore it in setting up our educational objectives. Shall we work to counteract it on the personal level through educational counseling or try to manipulate social change? It is not simple to propose corrective measures by either method; they have a way of trailing unintended consequences which quickly get out of hand.

What the girls need is more of the occupations where the much desired man-and-woman relationship may be maneuvered; teaching, the college woman's ubiquitous career, has become too disproportionately a woman's field to satisfy these needs. It restricts the teacher to the companionship of children and almost exclusively to feminine colleagues. We may not wish to organize propaganda for only married women teachers but we might at least make the hours and conditions of teaching more attractive for the young wives and mothers who have the needed companionship with men in their nonworking hours.

Psychologists have labeled the undefinable but undeniable sex differences in personality as masculinity and femininity. These two nebulous concepts are gradually assuming more concrete shape, although in searching for more precise definition, psychologists still have recourse only to the opinions and attitudes of the tradition. Recall, for example, the most masculine person and the most feminine person you know, and list their characteristics. Out of such listings of subconscious and unverbalized impressions two psychological entities have emerged, with a surprising amount of agreement about them. The "masculine character" has more self-assertion, aggressiveness, hardihood, fearlessness, and also more bluntness of manner, language, and sentiment. The feminine person is more compassionate, timid, fastidious, esthetically sensitive, probably more emotional, and is certainly a severer moralist; she is more enveloped in domestic affairs, art, the more sedentary and indoor occupations, and in ministrative occupations particularly to the young, helpless, or distressed.

In these two descriptions the role of the social folkways is very apparent. Masculinity is not only defined but confirmed and maintained by social pressures and expectations. Every individual possesses a good deal of both masculinity and femininity in his personality, and just how far he veers toward one or the other side of the scale will be determined by such variables as his family life, his occupation, and his formal education. If he has grown up in a broken home, with excessive or exclusive association with one parent only, or if he has had only brothers, or only sisters, his masculinity-femininity index will be affected. Physical traits, on the other hand—the pitch of his voice, the strength of his biceps, the height-weight ratio—have little to do with it.

Well-educated women tend to be emancipated from the cultural prescriptions and therefore are likely to be more masculine than the average woman. Cultured and educated men who have pursued vocational or avocational interests of the artistic or intellectual kind are strong on the feminine side of the test. In other words, as the woman rises in the educational world and uses her education to acquire traditionally male job experience, her interests and her temperament traits tend to follow the patterns of men. How could it be otherwise when she associates with them more frequently, when successful competition requires that she learn their attitudes and methods?

Likewise as the man climbs the educational ladder, profiting from the required cultural as well as professional courses, he is attracted by the pursuits which are generally reserved for women. A larger salary and wider professional experience give him more chance to take part in the leisure enterprises—travel, theater, music—and his mental habits inevitably tend toward the grooves marked out by feminine participants.

Yet the social and biological factors may be very intricately intermingled, and physiology may be more important than we can demonstrate. Animal experiments, for example, show that male sex hormones are effective in intensifying such a quality as aggressiveness, and dominance can be produced in females by injections of androgen. It may be, however, that the trait develops only because other animals react differently to the changed physical appearance of the subject.

Experiments on human subjects are not possible, but evidence is frequently available from the analysis of social data. It is probable that the more emancipated attitudes in women tend to be associated with the trait of masculinity; both may develop through environmental circumstance, such as excessive growth, a broken home, or being the only child. Certainly even the most casual as well as the more pretentious polls will demonstrate the remarkable sex differences in the self-regarding attitudes. When public school boys and girls rate each other for possession of desirable and undesirable traits, both groups attribute more favorable ratings to boys. The older the age the higher the ratings, although in these same school years the girls cooperate better, give the teachers less trouble, and earn better grades! Obviously, cultural factors favorable to men in the adult world are setting patterns of thinking even in this early school world.

Among adults, *Fortune*'s 1946 exploration found 92 per cent of men who would rather be men, but only 66 per cent of women who would rather be women. Could there be any more eloquent comment by women on their present depressed social, economic, and political status?

Yet a thoroughgoing equality and uniformity is not the only answer, certainly not the best answer to this feminine restlessness in women's traditional roles. Once we have disentangled the sex factors and prejudices from the long-standing attitudes and habits of both men and women, "there is no reason why women cannot develop independence in fields of their own choosing everywhere. What we need is not uniformity but added variability and stimulation for social inventions which will prove more adequate to our needs." [4]

After all, most of the fundamental human needs are the same for both men and women, and we can expect polls to reveal women's dissatisfaction with the larger opportunities of men to satisfy these drives. The fact we cannot afford to forget is that "no woman by virtue of being married loses her need for individual development and achievement, the chance to function as a person as well as a wife and mother. Nor does any degree of vocational success and recognition for the unmarried woman take the place of the need for intimate and satisfying relationships with people." [5]

The prevalent desire of so many women for the masculine role is perhaps one of the many lines of evidence which point to the significance of sex activities in the lives of men and women. The partners in sex life have different roles, different biological functions, and inevitably different psychological attitudes. More important, these diversities have created in the socially inherited ideologies a tremendous burden of lore and literature which serves both to nourish and to disturb the feminine ego.

Sex differences in the self-regarding accompaniments of the sex functions, the inner emotional attitudes toward self-as-man and self-as-woman, have been the topics of many learned essays and much of the fiction writing of all times. Here individual differences are more pronounced than in any other personal traits; they all but invalidate any generalities for either sex, a fortunate circumstance for the novelists. The accumulated literature—poetry, fiction, essay, biography—however rewarding in release and insight, has nevertheless misled the unwary reader in this one respect. The commonplace has never been worth writing about: it quickens no heartbeat, rouses no controversy, satisfies no longing, and creates no market. For popular consumption and entertainment, the bizarre and the erotic hold an ever widening edge.

Unfortunately (since they command so wide a market), modern sex fiction and autobiography have provided insights that have only a limited therapy; the indiscriminate application of their tortuous "truths" is as ludicrous as would be nationwide injections of insulin because of its dramatic cure of diabetes.

Lady Chatterly, Melusine, Natasha, and Sonia, the equally artistic reminiscences of Colette Audry and Marie Bashkirsev, together with the titillating case histories of the psychiatrists and analysts, have, to be sure, created an understanding and sympathy unmatched in the history of femininity. But their hypnotic popularity conjures up no guardian angel to warn the young and the unsophisticated that there are long, pleasant but monotonous valleys lying between these mountains of erotic feelings. The emotions described so pungently and at such length are, in most actual lives, quite minimal and fleeting; for the majority of womankind they are much less disruptive, less frequent, less intense than the novelists might lead one to believe.

Nor can the reader rely on ancient folk tale and drama for a record of Absolute Truth, good for any century, any culture; they reflect only the convictions of their particular epoch. Oedipus, for example, hoary father of the famous complex, was a very typical creature of his time, a time when Aristotle taught that the female nature was afflicted with a natural defectiveness and that women never suffered baldness because they did not use the contents of their heads as men did. In those times men and women believed with Pythagoras that a good principle had created order, light, and man, and that a bad principle had made chaos, darkness, and women. Physicians taught that only man could create life, since he planted the human seed in the body of woman, whose sole function was to nourish it and bring it to birth.

These myths have as much place in modern social thought as Cinderella and Snow White, no more and no less.

Scholarly analysis and interpretation of the whole great body of feminine psychology, philosophy, and history is essential for insight into a woman's status as an integrated personality in her present culture. But preoccupation with history, philosophy, and psychological introspection is justified in educational programs only as the outcomes contribute to current understanding. Not the origins of these traditional concepts, but how they actually affect the thinking, conscious or unconscious, of today's millions of women is the root question.

Again the educators must keep in mind the different socioeconomic classes, their proportionate representation, and the differences in societal functions, capacities, resources, and outlook of these millions of women. Is it the masses of average and normal women who are most sensitive to the effects of their long and checkered phylogenetic history, or only the few more privileged, more reflective, more frustrated? What shall be the educator's method of correcting or lessening these effects? How much attention can be diverted to them, and for how many women? These are some of the questions where the scholar's help is most needed in dealing with the riddles of sex differences in men and women.

"We become what we do," psychology is constantly reminding us, but we cannot escape doing what circumstances prescribe for us. Some free choice we do have, in proportion to the versatility of the environment, and the range of choice is wider for the wealthy, the more intelligent, and the young. But for those at the bottom of the social scale, for the dull of wit, for all those underprivileged masses living in the backward nations, *and for women,* it is narrowly restricted.

The only punishment for evil deeds is evil habits, and the punishment is not only for the individual but for the group, for the nation, for the species. In this perspective, women are now repeating the evils of the centuries of their subordination to men, of their own inaction, of their own acceptance of less worthy goals, of less freedom of choice, less opportunity, less self-improvement. "Her grasp on the world is thus more restricted; she has less firmness for projects that in general she is less capable of carrying out—in other words, her individual life is less rich than man's," argues the author of *The Second Sex.*[6]

It is man, not woman, who has broken through the animal level of the biological function of reproducing the species; it is man who has burst out of the repetitive present into genuinely creative (not merely reproductive) activity, who has achieved self-realization for himself and his race. In her heart of hearts woman feels the same urge to create, to surpass; she confirms all the masculine pretensions; she subscribes to man's values, admires his risks, embraces his goals. "Her misfortune is to have been biologically destined for the repetition of Life . . . when . . . humanity values the reasons for living above mere life." [7]

It is only in the present era that these social and historical differences in status are felt as disturbing, are beginning to cause unpleasant though effective eruptions. Modern medical skills, birth-control techniques and education, together with state solicitude in the matter of infant care and child training, have freed woman from the slavery of childbearing. The machine and the trade-unions have both played their parts in making her economically important, even independent. But much more than these, the naïve psychology of four centuries has given place to world-shattering insights into sources of feelings, beliefs, and attitudes, and the developing techniques of social analysis have laid bare the ruthless unreason of prejudice. Some of the resulting changes we shall consider in subsequent chapters.

... *3*

Social Change and Sex Conflict

THE busy little lasses of the 1850s were not to be found on a college campus, seldom even in public high school, but they were not without counsel. They read profusely, if we may judge from the reported sales of the *Letter Writers* and etiquette books and the number of them still to be found in old attics and antiquarian book shops.

Nothing could better epitomize the social self-consciousness of the emerging bourgeosie than these widely read admonitions. Forerunners of the later newspaper columns of advice to the lovelorn, fashions, and household hints, they standardized for their eager readers the minutiae of daily living. Indigenous manners and frontier attitudes were grimly rooted out and importations from the Old World, especially from England, were zealously cultivated. To farm and village, to all the rude houses in all the muddy streets, these cherished anachronisms were transplanted for the edification of the new American lady. They brought her a demure elegance and a tender conscience, impossible clothing and false modesty, and it has taken her a century to throw them off.

Here are some samples of the precepts by which she lived her social life:

In crossing a street a lady should gracefully raise her dress to the ankle, with one hand. To raise the dress with both hands is vulgar, except in places where the mud is very deep.

Ladies are not allowed, upon ordinary occasions, to take the arm of any one but a relative or an accepted lover, in the street and in the daytime. However, in the evening, in the fields, or in a crowd, whenever she may need protection, she should not refuse it. She should merely pass her hand over the gentleman's arm.

A lady in dressing for a ball, has first to consider the delicate question of age; and next, that of her position, whether married or single. The dress of the married or unmarried lady, however youthful the former, should be distinctly marked. Silk dresses are as a rule objectionable for those who dance, but the married lady may appear in a moire of light tint, or even a white silk, if properly trimmed with tulle and flowers. Young, unmarried ladies should wear dresses of light material—the lighter the better—tarlatane, gauze, tulle, fine muslin and lace. . . .

Well bred young girls are limited as to jewels—a string of pearls for the slender neck, a ring with the natal stone or an ornament of turquoises and pearls, a little gold love manacle about the wrist, that is all, and quite enough until after marriage.

Modesty was still a hazard to good health, and mental health had not yet been differentiated from physical health:

It is not well to dance every dance as the exercise is unpleasantly heating and fatiguing. There are several dances that should be abandoned by delicate women on account of their causing too violent emotions; vertigo is one of the great inconveniences of the waltz, and the character of this dance, the clasping of the partners, their exciting contact and the too quick and too long continued succession of agreeable emotions produce sometimes in women of irritable constitutions, syncopes, spasms, and other accidents.

Ventilation of the room is desirable, and for this purpose the grate should be kept open, and even a small fire employed to create a draft. Windows must be kept securely shut against the dangerous night air.

Ladies should not be sparing of flannel petticoats, and drawers are of incalculable advantage to women, preventing many of the disorders to which females are subject. The drawers may be made of flannel, calico, or cotton, and should reach as far down the leg as possible without their being seen.

"Nothing," runs the comment on these helpful hints, "could be more maidenly or in better taste." Supplementary advice was directed toward the gentlemen:

In conversing with a lady, do not appear to bring your conversation down to her level. Sensible women regard with contempt the man who appears to think they cannot converse intelligently upon subjects generally treated of in society.

Should the lady's shoe become unlaced, or her dress in any manner disordered, the gentleman must not fail to apprise her of it, respectfully, and offer her assistance. A gentleman may hook a dress or lace a shoe with perfect propriety and should be able to do so gracefully.

If those who have danced together meet next day in the street, or the park, the gentleman must not venture to bow, unless the lady chooses to favor him with some mark of recognition. If he does he must not expect any acknowledgment of his salutation.

No gentleman should use his bare hand to press the waist of a lady in the waltz. If without gloves, carry a handkerchief in the hand.

In making a formal call a gentleman should not sit with his legs crossed. Calls should not be made before 10 A.M., nor after 9 P.M. Some persons receive up to a much later hour, but this is bad taste. By nine o'clock, the ladies are thoroughly fatigued, and in no humor to entertain visitors.

Never allow a lady to get a chair for herself, ring a bell, pick up a handkerchief or glove she may have dropped, or in short, perform any service for herself which you can perform for her when you are in the room. By extending such courtesies to your sister, mother, or other members of the family, they become habitual, and are thus more gracefully performed when abroad.

At length the time arrives for the gentleman to make a proposal. If he is a good judge of human nature, he will have discovered long ere this whether his favors have been acceptably received or not, and yet he may not know positively how the lady will receive an offer of marriage. It becomes him to propose.

What shall he say? There are many ways whereby he may introduce the subject. Among these are the following: He may

45

write to the lady, making an offer, and request her to reply. He may, if he dare not trust to word, even in her presence write the question on a slip of paper and request her laughingly to give a plain no or yes. He may ask her if in case a gentleman very much like himself was to make a proposal of marriage to her what she would say. She will probably laughingly reply that it will be time enough to tell what she would say when the proposal is made. And so, the ice would be broken. He may jokingly remark that he intends one of these days to ask a certain lady not a thousand miles away if she will marry him; she will quite likely reply that it will depend upon what lady he asks. And thus he may approach the subject by agreeable and easy stages in a hundred ways depending upon circumstances.

Although the contrasts between the 1850s and the 1950s tempt us to silhouette the modern woman against her counterpart in the earlier century, there is of course no such person as The Modern Woman, except in the omnibus sense, for there are greater diversities today among women of various ages, classes, and countries than ever before.

There are, first of all, great variations in age. "Adults" comprise a group roughly from about 20 to 80 years old, with striking differences in interests, needs, and attitudes. One old-time philosopher asserts that in her first twenty years a woman needs mostly beauty, in the next twenty cash, in the next twenty intelligence, and in the next twenty health. Counselors today may use a less pat formula, but the educational preparation for the cumulative decades in a woman's life will be none the less varied.

To plan the education of the sixteen- and twenty-year-old for the future needs of the forty-year-old and sixty-year-old is all but impossible, but it is a responsibility which cannot be circumvented. It requires an extremely difficult venture into the field of prophecy to estimate what will be the ideologies, opportunities, problems, and imperatives of the world a quarter or half century later. It further involves motivating the emerging adult to learn many things which will not interest her until much later, and the task of persuading the adolescent to embrace a curricu-

lum which will presumably help her solve unpredictable dilemmas at thirty or forty or sixty will not be easy. Future benefits
are less urgent than present needs.

Neither the student nor her parent conceives of the formal
school years as only a prelude to learning activities that will
continue throughout life. They tend rather to view the four
long, expensive college years as providing all the necessary educational equipment for future competition and success. Teachers
and counselors are sometimes misled by their own academic and
objective points of view into assuming that the layman too
accepts the process of education as a continuing one.

It is pleasant to picture the adult woman employing her leisure
time in reading and enjoying the stimulating intellectual associations of other adult minds engaged in carrying on the world's
work. Experience suggests, however, that the paths which were
not followed in formal schooling, the doors which were not
opened in classroom courses, will remain for the most part
unopened and unexplored.

Adults may regret that as youngsters they did not have time
for the clarinet, or were not required to take Latin-American
history, but they are not inclined to make up for lost time in
their present leisure hours. Perhaps the adult is too self-conscious,
too impatient in the unaccustomed role of beginner, a role which
does not bother the child. Or perhaps the amount of propaganda
and effort required to pull adults into the classes they need has
been underestimated by the administrators of adult education
programs. In any event, until there is more widespread acceptance of the idea of continuing study for adults, those who plan
the education of women in realistic fashion will discount all but
the formal school years.

Educational "engineers" need the richer perspective to be
gained from a study of the opinions and attitudes of women in
different age groups. The woman of sixty, who finished college
with the Gibson girls, has the skepticism and disillusionment of
two world wars imposed on the childhood background of a world
without the automobile and the radio, almost without movies

She will have her characteristic resistances to the new educational blueprints. The woman of forty, who finished her school years and embarked on her earning career about the time of the great depression, will have more of economic restlessness and insecurity than the thirty-year-olds who interrupted their school years to earn large salaries during the war years and thus easily came to take for granted the makeshift economy of rationing and priorities.

No matter what differences may be present in their individual backgrounds, all the women of one decade carry the almost indelible imprint of the ideologies and social temper of their formative years. And it is only with great difficulty that they can revise their thinking to understand and sympathize with the ideologies of those above or below them on the ladder of experience. Nor would it be altogether becoming for them to assume completely the ideas and attitudes of a generation which is not theirs. Each must solve in her own way the perplexing problem of just how best to mix the newer and brighter colors of the modern idiom with the more stable and substantial tones of the older.

But chronological separations among women are not so important to the educator and counselor as the differences to be found among the various social classes. No blueprint for education can be discussed intelligently without a substantial grasp of social stratification, the proportionate distribution of the several classes in the American population, and some opinion about the degree of mobility from one class to another.

Until recently these classes could be characterized only vaguely and obliquely by means of the personal and subjective mediums of life and literature. The good novelist perceived quite sharply the personal traits of his characters, both as individuals and as members of a social group, so that readers who had a wide knowledge of the worlds re-created in fiction, in the theater, in the movies, attained vicariously a pretty sound knowledge of life in its many facets. They became familiar with the social hierarchies of community life, in America and elsewhere, and with the differences between the various centuries, regions, and social levels in terms of speech, manners, morals, ambitions, and feelings.

But in the last few decades the studies of the sociologists have described these classes still more sharply, if less esthetically. The data are quantitative and objective, neatly packaged for the use of educators and social engineers, but even the high school girl can learn the attitudes and problems of the various social levels, including her own, and can be made, if her counselors are wise in teaching her, an active agent in understanding and correcting the inadequacies and inequities of our times. In fact, her cultural literacy today demands this knowledge. "The first lesson in modern sociology is that the individual cannot understand his own experience or gauge his own fate without locating himself within the trends of his epoch and the life chances of his social layer." [1]

Recent dramatic methods of socioeconomic analysis have disclosed six well-differentiated classes in the United States. Such summaries, of course, suffer from oversimplification, for our social structure is too complex to be described accurately in large generalities. But the descriptions can help the casual observer to obtain a more realistic view of his milieu and are tremendously useful to the social scientist, in spite of the fact that their categories do not fit precisely everywhere from east to west and north to south, from old to young, or from rural to urban communities. Social scientists are not agreed as to whether the recognizable strata are more subjective than objective, whether they are becoming more rigid or more fluid, whether their present contours and characteristics will hold for a year or for a decade. The concepts are nevertheless not to be ignored by the educator.

Details from a number of sociological research projects have been combined for the following descriptions:

The Upper Classes. Less than 5 per cent of the population.

1. A relatively self-conscious, "high-society" group including the oldest although not always the wealthiest families. They be-

lieve in birth and breeding. Money is important to them because it allows them to live properly.

2. Families of more recently acquired wealth, high professionals, owners of capital, large merchants, manufacturers, and bankers are included here, and they spend money largely to acquire rank and power. They have control of local politics, own homes in the best districts, and travel widely. They are conservative and stable, and they have small families.

The Middle Classes. About 35 to 40 per cent of the population.

1. Upper Middle. Families now acquiring wealth, most professionals, independent small producers, executives, and merchants fill this class. They believe in money and in comfort and are aggressive in business and social life and in civic life and churches, holding as high as 75 per cent of positions in these fields. They believe in education and are largely college trained. They marry in the middle twenties, have at least two children, and seldom get divorces.

2. Lower Middle. Merchants, white-collar workers, small business men, a few professionals, some skilled and semiskilled workers. They believe that money and morals are the keys to all their problems. They tend to own their own homes, usually in desirable but not preferred areas, and to have stereotyped home furnishings. They usually own a car. They are often first-generation families, marry a little earlier than do the higher classes, and have at least three children. They usually go through high school and sometimes to college.

The "Working" Classes. Well over half of the population.

1. The semiskilled laborers, some white-collar workers, and some skilled workers. They are ambitious, believe in education, and use their money for neat-looking clothes, magazines, and other symbols of higher status. There are many broken families, and girls marry in the late teens and have about four children. They do little civic or community work. Approximately a third of the population.

2. Semiskilled and unskilled workers, families on relief, transients. They are passive and fatalistic, live in poor homes in the poorest areas, and have five or six children per mother. Their education is limited to elementary schools, and nine tenths have no active church connection. Few have telephones or cars. Their social life consists in visiting one another, attending movies, gambling, and drinking. Money is to be spent, not saved, and

is important because it shuts the door on the ever-present wolf. As much as a fourth of our people are found in this group.

Not only the class descriptions but more especially the proportion of the population to be found in each class is of the greatest importance for the educational planner and counselor, and he must also keep in mind the correlated data in regard to the proportion of children in each class (8 per cent of all the children are in the upper classes and 90 per cent of them go to college; 30 per cent are in the middle classes, with 15 per cent going to college; and 60 per cent are in the lower classes, with 5 per cent going to college).

How many members of the lower or lower middle classes will be studying such data and helping the upper and middle classes in the planning of their own educational progress? Which classes furnish us with our college professors and counselors, our high school teachers and administrators? From what classes are drawn the readers of this book? And the readers of all the books and articles on educational planning and counseling? Can parents know the classes from which each individual college draws its students, and do they care whether or not their daughters meet members of all classes? Or do they prefer to protect them from a too intimate knowledge of divergent classes? Is it not important that every intelligent woman be concerned with these facts and figures as she plans her own educational program and considers the program and problems of other women and other daughters?

In spite of all the facts and figures produced by the social scientists, most of the thinking about women's education centers around the popular social construct of *the* American Woman, which is based on the upper- or upper-middle-class woman. The older etiquette books were addressed to these women, and in the current women's magazines—*Harper's Bazaar, Vogue, Mademoiselle, Charm, Ladies' Home Journal, Woman's Home Companion, McCall's, House Beautiful*, and others—in both the editorial and the fiction sections and especially in the advertising sections, the woman described and pictured is from these two classes: in other words, a woman who represents only about 15 per cent of our population.

The women which the advertisements present are probably what Americans like to think they are or could be; otherwise the products wouldn't sell. "The illusions of society are often contradicted by cold figures, but the illusions have their own reality which, in a way, complements the statistical tables, and it takes a look at both to round out the scene." [2]

For example, only the approved occupations ever appear in the advertisements. These always exclude factory workers, domestic servants, shopgirls, beauty parlor operators, elevator operators, seamstresses, and waitresses. Curiously enough, the largest professional group of women, the teachers, do not appear at all, nor do librarians, social workers, or researchers. The office worker is well represented, and actresses, nurses, physicians, and models are also included.

But of course the dominant figure is the housewife. This creature does all her own work, but invariably looks completely beautiful and well dressed. The typical American family includes a "happy little woman, happy little children, all spotless or sticky in the jam-pot, framed against dimity curtains in the windows or decalcomania flowers on the cupboard doors . . . in a world without tragedy, a world of new two-door sedans, and Bendix washers, and reproductions of hunting prints over the living room mantel. It is a world in which the ingenuity and patience of the housewife are equalled only by the fidelity of her husband and his love of home, pipe, and radio. It is a world that smells of soap. But it is a world of ambition as well, the constant striving for a better way of life—better furniture, bigger refrigerators, more books in the bookcase, more evenings at the movies. To the advertisers, this is Americanism." [3]

Can anyone describe with any degree of accuracy what the women from the lower classes are like? We know of course that 60 per cent of our school children are hers, but what does she wear, and what are her clubs? What are her entertainments, her working hours, her ambitions? Are her social and moral codes different from those of the classes above her? What are *her* problems, her income? How many children are there in her family and how far do they go in school?

If we have not enough data on these questions, it will be very important and not too difficult for us to find out, each of us for herself. Drive slowly and carefully through some underprivileged residential areas, spend more time as a volunteer worker for a social agency, work a few days a month at the community center, ask for the political job that calls for ringing the doorbells in the foreign areas. The one thing we shall certainly observe is that there is no typical pattern. There will be the usual difference in moral codes, for some of these neighbors will be devoted followers of the more conservative religious sects and others will never have been inside a church. Differences will be apparent in taste and cleanliness, in outlook and attitude, as well as in range of income and efficiency in spending.

We may get some notion of the entertainment values and standards of these women from the mass media of movies and radio and comic books, which are easily available to all. Case histories may be read in the textbooks used by professional social workers. And some research studies have given detailed descriptions or analyzed a few of the more measurable differences.

It has been found, for example, that the lower classes accept more aggressive behavior and are more tolerant of fighting, for in the socializing process the immediate rewards in terms of gang prestige, freedom of movement, and property gain all seem to be on the side of street culture. Lower-class mothers usually marry at a somewhat earlier than average age and more of the children are breast fed and are weaned at a later age. Their toilet training is begun later and completed later. They take naps less frequently, are allowed to attend movies alone earlier, and may stay out later. They follow the more marginal sex codes. They are not expected to help at home, to cook or sew or help with younger children as early as middle-class children, but they are expected to get a job after school and to leave school for a job at an earlier age.[4]

The view that American education is a heroic attempt to raise to the middle class the great masses of lower-status children gains meaning as we see more precisely the differing values and viewpoints of the several classes. The objectives and the lessons which fit one class of children may not be appropriate for those of another status, and the question of whose child must be accommodated, whose child is most dependent on the school for all his education, becomes a vital one. Motivation in the lower layers lies only in the social and biological punishments of lower status, and failure is rarely a tangible fact but only a matter of evaluation, the felt difference (if you can feel it) between what you expect and what you get, what you demand of yourself and what you actually do.

All these matters become important when education sets up its goals and objectives. For how many classroom students are "Think!" "Be patient," "Be reasonable" ineffective admonitions? The full understanding of the different ideologies of socioeconomic strata in our society gives even more force to Thorndike's classic understatement that it often requires great ingenuity to maneuver a person into having a certain idea, even greater into a desirable act, and still greater to lure him into responding because of a desirable emotion or attitude.

It is in this realm of relative intangibles that educational thinking becomes most difficult and obscure. The technological changes which have affected women's daily regime are easy to comprehend, but all of them produce corresponding inner states of mind, attitudes, and feelings which are as significant as they are elusive. The codes of manners and morals, the attitudes of men toward woman as she gains greater freedom and mobility, her own attitudes and those of her children, have changed no less considerably than the more palpable factors in her life.

The key to the understanding and manipulation of these forces lies in the acceptance of their mutability. The faster tempo and the radical nature of the economic, psychological, political, and sociological shifts of the last century are its most striking features. Only with the greatest difficulty can modern woman keep abreast of the innovations most important to her, and she must reconcile herself to a continuing state of uncertainty in regard to them.

"Emerging" is the best we can say about these codes and ideologies which we had hoped would give us the stability we require. Evidently we must adjust our thinking to the concept of a growing world, full of complex social institutions and forces and trends, all of them developing at irregular rates of speed and overlapping one another's territories. If we can grasp this concept of wide differentials in the growth rate of movements and forces and can recognize the unequal effect upon them of political upheavals (wars and depressions) and of technological advances (television, the automobile, the laundromat, the atom bomb), we may still see an orderliness in our world, though of a different kind, and may be able to accept the possibility of control by newly devised methods.

For example, such factors as the success of the suffrage movement, the spread of coeducation, the taking over of many domestic duties by public service enterprises (food canning and preservation, clothing manufacture and care), and the technical employment expansion in two world wars have greatly increased the scope of women's activities and have strengthened and enhanced the roles they may play. The woman legislator whose husband and children took over the management of the home as well as the campaign may have been a rarity, but she was an actuality. Some hard-working women do serve as editors or designers at five-figure salaries and also enjoy a glamorous home and family life. Other women not only stand beside men on the assembly lines, but alternate with their husbands in the daily round of shopping and child care. The proportion of women in the labor force maintains its continuous upward trend.

To view modern times as a great tangle of trends and forces in constant flux may help us to resist the persistent temptation to shout "chaos" and "crisis," and then, as the crescendo flows out of us, to murmur "inevitable" and "hopeless." True, the present decade, *any* present decade, sees the forces in conflict rise to seemingly overpowering heights of complexity. Wars are not local but global; the color of margarine leaves a trail from the farm all the way to the senate chamber; prices spiral upward and taxes shower downward. And all the gruesome details are laid at our doorstep, with fresh headlines, every morning.

But these truths are not necessarily colossal; it is the headlines, not the facts, that do the screaming. A more academic approach is more rewarding, for it means taking a searching look at the nature of our values, at all the things we want, at the way they get us into conflict.

Values arise because preference is a fundamental human trait, and confusion is the price we pay for our preferences. No two individuals have exactly the same set of values, but in America each accepts the other's as very real, grants him freedom in pursuing them, and adjusts as best he can. Those values that occur most frequently, and are held most commonly, constitute the culture pattern, which no human being can escape.

Preferences or values are linked to the group memberships each of us holds, and we are each a member of many groups whose values are different, even conflicting. The individual will therefore be confronted with the problem of finding some of his values irreconcilable. He can assuage or minimize the discrepancies, but he cannot abolish them. Sooner or later he is forced to the conclusion that he wants a certain value only if too much of it does not eliminate something else that he also wants. He wants complete freedom, but only if he can have it in conjunction with as much security as he needs; he wants truth only if it also allows him peace of mind; education, but not at the expense of other pleasures; a career only if it will also permit marriage and children.

Every mature woman develops conflicts within herself as she functions first in one group, then in another. Her own pleasant economic security may receive a sudden jolt when she studies the struggles of the less privileged; her experience as a consumer may nudge out some of her conservatism; her scientific sophistication fences briskly with her Christian convictions. There must always be a hierarchy among values, and it is one's experience of conflict among preferences that leads to acceptance of the fact that no value can be absolutely supreme. It is an unappreciated sociological commonplace that absolute values would make it impossible to have any society at all.

It is in this perspective that we must consider one of the undercurrents of conflict that has been accumulating force from the beginning of the century: the attitude of men toward the newer freedom of women.

A hundred years ago there was so little variety in women's activities that most men were not conscious of having any particular attitude toward women's freedom. But as the new roles for women grew more varied and substantial, the attitudes of men toward them became more sharply differentiated, maturing eventually into a recognizable body of ideas and arguments, often tinged with strong feeling. Today these controversies call for partisanships on the part of both men and women. Not all men hold the unfavorable views, but on the other hand, not all women repudiate them. And allegiances on one side or the other frequently shift as both men and women identify the sources of their opinions and vary their perspectives.

The "War between the Men and the Women," as Thurber likes to put it in his captions, will continue to be a cold war, and the sociologists can pin down its boundaries quite precisely: conflict between the sexes is inevitable whenever customary roles and statuses are threatened. In this case it is the man's earning capacity, his political power, his freedom of opportunity, his monopoly on the places of eminence, that are now challenged by women. The humorists as well as the social scientists take different views of the outcome. Thurber quips that "the most frightening study of mankind is man. I think he has failed to run the world and that women must take over if the species is to survive." Kin Hubbard was skeptical, but that was some twenty-five years ago: "Wouldn't th' way things are goin' these days make a fine argyment for woman suffrage if we didn' already have it?"

"Men," explains Ordway Tead more seriously, "broadly speaking, immersed in their own aggressive drives for creativity and for ego-maximizing in a competitive society, do not seem ready on as wide a scale as necessary to realize the deep roots of the woman's dilemma. Hence they do not do what they might as husbands and as citizens to help alleviate the contributing causes. There are still vast accumulations of male pride, possessiveness, false social standards, self centeredness, and fearfulness of job competition, which aggravate the over-all social picture that women confront. These are a part of the social pattern they encounter. There is no solution, as affecting these negative masculine forces, which can come without frank collaboration and a truer equal fellowship between the sexes both in the home and in the marketplace." [5]

Simone de Beauvoir in *The Second Sex* puts the matter less delicately: "We shall not permit ourselves to be intimidated by the number and violence of the attacks launched against women, nor to be entrapped by the selfseeking eulogies bestowed on the 'true woman,' nor to profit by the enthusiasm for women's destiny manifested by men who would not for the world have any part in it." [6]

"Emancipation" is the traditional but inaccurate concept for describing the changing status which the years have brought for women. It implies a previous bondage which most women did not feel. They were not enslaved either by men or by circumstances. The status of all human beings is determined by their environment, is in fact kept in equilibrium by their living conditions, by the mutual compatibility of all their wants. In the earlier centuries the status of women was satisfactory to them, and they did not feel enslaved, because the circumstances of their lives permitted their wants to be fulfilled.

Mental attitudes grow out of social stimuli as naturally as physical tolerances emerge from climate, disease, foods, etc. Women, and also men, are now readjusting their thinking because circumstances in the economic and industrial world have changed. The women are more sharply affected by and naturally more sensitive to these changes than the men, who are preoccupied with their own new stresses: military hazards, business competition, family responsibilities.

When the Industrial Revolution began to minimize the roles of men in preparing food and clothing for their families and in educating the children, they met no resistance in assuming new functions: voting for government officials, joining business associations and trade-unions, participating in social welfare activities, occasionally going to war, and establishing new routines of work to earn the family living outside the home. But when similar pressures slowly encompassed the women's functions and forced them to new roles, they met strong opposition both from men and from many of their own sex. This is partly because the changes have occurred so gradually throughout the last century and a half that most women have failed to realize their actuality and the urgency of dealing with them. It is due also to a cultural lag which has led writers, clergymen, politicians, advertisers, even educators, to postpone the issues by assuming that woman's only significant role is homemaking long after she has become important in activities outside the home.

The resistances of men for the most part stem from competition in employment, and it is the large numbers of unemployed women, those "contented housewives," experiencing the competition only vicariously, whose opinions are most like the men's. Simone de Beauvoir, although she cannot excuse the men for their unfairness, scores the women even more vigorously: "The financier, the captain of industry, sometimes even the military leader, know toil and care, they assume risks; they buy privileges in an unfair market, but at least they pay for them in person. But their wives give nothing in exchange for all they get; on this account they believe in their indefensible rights with so much the blinder faith. Their vain arrogance, their radical incapability, their obstinate ignorance, make them the most useless nonentities ever produced by the human species." [7]

That is an extreme indictment, but the contented housewife really does do an injustice both to herself and to her working sister when she remains indifferent to the sharpening issues and laments the vanishing of eighteenth-century gentility. The gentlewoman of this century will emerge with all the poise and tolerance born of unfettered understanding. She will, if called upon to do so, banish the last trace of priggishness from her thinking and face with equanimity the woman taxi driver and the women's baseball teams. She will forgive the arrogance of men because of their long ingrown traditional advantages; she will nevertheless set about undermining these advantages because she must above all create for herself a new function to replace her lost opportunities for self-fulfillment in homemaking. Indifference or resentment she cannot afford, for either attitude would close the door to the creative spirit and to the needed understanding.

Men and women alike must examine their attitudes on this issue as impersonally as possible. How much in the arguments is emotion and how much is logic? How much is fact, and how much is only defense of one's personal stake in maintaining the status quo, or in altering it? Are we defending values that fit the changing times, or values that are artificially bolstered by vested interests, in much the same manner as commodity prices are kept above their natural levels by tariffs and subsidies?

Outworn slogans ("there is always room at the top") and obsolescent ideas ("woman's place is in the home") may be used to disguise the pursuits of special and aggressive groups who count on the inertia of the masses and the efficacy of propaganda. Unquestioned values are a doubtful asset, no matter how respectably ancient they may be. Values should be inventoried as often and as painstakingly as are material goods.

There will continue to be more heat than light in this controversy until men and women recognize the fact that woman's concern about her place in the modern world is not dictated by mere perversity or caprice. She has a real problem, created by social changes for which she is in no way responsible. She is truly troubled by her need, as great as man's, to find a way of maintaining her inner, psychic satisfactions, spiritually as well as materially.

For those women in that 50 per cent of our population who are church affiliated, religion still holds the answer. Many blue-collar workers have found their spiritual satisfactions in the collective drive for class and group advancement, although their children, and even their wives, may not be able to relax in this solution. But the white-collar workers, especially the ambitious and intelligent college or professional women, still cherish the individualistic spirit and hope to enhance whatever they may have of wealth, power, and status with esthetic or spiritual overtones.

For these women divine approbation and recognition of service are not enough; emotional demands for beauty, for peace of mind, are no longer satisfied with only religious ecstasy. Woman, even more than man, must express herself creatively in some service to society, and must have approbation and recognition *from other individuals* for this contribution. She must find fulfillment in the rituals and sanctions of society as well as in the sanctions of her spiritual faith.

With the range of roles that are offered to modern woman, what stands in the way of her satisfying all these drives? Love, appreciation, and approbation she could achieve through devoted service to her family, but the family will fail her after a few decades, and it might crowd out the contribution she could make to society through a career in one of the arts, which she needs for other satisfactions. She could forgo the economic or artistic recognition if she were allowed to build with others in the political arena, but this is too difficult for her because of the man-made pressures and prejudices against it. She could contribute to the material security of her family if she could count on getting back into economic production after her child-rearing period is completed, but she finds it too difficult to keep open her bridges into the outside world during that period of heavy responsibilities, and she is also hampered by the difficulties that any person over forty encounters in breaking into the employment field.

In contrast to the man's simpler problems of achieving self-worth and self-expression, woman's struggles acquire a truly heroic quality.

The solution is certainly not capitulation to convention and retreat into preoccupation with husband and home. This withdrawal from the struggle requires of her less energy and initiative, but it accepts a personality that is one-sided and stultified and that will become more so as age confirms it. It is a wasteful retrogression, a pernicious kind of isolationism, when the modern trend is toward one world for men and women, toward a fraternity of interests and activities.

Surrender is the unpardonable sin for women, because the thinking of our democratic society rests on the concept of individual worth. Fuller participation in every field—economic, political, artistic, and religious—is the only answer. The unions, the schools, the church, social service, and civil service offer the necessary means of fulfillment for women. That their progress toward equality of opportunity will be slow we take for granted, but that they stand ready in the face of opposition to make sure that every avenue of development is kept open is the least we can ask of them, or they of themselves.

No woman can forgo this particularly necessary feminine brand of restless openmindedness. Until a woman has passed her eightieth birthday, too much tranquillity is suspect; it smacks of weakness and regression.

Does all this ferment of change and conflict mean that education should continue to prepare the woman for her traditional role? Or for a role which would make her a happier and more productive member of society? Does it mean that we accept our traditional world as the best possible and divinely predestined? Is it the responsibility of twentieth-century educators to perpetuate it exactly as it has always been? Or do modern technology and modern attitudes toward the worth and responsibilities of each individual point in new directions?

Margaret Mead and others have preached the gospel of cultural relativism particularly in the man-woman relationships, and the sermon has been heard and for the most part accepted by literate persons everywhere. But the mere acknowledgment that the origins of the relations between the sexes are primarily cultural is in itself only a static doctrine. Donald Adams regrets that there has been "little writing of a creative kind which has really come to grips with the matter of how important this changing relationship is; almost no writing which can be described as constructive . . . little general comprehension among our writers that women in their struggle toward readjustment—a struggle which men forced upon them when they brought the industrial age into being—have now arrived at a crucial point, beyond which they cannot go without men's understanding and help." [8]

In the matter of sex differences and sex conflict the period of scientific exploration is passing and the task of the educator may take some new directions. The shift to the positive and creative phases will not be easy, and requires preparation of two kinds. There must be training for those who will write the new fiction, paint and compose in new idioms, set the new fashions in philosophy and behavior and love. But even more important will be the education of great new audiences for these artists, audiences of both men and women who can and will turn their backs on the false images perpetuated by the mass media to satisfy their appetites on more genuine fare. In undertaking this new and double function, liberal education faces a truly formidable task.

... 4

Education for Earning

IF WE were to choose the outstanding problem among the many which women face today, it would certainly be that of women's employment. This issue affects all the other attitudes, frustrations, and maladjustments in the life of the modern woman.

The lack of genuine parity in employment is by all odds the most sensitive point of controversy, the basic grievance of women, and it evokes the greatest antagonism and resentment from men as well as from that most helpful ally of the men's point of view, the contented housewife. The man whose pay check supports the family and the woman whose full time job is to cash that pay check, spend it wisely, and supplement it with her own faithful household tasks cannot tolerate having any mere petticoat competition draw the same salary for the same work. This sturdy team of breadwinner and housewife has needs much greater than those of the individual woman. The better this worker is, the more their own earnings are endangered. Her cleverness, her good looks, her very presence in the office, are a threat to their domestic security and felicity.

We venture to say that if every woman could be educated to a realization of the drawbacks and heartbreaks she will encounter in the employment field, more could be accomplished in solving her problems of mental health, of legal status, and of opportunity for wholesome personal growth than by any other method. An awareness of the importance of such education and the corresponding need for concerted action for equal employment opportunities for women are basic to effective strategy in every other area of women's problems.

It is logical and feasible to begin the study of women's difficulties with an exploration of their earning activities, for here it is easier to find the facts and to agree on methods and goals than would be the case with most of the roles which women play. It might be quite a task, for example, to arrive at solid agreement among women of various ages, social classes, and diverse religious convictions on the exact nature of the role women should play in building social standards or in establishing the arts on a firmer footing or in educating for a democratic world. But the economic goals for women are more obvious and more concrete: better working conditions, equal pay for equal work, access to the executive as well as the minor positions in business and the professions.

For the educational and promotional methods needed to achieve such well-defined and acceptable goals, readily available patterns can be found in our culture. One might speculate, for example, on what would happen if the same amount of money and energy, of sound psychology and clever propaganda, were put into a campaign to sell the seventy-five million or more American women on the idea of equal opportunity in the employment field as is lavished each year on advertising by the fashion experts, beauticians, and cosmetologists to sell the ideas of dress and grooming. If this hypothetical plan were really undertaken, it would, without a doubt, convince women (and of course men would be sold in the process) of their own importance as participants in the real work of the world. The consequences of such a campaign would transcend even the advertisers' powers of description.

Almost any program advocating change is bound to stir up controversy. The sources of resistance to the more realistic campaigns for equal opportunity in employment for women are not difficult to uncover, for they pervade all professions, ages, and classes of society. No woman need go farther than her own intimate family group and her own circle of business or professional colleagues to collect the evidence. Complacency, competitive envy, half-hearted laziness, evasion, equivocation—these, like charity, all begin at home.

Here are just a few of the "old familiars" proffered by the opposition: "If a woman is really good, she can get to the top as well as a man." "Why should women be paid as much as men when they aren't supporting families?" "We tried a woman in this department once, and she was very difficult." "Working mothers are the cause of juvenile delinquency." "I still think that someone has to take the primary responsibility for the home and that someone has to be the woman." "But you don't mean that you really think that women should be represented on the town council?" "After all, wouldn't you rather work for a man than a woman?"

All these objections stem from the theory still so prevalent in our society of the dominance of men. The sociologists have a special term for this ideology—the androcentric theory. This concept has become, throughout the centuries, so deep-seated and all-pervasive that it is almost impossible for any individual, however rational and objective, to escape its influence. To be free of this tradition would mean to have no qualification or reservation in favor of our present societal patterns, no feeling of security in the status quo, no insistence that there be only men in the coal pits or in the White House or in those positions which absorb the brunt of the stress and strain of competition. To be completely objective would also mean to disallow any argument for dilatory procedures in attacking the problems, to eschew those phrases which, though praising the excellence of the goals to be attained, lament the crudeness of forthright attacks on them.

Such freedom from prejudice is of course purely hypothetical, for no member of a society can pull himself out of the very mold which fashioned him. But the exercise is invigorating, and the search for that mythical unprejudiced individual is as sporting a proposition, it seems to us, as any other pursuit which the more tough-minded intellectual adventurer may engage in. If such an experience takes a woman only a little deeper into the interior of her own thoughts and feelings, it may be enlightening as well as frightening. From that adventure she may return to hunt out with more merciless skill the counterprejudices of friends and acquaintances.

Social scientists have traced the process of prejudice in many spheres of social life. They have developed the methods for exposing its roots both in the psychology of the individual and in the social constructs of the culture in which those individuals move. Intelligent planners should know the most modern and acceptable means for measuring and manipulating attitudes and for evaluating the effectiveness of a variety of strategies in different types of communities, with persons and groups of various ages, classes, and professions. This is no field for amateurs.

Women leaders who are interested in crusading for better employment opportunities have discovered that many avenues of attack are needed. All the factors involved—the workers themselves, the jobs, the employers, the markets— must be analyzed and reorganized. But fundamental to all of these factors is the essential nature, the values and traditions, of the society in which they are embedded. The intelligent procedure when one is faced with hostile attitudes lies not in the old-fashioned, belligerent onslaught, but in an efficient search for the causes behind the symptoms.

Much can be learned about the successes and failures of dealing with these accumulated and deep-seated hostilities by studying the analogous problems of race or religious prejudice. In many aspects, working women constitute just another so-called "minority group," and their difficulties in raising their status and improving their opportunities would find a parallel in those already uncovered by the extensive research on the problems of the Negro and the Jew. Formal training in sociology usually includes a course with such a title as "Assimilation of Minority

Peoples," in which the student may discover the sources of hostility and the implications of prejudice for the welfare of our society, as well as methods for eliminating them. The study of women's problems should be added to the course and more women students urged to take it.

Presumably the education of the younger generation is one of the most important forces in the eventual elimination of the attitudes which act as deterrents to our national and social welfare, among which would be included the prejudices against the professional or business woman who is finding it necessary to engage in work outside the home. She is working in order to fulfill either her financial needs or those of her whole personality These are justifiable needs, and they will become increasingly valid for larger numbers of women in the expanding technology of our society. A thoughtful campaign for equality in employment opportunities for women, using the best psychological and sociological methods, is therefore imperative.

If a social emergency should begin to cause pressure for a solution of this employment problem of women, as it does in times of war and other catastrophies, such a campaign against traditional hostilities could be carried out with less resistance than in normal times. There is so much fundamental dislocation during periods of crisis and unrest that change is the accepted outcome of the general upheaval.

Wars and other disturbances have proved most advantageous in supplying new outlets for the ranks of women workers. The Civil War brought women into the classroom and gave nursing its initial impetus. World War I established women as skilled factory operatives, and World War II vindicated the right of the married woman to work. Per contra, depressions or recessions are the most dreaded threat for women's progress. Full employment has not as yet stood the test of truly peaceful times, but whenever the test does come, women stand to suffer earliest and longest. Minority groups are the last to be hired, the first to be fired. Test polls will again show the sentiment against them, and all the long-forgotten, unfavorable legislation will be refurbished for passage. Twenty-six states proposed bills against the married working woman in the dying years of the depression, and only the manpower shortage of World War II rescued them in the nick of time.

Leaders in women's education have the responsibility for preparing our younger generation of students to capitalize on the situations that unrest creates. As always, the job of preparation should be the concern of men as well as of women, especially of men who are leaders in education, but common sense dictates that women will accomplish their ends more quickly if they take the lead themselves. They will discover that there is much to enjoy as well as to learn in such leadership.

Social action of this kind begins with an analysis of the underlying forces and the preconditions for success. These prescribe that the objective must be socially desirable and sincerely believed in and that while individual leadership may initiate the action, large supporting groups are essential to its fulfillment. Social workers have usually acquired experience in research, in testing their hypotheses with statistical studies, and in establishing alliances with sympathetic groups to search out the opposition and to effect strategic compromises. Labor unions are also accumulating experience and techniques for social and political action. Both these groups have been training leaders among women who could be of tremendous assistance in educating the new generation of students. Facts and figures, principles and procedures, are the necessary background for both understanding and action.

The Women's Bureau of the federal government makes available monthly four mimeographed pages summarizing the facts on women workers.[1] Not as alluring or as widely read as the monthly *Vogue* or other magazines for women, they are basic to a constructive or mature viewpoint on the whole field of women's employment.

The periodic snapshot of the immediate employment situation is never so revealing as the study of its long-time trends. In

December 1952 there were about fifty-eight million women over fourteen years of age in the United States. One third of them, or close to twenty million, are technically in the labor force—that is, either at work or seeking a job—and of these, all but a half million are actually working. The twenty million women workers represent 32% of all workers, men and women. In 1900, women comprised only 18% of the total number of workers, and even as recently as 1940, only 25%. Their peak year was, of course, 1945, when the increased need for workers pushed the figure up to 36%.

Considered in the longest possible time perspective, women's employment is the final step in the two-century-old revolution—both industrial and social—which has drawn all manufacture out of the home and into the factory and has transformed the guilds into labor unions. The technological unemployment which has overtaken the woman in the home is fully as real as that of the weaver or the coal miner who has been displaced by the machine. The forces which have created and the consequences which have resulted from the relentless social revolution are most vital to woman.

Technological improvements have released her from such tasks as still remain within the home. She gets diaper service, lives on canned vegetables and frozen fruits, and buys ready-made clothing for herself and her family. The time thus saved enables her to design and sell clothes commercially, do social work, or teach school.

The decline of the birth rate has reduced the proportion of her family-occupied time and has helped to transform her whole philosophy of life and mode of daily living. The last of her children is born when she is, on the average, not yet thirty years old. At this age, with more than half of her total life span before her, she quite understandably still feels the urge for self-fulfillment in the outside world.

Broad educational training in the public schools has brought a wider variety of occupations actually within her grasp. She travels freely and is therefore not dependent on local employment or apprenticeships for her work and her training.

The trend away from the farms toward urbanization and away from the small town toward suburbanization has broken her isolation, awakened her desire for outside work, and supplied the means for satisfying the desire. It has provoked her appetite for more of the world's goods and given her the means to acquire them for herself.

Mass production has opened many old and new jobs for the erstwhile housewife; she has become a skilled operator on many an assembly line. Electric motors have taken the place of brawn and muscle and have eliminated one of the greatest sources of her unequal competition with men. She types, takes dictation, and runs the business machines; she gives manicures and permanent waves.

Obviously modern woman is both pulled and pushed into the labor force. The pull is the opportunity for employment at attractive wages under good working conditions. These opportunities are at a maximum in boom periods, in metropolitan districts, and for the younger woman who has mobility, versatility, and skills. They are at a minimum in depressed periods, in rural areas, and for the older woman who has been too long absent from the labor market. The push is economic necessity, insufficient funds to meet the new family needs, and the rise in cash outlay needed to maintain current higher standards of living and of leisure.

Simply stated, women work for essentially the same reasons that men do. "Women's wages are part of the purchasing power of the community," the Women's Bureau reminds us, "and for maximum prosperity America needs both men and women workers." The one clear reason why women now seek gainful employment outside the home is the same reason that their mothers and grandmothers had for the daily round of tasks performed inside the home. Then as now, women worked to provide the things that were needed for daily existence. In pioneer days women cultivated and preserved the food for the family; they wove cloth and sewed by hand the garments worn by themselves and their families; and they performed the multitudinous and laborious housekeeping tasks. In the modern industrial economy, women work to help earn the money needed to purchase food processed outside the home, to buy clothing made in factories from machine-made materials, and to procure the labor-saving devices which remove drudgery from the upkeep of their homes.

Eight out of ten women assert that they work to earn a living. If they live in family households, ninety-eight out of every hundred contribute regularly to household expenses. Well over half of the women in trade-unions report that they spend every dollar of their wages for daily living. "In the face of these facts," Frieda Miller, formerly of the Women's Bureau, has argued, "there would seem to be no doubt that women are entitled to the widest opportunities for training in order to make the most of themselves as employed persons and to discharge their financial obligations to their dependents." [2]

Framing sound policies for educating women calls for an intimate look at the composition of the women's labor force. Of the fifty-eight million women in the United States, the proportion who work has been steadily rising, in fact rising phenomenally in the past half century. The figure was 10% in 1870, 17% in 1890, 25% by 1910 (holding through World War I and the depression of the thirties), 27% in 1940, 31% in 1950, and 33% and 34% in 1951 and 1952 respectively. Where do they work? How old are they? What are they paid? What are their problems? The answers to these questions should certainly be of interest to educators.

There tends to be a concentration of women workers in the younger and the older age groups. Half of the women 18 to 24 years of age are in the labor force. Only about a third of the women in the next age group, 25 to 34, are workers; but two fifths of the women from 35 to 54 are on the payrolls. There has been a 60% increase for the middle-aged group in the last ten years, and in the same period the percentage for the still older group, 55 to 64, has more than doubled.

The important fact indicated by these figures is the great rise in employment among the older groups. In earlier decades it was usual for women aged 20 to 24 to have the highest proportion of workers, but top-heaviness in employment of the younger group has been steadily diminishing. After World War II, when the soldiers were reunited with their young wives, most of the decline took place among the ranks of the young women, accelerating the growth in importance of the older workers.

Prophecy can be read from these figures. Young women without children who enter the ranks of the employed tend to stay on through their middle years; young married women who drop out to rear their families come right back to the labor market when the children are older. Young women are not only conscious of their current needs, but they are also growing concerned about their later vocational needs; they will expect educational leaders to anticipate their requirements.

In 1950 more than half of all women workers were married, 33% were single, and 16% widowed or divorced. It was the World War II years which brought the greatest gain in married workers—from 36% in 1940 to 44% in 1944, and on up to 51% today. One out of every four married women is in the labor force; of more than seven million couples both spouses were at work in 1950, which is exactly *double the number for 1940.* The Women's Bureau assures us that these seven million working wives constitute one of the most *overworked* groups in our total population. The high school senior needs as good a grasp of these basic facts and of the social attitudes and sacrifices involved as she does of the more specific principles or skills of her chosen vocation.

In 1940 there were only 3 of the 451 occupations listed by the United States Bureau of the Census in which women had not worked: locomotive engineer and fireman, and fire fighter. By this time some adventurous women may have closed even this small gap. Other pioneer women have made history in public life, business, and the professions. There have been many women in the diplomatic service, even an ambassador and a minister.

Eleven women are in the national congress and 236 in state legislatures, and many are mayors in both large and small cities. Women edit magazines and newspapers. One woman is vice-president of an airline, one was in charge of manpower in Washington, and one is president of a giant department store. There are many women lawyers, judges, and physicians. And we are never allowed to forget those four women cabinet members among the four or five hundred men cabinet members of our republic's long history.

Although the scope of women's employment has broadened, the Women's Bureau reminds us that it is the woman lawyer, the woman scientist, or the woman business executive who is the exception in the present world of women's work: "Less than 500 women are employed in each of the more glamorous occupations such as airplane stewardess, actress, radio commentator, photographer. Even after 100 years of emancipation women represent less than five per cent of such high-grade professional groups as doctors, dentists, engineers, chemists, architects, lawyers and certified public accountants."

It is easy to understand why the professional group, constituting only 8 per cent of the total labor force, has claimed the largest part of the attention of mothers and their teen-age daughters; even the teachers and the curriculum makers are often preoccupied with this group. Those of the professional group are themselves the leaders among employed women; their occupations are enticing; they make news, and usually good news; they need and deserve our most generous attention. For total planning, however, the general distribution of the other 92 per cent of working women has at least an equal significance.

Circumstances have caused women to become concentrated in a relatively few occupations, roughly, in order of frequency, as follows: clerical (typists, secretaries, and other office workers), operative (especially apparel), service (beauticians, waitresses, housekeepers, servants), professional (teachers, nurses, technicians), and sales. The actual percentages of people in a few of the categories will demonstrate some of the occupational differences between men and women in the labor force.

	Per Cent of All Women Workers	Per Cent of All Men Workers
Clerical and kindred workers.......	27	6
Service workers	21	7
Managers, officials, proprietors.....	6	12
Craftsmen, foremen, etc............	1.3	19
Laborers	0.6	10

Further analysis would show that in the small proportion of women classified as laborers, or as foremen and craftsmen, the variety as well as the number is restricted in comparison to the situation for men. This greater homogeneity of the women workers makes vocational planning, which of course is quite a different thing from educational planning, a bit simpler for them.

For how many of these jobs do women need specific training *in the schools and colleges?* For the professional group and for most of the managers and proprietors (about 14%), higher education is quite obviously a prerequisite. A minimum of typing and stenography is also clearly indicated for some, but not all, of the clerical group—perhaps for a little more than half of the 27%. For the 60% who are operators, laborers, service workers, and saleswomen, only on-the-job learning is necessary. In other words, about 30% of the more than nineteen million workers need vocational training in their formal school work, which means that 70% (about fourteen million of them), plus all the nonworking population, or roughly more than 80% of all the young women in our secondary schools and colleges, need primarily general, not specifically vocational, training. This figure is only an approximation, but it gains some credence from the economists' conventional statement that 80% of all jobs can be learned in three months.

Several questions arise that are of particular importance in the education of professional workers (teachers, nurses, technicians, managers, and proprietors): What proportion of their formal college work should be assigned to their job requirements?

What part of their formal education is most responsible for their ascent from the routine to the more responsible and remunerative positions?

Preoccupation with the training aspects of women's employment has crowded out some of the other questions which are pertinent, if our objectives include not only larger economic income but also higher psychic income, greater satisfactions, and better adjustments. Vocational guidance might ignore the following questions, but true educational guidance cannot afford to neglect them.

1. Are the earnings of women workers sufficient to maintain them at acceptable levels? Professional and trade-union workers are perhaps fairly well accommodated in this respect, but what about the waitresses? And how much does the mistress pay her humble household help? One remembers the statement of Eliza's father in Shaw's *Pygmalion*: To the question, "Haven't you any morals?" he replies, "Certainly not. I can't afford them." Can the waitress "afford" the appropriate standards in morals and manner? The typist riding the subway, the model with her hatbox, the salesgirl with her bright lips and ready smile—do they earn enough to resist temptation? Do they receive regular advancement and seniority status, equal pay and equal privileges? Especially as the higher age groups fill the working ranks this question becomes more pressing.

Minimum wages, health, working hours, and working conditions are of vital concern to all women. Most of the gains in these directions have been won by women in the trade-unions. They have worked consistently not only for higher wages but for safety at work, paid vacations, health insurance, and maternity leaves, and through their efforts women have been given important opportunities to develop their capacity for leadership. But as in so many fields for women, "most of the road lies ahead." Nor are the attendant difficulties minimized by past successes. In the nineteenth-century campaigns, it was fairly easy to enlist support and sympathy from at least a few of the prosperous and privileged members of society. But when the standards of living improved and the tenements and sweatshops disappeared, the problems became less dramatic, and the benevolent attitude toward working women changed. Too often it has been replaced not only by indifference but by the conviction that enough has already been done, that equal pay and good working conditions are accomplished facts, and that there is no need for further vigilance or improvement.

2. Are working women, especially the widowed, divorced, and separated, efficient in organizing their domestic activities to maintain comfortable family life? Does society provide adequate subsidies for their dependent children? Do they maintain their home life at the expense of health and leisure? Unfavorable answers will call for educational correctives on an extensive scale.

3. Should we not also be justifiably concerned with the non-working women? This group includes not only the younger women awaiting graduation and the opportunity to join the labor force but also the three out of four married women who are perhaps not using their skills and their knowledge to the greatest advantage of society as a whole and for their own optimum development in wholesome living. The fact that honest and significant answers are hard to come by does not relieve any woman of the obligation to explore this question. Many may feel that child care and the best kind of family living demand home service beyond that which they can give if they hold a job. But one principle must surely be defended: There should be no restriction of opportunity on any housewife's freedom to earn. "Surrender to a less than rounded vision and employment of one's creative powers in the home is often the easiest way," Ordway Tead asserts, "for it mollifies the husband, pleases the children, and takes less energy and initiative merely to keep the home fires burning. Always to take from life less than it can offer of richness and personal unfolding is to deny one's very selfhood, or at least to hold it too cheaply." [3] If such a decision is to be made, it must at least be made voluntarily, but with our present attitudes and mores, we are far from achieving that freedom.

77

4. Why are many able-bodied women not working? Some are deterred by the generally unfavorable attitude which is reflected especially in the opinions of their husbands and friends. Some are resigned, glad to follow the line of least resistance. Many of them prefer their leisure. Shall we say that they are lazy? Or shall we say that they are happy in their present status, perhaps in their civic work, and that they prefer this leisure to the things that money could buy them? One is tempted to ask them to account for all the hours of this leisure time.

Many of the members of this last group would not be able to find congenial employment because of the discrepancy between their abilities and their opportunities. Perhaps others feel that to seek employment might not be prudent economy, since the cost of household service, clothes, and transportation might exceed what they could earn. Many of them are actually doing a full-time job of furthering their husband's or even their children's careers. One thinks especially of the clergymen, statesmen, and the many officials and administrators who need much more than a mere hostess and whose wives are happy in providing this full share of the family services.

The more specific problems of women in the labor force may be summarized in terms of women's disadvantages in contrast to the more favorable position of men. Some of these drawbacks are the result of societal attitudes and prejudices, and others are matters of more immediate circumstances. Women in general do, of course, enjoy many prerogatives. Their time and opportunities, and perhaps even capacities, for enjoyment surpass those of men. However, the social scientist recognizes five distinct handicaps of the *working woman*:

1. She receives lower pay for the same work.

2. The jobs of higher salary, skill, and authority are closed to her.

3. Her husband's employment takes precedence over her own and thus decreases her mobility and her market.

4. Continuous advancement in her job is interrupted by her homemaking period.

5. Homemaking, her fundamental responsibility, offers no regular pay and gives no prestige.

These disadvantages are, of course, very much interrelated, although for certain groups or individuals one or more of them may not actually be in operation. But they are the handy and essential framework on which all the productive thinking in women's employment relations must be built. They constitute the A B C's for the college student in understanding her future prospects.

The subject of lower pay for the same work is more than a mere argument in ethics; it is a problem whose roots lie in the very nature of our competitive society. That the general wage levels for women are lower than those for men and that the predominantly women-employing businesses are the low-wage industries are well-known facts. This unfavorable competition began when women first entered industry. As a minority group they were exploited as is any new group entering industry—as were, for example, the immigrant workers of the various nationalities and races. But in the case of women, the differential has continued even after industry has come to depend on women's work to a very considerable degree.

When the occupational achievements of men and women are compared, the best-paid college-trained women rise no higher in the salary scale than the average noncollege male. Like the college-trained man, the college woman does indeed hold far more of the professional jobs than the average worker, and her annual earnings are higher—a $2689 median for 1947 in contrast to the $1000 median for all working women. But "at this point all resemblance between the economic success of career women and her male colleagues comes to abrupt end," for the median salary of the men graduates was $4689, exactly $2000 more than the women. Two thirds of the college women were earning less than $3000 a year, a bracket where only 14 per cent of male graduates were found. "In the higher brackets to which most men were accustomed . . . there were practically no women at all."[4] In 1949 the working women among the alumnae of seven eastern women's colleges reported an average salary of $3790 fifteen years after graduation, while the husbands of their married classmates earned an average of $9800.

The extremely high turnover among working women is partly responsible for their lower pay. Often they remain in an occupation only a few years, and are therefore more frequently rated as apprentices and beginners. They fail to gain tenure or to receive the benefits of gradual raises in pay to which seniority would eventually entitle them. The woman employee may at any time leave her job to marry, to move to another town with her husband, or to raise a family.

Employers find this short duration of time on the job a great expense to management. They hesitate to promote any woman into a real career because of the loss to them in time and training when she is forced to leave their employ. Then, too, women who are capable and ambitious often have little bargaining power, because they hold the only jobs available to them in the town or part of the city where their husbands happen to live. Anchored as they are to their families, they do not have the mobility to take advantage of better opportunities in distant localities.

Such handicaps at least partially account for the second of the disadvantages of working women, the fact that positions of greater skill and authority are so much less accessible to them than to men. Both skill and prestige are products of long service. There are too many situations in which the woman will not be a permanent worker, and the fact that she is not a free agent, geographically speaking, weakens her ability to compete. A more important reason, however, is surely the psychological disinclination of men to work under the direction of women. Even the women, at least substantial majorities of them, do not feel comfortable in being subservient to members of their own sex.

These are matters for the industrial psychologist, although interpersonal problems arising in the field of labor relations are found as frequently in groups of the same sex as in mixed sex groups. The attitudes and prejudices are felt sometimes in a direct and personal fashion, but more often in an indirect and objective way through the deeply imbedded mores and institutional practices in the business, professional, and social world. For example, Allport explains that women are superior to men in interpreting attitudes because "her success depends upon the attitudes of people toward her. It is important for her to know for example whether her male associates in business have an antagonistic, jocular, patronizing, or fairminded point of view regarding her presence in their profession." [5] What male labors under this added handicap in his business or professional dealings? Much business is transacted during the time that men spend together in their unofficial social contacts, but membership in many of their clubs and luncheon organizations is not open to women.

A clear statement of this kind of handicap for the woman chemist runs as follows:

Since she is rarely given executive or supervisory positions, the woman chemist must develop, if she continues to develop, in individual research. She is apt to receive generous aid from co-workers, as are most scientists, but her achievements are essentially restricted to those of an individual working as well as thinking alone. She will also find her work hampered by the fact that industrial companies prefer representation by men. Even when work is independent and involves little or no supervision, as is the case for sales, sales services, and technical service, the company very definitely desires a male representative. Thus a woman chemist must obtain much of the practical experience and most of the professional contacts necessary to her research work vicariously if at all. In a sense she is left to carry out research in a vacuum or, at best, to base her plans on second-or-third-or-fourth-hand trade information. When the woman reaches this dead-end, she finds that she remains stationary in her position while men who were her co-workers are advanced beyond her. [6]

And later, in the same article:

The first impasse to normal job development is found in the dictum: A woman cannot supervise a man. Thus no matter how well suited to executive work a woman chemist may be, no matter how well her personality may be adapted to getting along agreeably with both sexes, and no matter how successfully she may have supervised the work of women under her, it is unlikely that she will be awarded any executive or administrative post which entails supervision of men. And since the present personnel of the field is predominantly male, the woman chemist is thus almost automatically barred from achieving a near top-flight position.

Some men feel that women use their feminine qualities to gain such advantage for themselves as promotions, favorable hours or assignments, and other privileges. Perhaps the men who do not sense this may be the very ones who most readily succumb to feminine blandishments. On the other hand, some women workers overcompensate for their femininity and work more industriously than is becoming. At any rate, both men and women workers could profit by a better understanding of interpersonal relationships as practiced by each sex. The "frail act" of the woman and the bullying tactics of the man are equally out of place in good working relationships. Many of the usual grievances are as characteristic of men as of women, but that fact in no way relieves the ambitious woman worker of the necessity of being aware of them and of trying to avoid them.

When the elusive field of interpersonal relationships and group dynamics is further developed, as it will be for the present generation of students, these attitudes will more easily be identified, and professional codes, either more or less explicit, will be evolved for dealing with them. Whether or not to "date" the boss, either the foreman or the forelady, will probably be discussed pro and con in the orientation pamphlets for new employees of future decades.

The Women's Bureau has summarized the prospects for advancement, as gleaned from interviews with successful women in a variety of business and professional occupations:

On the one hand experience has proved that there are few types of jobs which women, simply because they are women, are unable to do well. On the other hand, attitudes change slowly, and women have lagged behind men in attaining the more responsible and better paying jobs.

Department store work is considered a "woman's field" and so offers more chance for progress, but relatively few women in proportion to men hold jobs in top management. Women hold nearly all higher level jobs in personnel, counseling and training. They have advanced in the fields of buying, merchandise management, sales promotion, publicity, and advertising.

In factories men hold 90% of the upper level production jobs. Very few women get beyond the forelady classification. Higher level jobs most easily acquired by women are in personnel and employee welfare.[7]

In the matter of employment success, a statement from the recent extensive study of college graduates, *They Went to College,* suggests the ineffectiveness of educational guidance in the face of societal pressures:

It makes no difference at all in earnings to have specialized or to have taken a general course. Nor do most of the other factors . . . activities, self help, church . . . make any difference. The women graduates are equal in their unequal pay; college helps them rise well above the earnings of the average woman, but nothing they can do or study in college makes them rise nearly so high as the men. There simply seems to be a ceiling on women's earnings—and the graduates of all types, of all family backgrounds, of all schools, and of all kinds of courses seem to run into it. It can be said here for once and for all that the matters we are discussing because of the effect they have on the earnings of men graduates (activities, self help, curriculum), have no effect whatever on the women.[8]

Another of the economic disadvantages, the geographic immobility of the married women, may be counteracted by judicious choice of training. The woman student must first acquire a sophisticated awareness of the problem and all that it implies, as well as a healthy and objective attitude toward it. Thus she will learn to anticipate this obstacle and deal with it in advance by selecting those occupations which are least affected by it. For example, the work of an interior decorator normally requires an urban milieu, but the student who prepares for it may find herself in a rural or small town area which cannot support such a "luxury" profession. On the other hand, employment as a medical technician is available wherever there is a practicing physician. The hairdresser can set up shop with profit in almost any community. Teaching and typing are less dependent on favorable geography than editing or acting.

Much more attention should be given in vocational guidance to husband-and-wife teams of workers. With the larger number of student marriages, curriculum planning for business or professional teams may eventually assume its proper importance. A pair of physicians, one specializing in surgery and the other in internal medicine, or one in pediatrics and the other in ear, eye, nose, and throat, may have great success in working together. A barber and a beautician might share a joint establishment. A business manager and a dietitian might combine to create a highly successful restaurant. A printer and a commercial artist might make a good combination, or a minister and a social worker, or a contractor and an accountant.

A barrier to these cooperative ventures is often found, however, in the nepotism rules, and the career woman is therefore pulled toward the urban areas where there is a multiplicity of companies and institutions for whom she may work. Both popular prejudice and managerial prudence frequently operate to bar having two employees from the same family on one payroll. The practice has been widely codified, and continues to work much hardship. Again it is better understanding and training in all kinds of interpersonal relationships which will safeguard both employee and employer from the genuine dangers of these dilemmas.

In assuming the role of gainful worker, the woman has not been able to shake off entirely the remnants of domestic life with which biology and long tradition have entrusted her. She is still unique in her dual capacities, and whether or not the working woman, preoccupied with domestic interests, can give as much to her work and earn advancement as deservedly as her male colleague is a difficult question to answer.

The satisfactions available to the woman worker in a society which clearly favors the male earner can hardly be identical to those of the man. This social pressure is felt more or less keenly by the individual worker according to her age and her future plans, the nature of the work and her training for it, and her responsibilities toward family and community life.

To be sure, men also vary among themselves in the spirit and energy with which they enter into their jobs. Perhaps we should limit our generalizations to saying (1) that married women workers may be expected to contribute a somewhat smaller margin of time and energy to work outside the home, and (2) that the husband of the woman worker will still be able to claim for his job a larger margin of the family budget of time, interest, and energy than the wife.

Certainly the married working woman, or any working woman who maintains a home, will find herself working harder and longer (and perforce more efficiently) and having less leisure time than other women. This leads to that significant truism that "married women who work outside the home constitute one of the most overworked groups in our society today."

Hard work happens to be the price which this particular pioneering movement exacts of its leaders, and even as this is written, evidences of relief are cropping up among some categories of husbands, especially among the younger generation and the intelligentsia. The problem is eased also as both women and men become involved in building and maintaining more efficient household units. Men have already been demonstrating their aptitudes for household engineering, and they show as much professional pride and pleasure in streamlining and improving and organizing within their homes as in their business or professional activities.

Another of the economic or ethical riddles growing out of increasing competition is the question of whether married women workers are entitled to jobs when men are unemployed. The older generation may remember the lessons learned in the 1930s when the fifteen million unemployed forced talk of the "needs test" to everybody's tongue. Gladys Dickinson, speaking for the

Women's Bureau, reports, "Our society doesn't think of saying to a young man when he applies for a job, even in a depression, 'Well, now, can your father support you? Do you really need this job?' It is expected that a man should have a job. And I think, as we do not apply a needs test to men for jobs, that we should not apply a needs test to women." The solution awaits, of course, the attainment of the hitherto unrealized goal of all workers: full employment with jobs for all who want them.

There are some storm warnings out for the college graduate in the bold plans for expansion proposed by the President's Commission on Higher Education. This report urges an education for all who can profit by it—an enrollment of as many as four and a half million students for 1960, in contrast to the two and a half million in 1949 and the three million expected in the 1950s. Obviously, this is a gain proportionately much greater than the gain in the general population. Even with present-day enrollments, we can expect to have at least ten million college graduates in the market for jobs by the 1960s in contrast to the four million college-trained workers in the 1940s. College-bred populations (including those who attend only two years) of thirty to forty-five millions, or as much as 25 to 35 per cent of the labor force, are easily foreseen, whereas only about 10 or 15 per cent of the jobs in the entire labor force require or attract college graduates. It is not difficult to calculate the surplus of candidates for the professional and white-collar jobs.[9]

Neither government nor industry nor the professions can absorb the college-trained personnel as fast as the proportions of people in these professions are being accelerated in the general population. Furthermore, the general population itself may not be growing at the rate anticipated in the president's report. The problem requires more than a thorough study of the supply and demand for college-trained men and women; it is not a purely vocational problem, but one that is full of social, economic, and political implications.

What would happen if we had by 1960 an oversupply of

frustrated intellectuals? What justification for college education can we give our students beyond the cash dividends which are now the chief motivation? How can we make the intangible social and cultural values of education more obvious to college youth—especially if they are not entirely clear to ourselves as educators and counselors?

One antidote for the oversupply would be an immediate extension in the practice of part-time work. For many a woman this would provide the perfect solution for reconciling the dual claims of home and job and for maintaining her techniques and interests during that period when she is most closely tied to the household. This would mean major adjustments on the part of employers, although there is already a large accumulation of experience in such procedures. When two individuals must be trained to work at the same typewriter or in the same spot on the assembly line, management's personnel expense is almost doubled; hiring, teaching, supervising, promoting, paying, and keeping the records must cover twice as many employees. This is a formidable obstacle in our highly competitive industry. Perhaps it might be offset by larger quotas of accomplishment, fewer "coffee breaks," and greater all-round efficiency in the shortened working day. Perhaps compromises in the hours might be effected, with two 6-hour employees giving management a full 12-hour day for his capital investment in machinery and office space.

Already there is a trend toward shortening the work week, and a 24-hour week, or a 30- or 32-hour week might well prove a profitable and feasible contract for employer as well as employee, for both men and women. There is already a trend, too, toward greater flexibility in the hours of the daily shifts of industrial and business workers, with traffic facilities, retail store hours, and even church and recreation schedules geared to accommodate several work groups.

Cooperation between man and wife, both working outside the home for only thirty hours, could make housekeeping a relatively light task for both and might prove a richer life experience for everyone. Better organization in all parts of the industrial machine, the business enterprises and the services, may likewise provide striking advantages—more profit to management from the extended use of expensive equipment, better distribution of traffic and fewer crises in transportation, more enjoyable use of all the entertainment and leisure-time facilities because they would be less crowded. Rich experiences in individualization might also be in store for the personality of the future, even the ultimate loosening of the tightening vise of standardization. Greater flexibility in the working hours might bring parallel fluctuations in behavior and attitudes; the regrouping and deploying of workers might cause the development of new affinities in tastes and interests, even in ideas and values.

There is no all-embracing resolution to the manifold issues of gainful employment for women; in fact, it may not even be possible to formulate clearly the proper question, to envisage all of its implications, and to phrase it in terms of current social and economic concepts. What is the real significance to women of their employment, and how can education deal with this significance? Does employment yield a psychic income, as well as monetary income, which nourishes one's self-respect, ideals, and ambitions? Is there a ceiling for this psychic income for women but not for men?

Has employment any intrinsic worth to the individual woman or to women as a group, and can education help women discover what this worth is, how they may acquire it, make full use of it, and teach it to new generations? Is this transcendent worth available only to the minority of workers, for example, the top-level manipulators or those in the intellectual occupations? Is there a hierarchy of values, corresponding to the several categories of workers, some of which are intrinsic and internalized, and others extrinsic and self-alienated? Must education set up a hierarchy of training for its women students and teach different moral and esthetic values to parallel the various degrees of intellect and skill?

88

Women both as groups and as individuals have been so immersed in the struggle for employment opportunity, so preoccupied with all its domestic involvements and psychological attitudes, that these more enigmatic aspects have not received the needed attention. We are not, of course, questioning woman's ever-present need for employment; insofar as she must have work to provide her material "living," she has no choice. However empty of worth and meaning her life and her work may be, her purse no longer has to be empty; but her search for the old-time values in work may be anachronistic, for without her share of legitimate work she is herself an anachronism. Women cannot go back to a more meaningful kind of work in the household or even in the family. The "sphere" to which nature was once supposed to have committed her has vanished. No one group in society can reverse its own inevitable trends and journey back alone to the good old times, however tempting this solution might seem.

On the contrary, just as political revolution may start when too many people suffer physical hunger, so a reversal in thought and attitude may begin when the existing ideologies seem hollow and empty and fail to give satisfaction to large sections of the population. Spencer's dictum that social changes are made by the hungry and resisted by the well fed is as true in the psychological as in the material realm. Widespread personal frustration is the starting point for new trends, but only insight, ingenuity, and creativeness can turn these forces in the direction of practical social solutions. Who but the women themselves can furnish these insights, this creative power? What educational forces will generate them?

We acknowledge the great emphasis, born of insistent desire and economic need, on vocational education in our schools and colleges. We know that our society itself has shifted from a liberal capitalism of small properties to a corporate system of enterprises on a giant scale. Society now demands that education prepare not the good citizen for the old-fashioned way of living, but the successful earner for an industrialized society with security as its goal. Education functions now primarily as the link in the occupational mobility between generations.

We accept the fact that women cannot reverse any of the long-term societal trends and that they may expect, therefore, to be drawn more deeply each year into the labor force. Also, we perceive that the large majorities of the workers in this force, both men and women, but more surely women, will be occupied exclusively with the noncreative impersonal routines, will be managed and manipulated, with more and more alienation of their personalities from their gainful employment.

Fewer and fewer will be the individuals who can develop their personalities through the employment of their skills, who can express themselves freely or creatively in their jobs. No matter what values we assign to employment in an effort to personalize or glorify it—whether we speak of Christian virtue, dignity of labor, self-expression, service to mankind, or joy of creation— they are all out of date and foreign to the labor and employment situation which predominates overwhelmingly in our social structure of today.

In this modern world, then, where work pays off in income, status, or power, is there any possibility at all of educating women to find in their employment some of the things which contribute to self-fulfillment? Or is this term itself a glib phrase, another false dream, useful only to some unidentifiable manipulators?

Self-fulfillment in itself is not an insubstantial and irrational dream. It is psychologically the necessary consummation of the life-giving energy and drives—the "conscience" that must be satisfied, that cannot suffer community disapproval, that cannot escape the values implanted by social training.

Self-fulfillment is indeed one of the key words, perhaps the one of utmost importance, in education today, but the separation of self and work which our preponderantly mechanized society imposes largely denies its development *in employment*. We are not surprised, therefore, to find in our vocational guidance a minimum of attention on the intrinsic values of work. Vocational guidance—which is different from educational guidance—as it is practiced today must give emphasis to discovering and matching the individual abilities to the requirements of the job. Education for vocations likewise serves its own purposes, and as we see these purposes more clearly, its limitations also stand out in sharp relief. Some other kind of education, whether we call it liberal or devise some other name for it, must meet the needs for self-fulfillment in the society of today.

The first Industrial Revolution substituted coal for muscle and approaches its climax in the automatic factory. But the second and much more profound revolution, the substitution of electronics for brains, has barely shifted into its lowest gear. The triumph of the business machines earns for man and for woman not things but time. As the wheels of the new technology turn faster and faster, a new economic system must also evolve, matching revolution with revolution, paralleling each new invention with new concepts in economics, ethics, and esthetics. Almost before man can anticipate it a new problem will overwhelm him—not how to earn a living, but how to live.

. . . 5

Education for Dating and Mating

For youth, interest in sex is insistent and dominating, with strong emotional overtones; for the older generation, this interest is more marginal and occasional, subject to management and direction. Because of the divergence in orientation—toward experimentation and expression by the one group and toward control and education by the other—unusual subtlety and skill are called for on the part of educators. Otherwise they will seem arbitrary and unsympathetic, which may cause the younger members of society to become frustrated or rebellious. Furthermore, the subject is one which cannot be side-stepped in an educational program for youth; training for health, citizenship, vocation, or philosophy may be delayed occasionally, but sex demands the right of way.

In the high school and college years romance overrides realism, feelings run high, and opportunities for meeting the opposite sex are more continuous and more natural than they will ever be later. During these years, emotional tensions and episodes are more frequent and habits of controlling them are not yet developed. Kinsey has reported that men reach their maximum sex drive in their teens and are already showing a decline by the time they graduate from college and consider themselves old enough to marry. The schools must see them through these years when they are most impetuous and least encumbered with restraints. Perhaps it is fortunate that women mature more slowly and reach the peak of their sex drive well after the college years.

While the older generation takes a long-range view of the whole subject of sex, the teen-ager usually sees the matter at short range, but much more vividly. The adult is preoccupied with education for marriage; the student agonizes over the fact that she has no date for next Saturday night. Of course any girl is interested in how to estimate a man's possibilities as a marriage partner, but she is much more immediately involved in two other problems: how to assure herself of as much romantic attention and experience as all the other girls of her generation, and how to have an active and enjoyable social life with the men of her classroom and campus. Mothers and counselors usually find themselves, willy nilly, in the throes of these short-range problems with the long implications, but teachers and curriculum makers are a little farther removed from them and need occasional reminders of their existence and importance.

Women students spend more time than their elders realize in worrying about finding pleasant companionship with men. Formal and informal school and campus functions demand at least acceptable, and if possible interesting, partners. "Desire for popularity with men" took precedence over any other source of anxiety on one campus and was an admitted characteristic of more than half the freshmen interviewed, with no diminution of concern even by the junior year. Failure to establish acquaintanceship in general was the most fertile source of apprehension among college freshmen. It overbalanced anxiety about morals and standards of campus behavior, concern about class work, vocational choices, home ties, finances, sororities, and general feelings of inadequacy. Freshmen women also expressed many feelings in their interviews which were classified under the heading "disillusionment with the intellectual interests and social gallantry of men."

Mothers as well as daughters know that high school and college dates are the preliminary but determining factors for the matrimonial future. The girl who has many contacts with boys of her own age has only the problem of choosing the right one, or of working the right one up to the proper degree of interest and attention. In contrast, the social life of some girls centers around other members of the same sex, young or old, with a minimum of acquaintanceship among men. Other girls have quietly paired off with one boy throughout their adolescent years, and their usual question is "How soon?" Problems are far from identical— there are the too shy girls and the too aggressive, the too sophisticated and the too naïve, the too pretty and the too plain.

"Dating," as it is applied to school and campus activity, has a double meaning. First and most important, it is frankly an end in itself, a kind of social entertainment, a typically American way of spending an evening. Second, dating is a means to an end, a method of exploring and experimenting, of investigating the possibilities of the opposite sex with a view to choosing a life partner. This latter meaning is more technically "courtship," the first definite step in the marriage relationship.

Student standards may be branded by adults as artificial and transient, but that does not mitigate their relentless pressure on growing personalities. A topnotch masculine "date" for the coed must belong to a better fraternity, be active in campus affairs, and dance well; he must have spending money and an automobile; and he must be well dressed and smooth in manners and appearance. The corresponding feminine qualifications are good clothes, ability to dance well, and a smooth "line." True, many a college girl is happy to settle for less, and may even prefer a less obvious display of attractions. Many are also aware that these are surface qualities only, but nevertheless indispensable as current social coin.

Gregariousness has made itself felt so forcefully that the presence, the attention, and the admiration of other people in all the accepted social patterns have become necessary in our American culture, and never more so than in the high school and college years. Every human being is afraid of loneliness. Self-esteem is measured by social approval, and the ultimate questions must be "Can I love?" and "Am I loved?" For the campus adolescent some of the usual questions are "What if I don't feel excited about men?" or "Why am I so much more emotional than he is?" or "Must I kiss every time it is expected?"

Deans and personnel officers on either the coeducational or the one-sex campus are well aware of this situation and have explored all phases of it. They know that social behavior must be learned in a social environment, motivated by natural impulses, sustained by appropriate satisfactions, and judged by current social standards. Because of their wider experience in working with youth, school and college administrators often have more objective attitudes toward adolescent needs than parents, a better understanding of them than society at large, and more zeal than most other groups in designing activities to meet the needs. Both the campus researches and the sociologists' analysis of the general cultural milieu are needed by those who make the blueprints for education.

The biological and chronological aspects of the girl-boy relationship have been outlined expertly by Scheinfeld.[1] The basic fact is that the schoolgirl reaches physiological puberty about two years earlier than the little boy in her classroom, which means that she begins to sense the problems of romance, of social and sex relationships, long before the boy faces them and before she has the preparation that the boy will have in mental development, education, and experience when puberty catches up with him. Sex experimenting is more hazardous for the girl, and the "double standard" makes any indiscretions more consequential for her future social standing.

Although these factors are mainly responsible for the universal policy of restricting, at least in some degree, the freedom and activities of girls, the roles of sex differences and of social pressures are not clearly understood or frankly discussed among young adolescents. Men and women, youth and age, have much to argue and much to gain in arriving at the scientist's clear-cut dictum: Biological drives can reach their psychological threshold only in socially determined form.

Age limits for the various stages of sex companionship in our culture have been well differentiated. In infancy and babyhood individuals are interested only in themselves. In early childhood they seek companionship of other children regardless of sex. When they are about eight years old, boys prefer to play with boys and girls with girls. From ages ten to twelve, antagonism between sex groups is usually the rule; but at thirteen to fourteen, girls become interested in boys and try to attract their attention, while the boys tend to remain aloof. From ages fourteen to sixteen, boys begin to reciprocate the interest in the opposite sex, and some individuals even tend to pair off. For young people of sixteen or seventeen years and beyond, social dates in couples become the general practice. Exceptions of course tend to occur, and there are variations according to the culture—English, French, north, south—but the pattern just described usually prevails in America, and counselors and educators do well to keep its general outlines firmly in mind.

Frankwood Williams has written eloquently on this problem of the development of heterosexuality. The girl, up to her high school or, in a few cases, early college years, has not been heterosexual but rather asexual. Her sex attitudes have not been fully developed, and there are many circumstances and symptoms to be studied before it can be predicted just where any one girl will find her place on the scale of sexual development. The adolescent years are of the greatest importance in the sense that if

. . . hetero-sexuality is not accomplished in these four or five years it never will be accomplished in a normal way. These years hold the only chance the average boys or girls will have to establish their hetero-sexuality. Once prevented, it can never come naturally and normally again. . . . Hetero-sexuality cannot be obtained in a vacuum. It cannot be attained by itself. It does not just happen; it is a development and growth that is nourished and continued by what it feeds upon. Hetero-sexuality will be established through contact and experience with those of the opposite sex. Anything, no matter for what purpose, that tends to make this contact too difficult is not in the interest of the child, or the parent or society.[2]

Two factors are of utmost importance in helping children achieve healthy heterosexuality. The first is the skillful planning of recreational activities in community and family, with the father as well as the mother sharing in the responsibility and the fun. These group functions not only teach the child new sports and skills; they also turn the unfolding personality gently toward the mature attitudes and adult values which it must ultimately embrace. The second factor is the development of a carefully graded instruction schedule in the physiology, psychology, and sociology of sex. The curiosity and emotions of the child must always be anticipated, so that no morbid imaginings, no warped misinformation, will haunt his dreams by night or by day.

Unplanned leisure hours spent with casual companions in unsupervised idleness often ferment their own insidious poisons. The feverish reminiscences of biography and fiction detail all too clearly the common childhood diseases of mind, will, and feeling which may infect the unprotected victim. But modern woman, as she entertains herself by dipping into this particular literary genre, must ask herself whether these esoteric gropings are not, like rickets or smallpox, the mark of a backward people, a retarded culture. If they can be accepted as true and accurate reporting of the inner life of the typical youth in our era, then there is indeed cause for alarm. But modern therapy can inoculate against them as well as against the old-fashioned diphtheria and scarlet fever. Trained youth-leadership, a flourishing children's literature, appropriate radio and television programs, and widespread recreational projects can crusade for mental health exactly as public clinics, visiting nurses, and school programs have done successfully with physical health.

Education cannot shirk its responsibilities here. Fathers and daughters, sons and mothers, men and women at every age can and must develop more shared interests and more common values. There is no need in our enlightened and democratic society for the happy flowering of parent-child relationship to be blighted by the self-conscious complexes of other times and cultures.

Mothers and daughters, as they look at various colleges, would do well to note what steps are taken for women students to meet suitable men of their own age under favorable circumstances. To be sure, all places and activities on the coeducational campus—the classroom, the laboratory, the church, the clubs, centers for eating and studying, athletic events, theater and choir rehearsals, even travel to and from the campus—serve as meeting, and therefore "dating," grounds. In addition, dances of all types, tennis, hiking, bowling, mixed swimming, record hours, fireside forums, bridge tournaments, picnics, and of course movies, lectures, concerts, and other entertainments supplement these opportunities.

Besides all this, there are also the mixers that flourish, especially in the fall, among the homesick freshmen and unattached sophomores. In fact, the enthusiastic informal mixers of October and November taper off into the tired and discouraged committee meetings of March and April because of their own too great success! The participants have paired off happily and have progressed to their own more preferred clubs and social preoccupations. The blind dates arranged for the freshmen by the social committees, and the "exchange dinners," where half the residents of one living unit change places with half the residents of another unit, usually accomplish their purposes early in the year and meet a good deal of resistance after the first semester.

The one-sex college necessarily organizes for acquaintanceship and dating on a different basis, but in these days of easy transportation and high mobility, difficulties in filling quotas of men and women for both "import" and "export" needs are not prohibitive. At least, the marriage rate for the women's college graduates does not lag behind that of the coeducational school graduates, so it is obvious that many circumstances other than the segregation factor, especially religion and socioeconomic level, also affect it.

In some colleges less attention is given to this dating problem because of the rich social life which students have with their own families, in their long summer vacations and their week ends at home or in nearby cities.

Whether the mother expects the daughter to meet her future husband in her own living room or on the campus may become one of the major factors in choosing the right college. Sociologists find, for example, that people in the lower educational and class levels are more likely to meet in secondary contacts such as business, travel, or commercial places of recreation. Those in the upper middle class, where class consciousness is stronger and contacts are more exclusive, are more likely to meet in the primary contacts such as private homes, churches, and clubs, as well as the college classroom.

In contrast to courtship, dating as an end in itself—whether in high school, on the campus, or within the home—can best be understood as a phenomenon of our modern times. As the concepts and mores of romantic love were widely disseminated by the new mass media, parental control through "arranged marriages" decreased.

Comparison of the European customs in courtship with American customs brings our own folkways into salient relief. Especially in the last fifty years many factors have helped to determine the trend. The American coeducational system, utterly alien to Europe, and the ubiquitous American automobile, still uncommon in England and on the continent, have been important contributing factors in the breaking of the former rigid family controls. Courting activities, like everything else in our shrinking family life, have been taken out of the home and into public parks, night clubs, roadhouses, swimming pools, and movie theaters, and more especially to the campus nooks and walks and "joints."

Motion pictures and light literature have reinforced the trend away from the older, more formal and businesslike patterns toward the present activities of romantic love. Before the present era, these relaxed and experimental dating relationships were confined to the wealthy and aristocratic classes. They could not prevail generally in any culture without the growth of wealth and the rise of the middle classes to positions of relative security and leisure. Old restraints could be thrown off only as the growing urban industrialization developed anonymity, independence, and individuality. Old-fashioned courtship was based on self-conscious qualities of family, class, ancestry, and economic power; but dating takes into consideration primarily personal qualities such as similarity in taste, reading and sports, physical attractiveness and dress, dancing ability, popularity, hero worship, and of course that elusive but important quality, school or campus prestige, or "rating."

Dating also differs from "courtship" in that the latter assumes one constant suitor, whereas in dating, the girl is expected to attract many admirers from whom she chooses now one, now another, as social convenience dictates. Sometimes it is expected that the campus newcomer will find, before Christmas, one person with whom to "go steady"; more frequently only juniors and seniors "go steady," and freshman and sophomore women must have a demonstrable variety of acquaintanceship. For purposes of exploration, double dates are useful and in some places *de rigeur*. If being extremely casual is the rule, the "principle of least interest" is much in evidence, with the partner who cares the least enjoying the greater prestige.

The "line," which so amazes, distresses, and befuddles the adults who are privileged to listen to it, is probably a development based on this principle of least interest, for it may be at the same time protective, enigmatic, and useful in keeping the situation both flexible and under control. It is emotionalized rather than sentimental, dramatic and full of cliches, slang, and current radio and movie quotations, which double as epigrams and smart repartee. It is a kind of twilight zone between revelation and concealment of romantic interest. It has versatile uses, all of which youth exploits to the full, and is therefore as indispensable as the reversible raincoat. To understand the nice discriminations in parrying the line, in maintaining both enthusiasm and dignity, is an important item in the current education of America's young women.

100

Modern dating, especially in the campus setting, has been described as a dalliance relationship largely dominated by the quest for the thrill. It is regarded as a proper amusement, especially by the male, for whom it is probably becoming an appropriate behavior form. He has already reached physiological maturity but not economic independence, and therefore his interest lies mainly in the preliminary and less responsible segment of the total dating configuration. He cannot yet support a wife, much less a family, and therefore hesitates to accept serious courtship duties. In fact, the dating procedure calls primarily for the use of techniques to avoid lasting attachment or involvement. In the meantime, however, it is not all "schmaltz," not without some substantial benefits, for dating serves to broaden experience and enrich the personality.

Dating contributes to poise and balance and the ability to adjust to all types of people in all kinds of circumstances. It gives practice in discrimination for the later process of choosing from a wider acquaintance the most suitable mate. It may even help to reduce naïve emotional excitement, release emotional tensions, and make rational foresight possible, although only careful planning and wise guidance can provide the favorable circumstances which will produce these desired results. Contrary to the eighteenth-century practice of frowning on dating, new conditions of life have dictated new policies, and it is now the function of the high school and the college to encourage dating rather than to be overprotective or to resist this most important urge and activity of the adolescent years.

In a heterogeneous society such as the United States, one cannot expect homogeneous patterns. Dating practices therefore vary widely from one community to another and especially from one campus to another, both in the subjective attitudes of the individuals in the different groups and in the more concrete behavior codes. The ratio of men to women is perhaps the factor of greatest consequence, ranging from the 50-50 proportion to complete segregation and dependence on week-end emigration and immigration. The presence or absence of fraternities and sororities, the size and location of the campus, its urban or rural setting, and the homogeneity or heterogeneity of its student body affect the dating customs. In some cases there is a clearly defined hierarchy of student groups, frequently inherent in the social fraternities and sororities or in various types of housing units. "Class A" men date only "Class A" women, according to the unwritten but well-understood norms of campus prestige which grow out of "campus politics" and the "bull sessions" within one's own sex groups.

Our complacent attitudes toward the whole dating complex have evoked criticism from other cultures as well as from the conservatives in the home culture. The British Geoffrey Gorer, in an ironic mood, describes dating as a particular kind of patterned precourtship behavior peculiar to the inhabitants of the United States. Subjectively it is, says he, the "most important and enjoyable occupation of the peak period of one's life, twelve to twenty-five," and he goes on to add that in retrospect it acquires ever-increasing charms, surpassing both present and past reality, so that even among adults many attempts are made to provide a simulacrum for those whose years have removed them from reality.[3]

Janet Kelly has uncomplimentary comments to make on the adolescent quality of the activities of alumni in their relations to the college traditions and warns the colleges and the fraternal organizations that they may indicate "regressive tendencies." [4] Perhaps these patterns of shifting affections and the lighthearted freedom of dating days become so much a part of the youthful way of life that later supposedly "permanent" ties are not proof against them. At least the much higher divorce rate of Americans as compared with Europeans suggests this explanation.

Dating is just another of the amenities, the luxuries, to which campus life introduces the student, one which perhaps neither the man nor the woman may ever be able to afford again. There is an unrealistic haze which sometimes only a woman's later disappointments in the business or professional world can dispel. She learns, too, that as her own education and earning power increase, the size of the income which her partner will require to win her also increases, and that this decreases her attractiveness to eligible males. At least, we may say that she was in the process of learning this important truth until, as the aftermath of World War II, the "G.I. Bill" reversed the norm and brought to the campus the veteran student, partially supported by the working wife. The ubiquitous married couple on the postwar campus has made a tremendous impression on the undergraduates.

In both courtship and dating, tradition has accorded the greater initiative to the male. This was always a partial myth, and shifting circumstances are gradually nibbling away the foundations of the priorities of the man. The popularity of the "Dutch treat" and the ever-present "pay-back" date, Sadie Hawkins dance, and Gold Diggers' ball testify to the gradual breakdown of another of the courtship traditions, the right and privilege of the male partner to underwrite the finances. But in more ways than this the modern coed is showing the initiative in the partnerships. She has no hesitancy in revising and reorganizing the plans for the evening; she suggests alternatives, and she is also developing greater skills and freedom in suggesting the dates themselves.

It is more realistic to recognize that it is the partner with the greater aggressiveness, either man or woman, who takes the initiative in stimulating or decelerating these dating contacts. But even more important, it is likewise the marriage partner with the greater insight and maturity who will assume the burden of adjustment in marriage. This often means an almost prohibitive cost to the adjusting personality, perhaps in early dating and certainly in the later union, and unfortunately the more inflexible partner achieves his own personal fulfillment at no comparable cost in suppression and denial. It is good to find these things out as early as possible, to experience a range of subjective feelings, both dominant and submissive, and to practice constructive quarreling with a variety of sparring partners. It is not enough for the woman alone to acquire this education; the man must have it also to assure a happy outcome for both.

Waller explained some of these undercurrents of mating in the dating process as follows:

A very important characteristic of the college student is his bourgeois pattern of life. For most persons, the dominant motive of college attendance is the desire to rise to a higher social class; behind this we should see the ideology of American life and the projection of parent's ambitions upon children. The attainment of this good life necessitates postponement of marriage since it is understood that a new household must be economically independent; additional complications sometimes arise from the practice of borrowing money for college expenses, and yet persons in this group feel very strongly the cultural imperative to fall in love, and marry and live happily in marriage.[5]

Popenoe recognizes a further characteristic in the mating relationships called the mating gradient, which is the widespread tendency of women to marry above their own level and of men to desire to marry below. Men usually marry women of either equal or inferior education, while women tend to marry men of equal or superior education. Even more important, as men grow older, they tend to marry younger women.

In spite of all opinions to the contrary, the shadow of the old double standard lurks in the darker corners of courtship and over all the man-to-woman relationships this side of marriage. It is not only that man still holds his greater freedom in social standards, but also that woman has the more passive role, is less a free agent, not so easily able to choose her male companions or her husband, and therefore the more likely to suffer from the frustrations of inaction as well as the censure of society.

But neither men in their more active roles nor women in their more passive and vulnerable situations have been able to keep the older patterns from disintegrating. "The present state of our love and sex mores," wrote Folsom in 1943, "is chaotic, inconsistent, and transitory," and in our present, post-Kinsey era, this may be even more true. Most of the older traditions and controls in courtship, largely inherited from nineteenth-century England, have broken down, and the newer generations of lovers have not worked out their new codes and sanctions. Perhaps women should be glad of this; perhaps it will enable them, if they choose, to take the lead in forming new codes more favorable to themselves. One crucial factor will be their expanding financial independence, of which all men will become increasingly aware. The women's attitudes will shift from the ethical to the economic.

If we cannot yet see the newer patterns, we can note some of the negative trends—the decline in the efficacy of religious sanctions and the influence of the increasingly available contraceptives. What Waller calls the "dominance of the thrill," the search for excitement, the emotionalization of every experience, has had its effect on dating, and much social interplay has the purpose of communicating, buying, or selling the thrill, of enhancing self-esteem through attention and admiration.

Love has been slowly moving out of the domain of the poets, the spontaneous, mystic, and deeply personal, and is being frankly manipulated in two very different directions: toward the sentimental and overcharged stereotypes of the movies and the pulp magazines for cheap mass consumption, and by modern social scientists toward a psychologically and sociologically acceptable concept which is every year given more human warmth and spiritual depth. Youth today can scarcely avoid making the choice, or the compromise, between the movies or the pulp magazines and the marriage course, and the latter is not without its own peculiar glamour.

Romantic love is defined as the shifting of the center of affection from one's own parents and family to a specific member of the opposite sex and another family. The process begins with the first date and ends with marriage. The psychoanalyst pronounces that productive love implies care and responsibility not only for physical life but for growth and development of all human powers. For the philosopher, love is a kind of growing, and thus love, inclusive of sex, needs marriage to protect and nourish its values. For human progress, the lover must see his mate not merely as a male or female for sex satisfaction alone, but as a person who induces respect and self-control for the sake of human fellowship.

These latter views are propagandized in the schools by conscientious social scientists who believe that marriage, to be a completely satisfying experience to each individual, must be put to work in building family life and society. Sex and moral educators rely more and more on the idea that exclusiveness beautifies and ennobles intimacy. Mutual confidence grows from the realization that sexual impulses are under control.

In spite of the efforts of Hollywood, there seems to be some indication today that youth and beauty are not the only stimulants to love and that these ideas have been a little oversold. In this we probably see the benefits which our young people are deriving from the franker attitudes and more freely available information on both the biology and the psychology of sex life. There have been many excellent books which have enjoyed a wide, if sometimes surreptitious, circulation. Many parents have been enlightened by the books intended for their children.

Also, there have been many excellent courses in both high school and college which have served not only as a needed source of information but also as an important emotional outlet for youth. The courses teach a much higher evaluation of personality, intellect, and health as ingredients, if not of romance, at least of successful marriage. Students are more likely nowadays to check such qualities as good nature, competence, and cheerfulness as prerequisites for the marriage partner. They apparently enjoy a pleasant, romantic stimulation from their group and individual discussions of budgets, housing, contraceptives, spaced births, interior decoration, mother-in-law relationships, and other topics for which their formal courses and current reading have given them an adequate vocabulary and a lively interest.

Perhaps it is not too much to hope that from these new courtship activities and ideologies may grow the true affirmation of the sex function, both biological and psychological, not merely as a step which may lead to something higher, but as an integral part of that higher value. Obviously it is too much to hope for unless the women who hold these higher values get behind a kind of "sex and semantics" movement to make the younger women articulate and self-conscious about them.

There is no denying the fact that current light literature remains optimistic and cultivates almost exclusively the well-established idiom of romantic love in our culture. Love is always triumphant and always ends well. It is always wholesome, genuine, fresh, and uplifting, and it is the only reason for marriage. If it should fail, there is only one solution—throw the whole thing overboard and begin all over again with another partner. The aim of life is perfect happiness through love; there is only one kind, and if you cannot get the deluxe model, with a lifetime guarantee of perfect functioning, nothing else is worth while. Especially in the movies these escapist values are constantly presented, in technicolor and with the most glamorous stars. Who could question the obligation of education to provide a vigorous program of counterpropaganda?

Illuminating for such a program is the material from recent sociological exploration based on actual school and campus data. Like the human body, formerly too intimate and sacred for laboratory dissection, romantic love has finally yielded to the scalpel and the microscope. Now from the case histories of hundreds of college men and women, the typical romantic episode of the campus can be depicted, analyzed, and viewed with revealing objectivity.

There is an impersonality about love affairs when they are carried out to two decimal points that is very refreshing. To the sensitive college woman, smarting from another romantic rebuff, a study of the composite curve of dating from onset to termination may be as good as a tonic. In her frustration she finds it heartening to learn that more women than men on the campus suffer from parental disapproval of their dating behavior, that the average student has approximately 2.2 love affairs of which 75 per cent are broken off, that the readjustment curves show at least half of them terminate without serious emotional turmoil

107

or trauma, and that it takes the women longer to recover than the men.

There has even been a formal college course in dating, covering quite completely all its social and general implications. It makes clear the relationship of past dating experience to the eventual choosing of the marriage mate and explores the possible significance of dating in successful marriage experience.

Men students, even men counselors and teachers, are amazingly unaware of the major role played by women in campus social opportunities and training. Perhaps because of the initiative allowed the man in person-to-person romantic relationship, insights do not come to them readily in this woman's realm. Unaware of their own borrowings and dependence in manners and morals, they blithely counsel *laissez faire* for their feminine partners. Why all the fuss about women's rules and regulations? If women are now on the assembly line and in the market place, if they can argue economics, lead the cheering sections, and edit the campus paper, why can't they stay out all night when they feel like it, just as men do? Why cannot the women students come over to the men's houses for their dates? Why are there so many committees and counselors, so many career conferences and charm clinics?

In all her social relationships, in her housing unit and anywhere else on the campus—and especially in the coeducational college—the young woman needs differential treatment from campus counselors trained in her special outlooks and needs. When the freshman steps into her residence hall, into her social engagements and her dates, she cannot possibly shake herself free of the accumulated traditions and current attitudes toward women in the outside world. Like her counterpart in the men's quadrangle, she is acutely aware of the society that will eventually sit in judgment on her personal qualifications and determine her future success. But her success is much more largely in terms of her social relationships than is the man's; her personal attractiveness, grooming, manners, and ethical standards are far more important than his in the eyes of the judges. For him, business acumen, technical proficiency, and earning power are some of the more important ingredients; and he is firmly oriented toward these, impatient of any others.

The freshman girl is also more dependent on her family for her spending money and her wardrobe, for social contacts and encouragements. It is more becoming to her to continue dependence, while the man cultivates (or affects) independence. Her family recognizes, even if she does not, the social and moral dangers of the campus, the slender threads of social prestige, the importance of safeguards against social failures and against the irretrievable losses from one discovered ethical or social misstep. Her family therefore demands protection through planned social opportunities and training and a campus-administered moral code even stricter than they themselves have enforced.

Parents do not make comparable demands for their sons, except indirectly. Following the mores of the general society, they count on having good morals and manners for their sons stem from the standards upheld by the women. Young men would resent, as would their fathers, any more obvious controls. The campus morale and high standards must be achieved for men as well as for women by rules, regulations, and social training for the women students.

In the women's residence, life is more complicated than in the men's, because there is more laundry work and cleaning, more shampooing, sewing, shopping, and cooking—everything necessarily regulated for the convenience and efficiency of all. There is more social awareness, therefore more gossip and personal tension. There is more sensitiveness to social success and failure, with consequent emotional fluctuations and therefore more tears and giggles, more need for personal counseling. The richer social activities—parties, dating, and entertaining of men—necessitate elaborate planning and training and a convenient framework of rules, officers, and committees. Because there is more naïveté, temptation, and far-reaching consequences, there must be more protection.

Throughout their college years, then, in addition to their classroom interests, women must divide their attention between the social activities and the campus standards. Men need the same workable body of skills, facts, insights, and attitudes; but unconsciously they refer to the women in these matters, leaving themselves freer for classroom work or for campus politics which will promote their career interests. Women student leaders conscious of their responsibility and well-indoctrinated with the right principles are the best means for making such principles prevail, for maintaining good morale.

On one coeducational campus, women students listed the following minimum equipment as a practical guide for success in dating:

Keep abreast week by week of all the town and campus entertainment facilities, the free and cheap ones, such as swimming, record hours, bridge tournaments, as well as movies, dances, concerts. Know the cost of each, the hours, and whether they are likely to be big and impersonal or small and intimate.

Know the campus codes—whether you walk or take a cab, what you wear to different places, how much is usually spent on more formal and more casual dates, whether you walk along the streets holding hands or otherwise display feelings in public, where and to what extent drinking and smoking are accepted on the campus.

Know what men of different ages and social classes expect. Some expect "Personality" and a "line." Most of them want attractiveness, good nature and friendliness, a sense of humor, interest (either genuine or assumed) which follows their own indicated interests. There are always some men who want intimate physical contact immediately, which means thinking through beforehand how far the girl is willing to go in order to keep her popularity, estimating what she stands to lose or gain, and planning various controls for the treatment of advances when they become unpleasant.

Know the psychology of men. Men too are often unstable and uncertain but their code demands that they conceal those attitudes. They are also, like the girls, "looking around" and usually prefer, as do the girls, to develop a number of casual contacts before choosing "steady" company. Although their code demands that they take the initiative, they are also alert to certain kinds and degrees of enthusiasms and suggestions as clues, and in some circumstances to even more forthright overtures from girls.

Know the problems, attitudes, and interests of men, especially their vocational problems, sports, and the business world, at least to the extent of intelligent listening, and with more depth if at all possible.

Know the physiology of sex, that men are more easily stimulated than women, and that it is therefore not fair to "lead them on" early in the evening and pull up short later on. There are excellent books for girls of all ages on sex, and there is no excuse for any girl who hasn't read at least two or three good ones.

Pause occasionally to take stock: How many men do you know well enough to pass judgment on whether or not they would make fit marriage partners? How can you, otherwise than by using your body, enhance the feeling of pleasure of the boy who takes you out?

Such guides are reduced to a more formal pedagogy in the courses on marriage and family living which are found on almost every campus. The years just before World War II and the early years of the war itself witnessed a great demand, generated and sponsored largely by the students, in marriage courses, which had been inaugurated in the mid-twenties by Groves at North Carolina. Many of them were extracurricular courses, with large classes, no credit, and no academic prerequisites. The motivation behind them was genuine, and the movement and the interest spread rapidly. For the unrest of the period they often furnished genuine release.

The postwar period saw the end of this movement as an extracurricular fad; the courses became less improvised and extemporaneous, more standardized and substantial—especially in such departments as sociology and home economics. This was of course made possible by the great increase in subject matter, in contributions from the researches and analyses of sociologists, social psychologists, and anthropologists, and in funds from the national foundations for the study of marriage and family relationships and for research in social hygiene, divorce, the class

111

structure of society, the socialization process in the schools, and adolescence in general. The development of better group techniques for instruction and discussion have also helped in the rapid development of courses in this field, for in these classes, as in no others, the projection of the student's personal problems and thinking in the classroom situation is a vital part of his instruction and progress.

A substantial backlog of literature has now accumulated and is no longer read furtively, but is introduced for coeducational class discussion in such courses and departments as personnel, social work, education, child development, law, philosophy, and ethics. Such literature is read widely by both the older and the younger generations.

It is obvious that many different kinds of marriage or family courses will be required to meet the needs of the present generation of high school and college women. Different treatments will, of course, be called for, depending on the class level, the department that offers the courses, the personality of the instructor, and the size and character of the student body. At any level, however, they are an essential ingredient of women's education. "What we are today calling education for marriage and family life," says Lawrence K. Frank, "may be recognized as the first steps toward a reorganization of our culture, something of far greater significance than all the contemporary political movements, programs and conflicts that now engross our attention." [6]

Information and analysis of all social processes, and the greater sophistication of the masses of our people in these processes, are without doubt the best means for undermining the false system of values in our current conception of romantic love. In a cultural milieu which accepts the ideal of romantic love as the ultimate evaluation of marriage, these courses cannot ignore the part that affection plays in marriage success, but they can at least instruct young people in the art of wiser initial choice and greater wisdom in the day-to-day living of marriage. They can also do much to tone down the exaggerated expectations which both the young men and young women cherish.

112

These marriage courses, both in high school and college, do much to bring about a considerable shift in emphasis from emotion to the more substantial and practical values, but in relation to both the objectives and the resistances, progress is slow. With the organized devotion of merchandising and newspapers, and with the tight grip kept by all the mass media—radio, movies, and the special youth magazines—on the romantic image, one hardly dares mention that other times, other cultures, have managed very well with less romance, with less glamour in the marriage ceremony, and with a more businesslike consideration of the contractual details and implications.

Why not teach, at least at the college level, that girls can be as selective about their husbands as their jobs? No young man says, "My interests and aptitudes are for agriculture, but I'll have to plan to live in the city because my fiancee is a statistician." He does not even think of looking for another girl who might be majoring in 4-H clubs. Nor does he think about changing his own vocational plans; he keeps right on studying about farm financing and fertilizers and lets the budding statistician do the worrying, if any.

Conversely, there is no need for a girl who has specialized in mathematics and statistics to marry a farmer and retire to a Texas ranch or the most rural section of Iowa or Vermont. There are hundreds of young men in any one of a dozen other vocations who would keep her in the city where she can find congenial work. There is a satisfactory variety of temperaments and personalities in any of the vocations and she can find that "one" who fits her individuality as well in nuclear physics as in soil conservation.

But she cannot rid herself of the obsession that there is "only one," and she is mortally afraid that somebody else may get him. She has too often been told that "a bird in the hand is worth two in the bush," and she dreads that fatal twenty-to-thirty decade when her attractiveness fades so rapidly! She needs to weigh her drive and talents for mathematics against her drive and talents for the details and satisfactions of homemaking, and if the scale tips toward statistics she should summon the courage to cross agriculture off her list and begin to look around with a somewhat different purpose.

In other words, modern times have made it necessary for the young woman herself to exercise the judicious objectivity which was formerly the function of her parents, her family. The "arranged marriage," formerly maneuvered by solicitous and hardheaded parents, must today, in our culture, be arranged by the young people themselves, and their education must help them toward success in the process. It has now become a task of vocational guidance, provided largely by the schools, or certainly a part of educational guidance, to call the attention of young women to such factors as these.

Imagine presenting these arguments to a class of starry-eyed eighteen-year-olds some sunny May afternoon! Better to pick a damp March afternoon or a brisk October day, and to begin by stating firmly that there will be a question on this material on the final examination. Just think of a magazine story that ended, ". . . and so they went on to graduate school and then obtained research fellowships. At twenty-eight she married a man from her own branch of government service and had only two children; but not until he was *thirty-two* and a full-fledged atomic scientist did he find a homemaking enthusiast who gave him the wonderful home and six children he had always longed for."

"Why *will* they get married?" lamented a graduate dean, and he was speaking of men, not women. If the graduate schools do not get their fair share of the best minds and personalities, it may be partially because the attractive young wives and family responsibilities of these students have denied them the continuous and leisurely maturing process of the true devotee to scholarship.

In all this we see the usual fault of the mass communication media: their steam-roller tactics force standardization. No voice can be heard that raises the question of whether or not the high school and college marriage courses can be used to prepare adolescents for the life experiences they will face, without by this very procedure urging them toward early marriage. Classes devoted exclusively to marriage, with the emphasis inevitably on the earlier and the more absorbingly domestic years, elicit such spontaneous enthusiasm from the eighteen-year-old men and women students that the courses tend to promote a kind of spurious value for these experiences and these years. The counterbalance for their powerful pull will surely require more than vocational studies and skills.

The drive toward social and sex competency is strong. The drive toward individual fulfillment is also strong and if denied will lead to serious maladjustment later. This drive for self-fulfillment needs to be identified and brought to full consciousness as early as possible. To do this, the subject matter must be truly liberalizing, built upon our present-day civilization and not on any nineteenth-century or European substitute, and attractively presented by powerful, not pedantic, teaching.

... *6*

Education for Homemaking

IF THERE are any doubts about the significance of the home economics movement in the unfolding of our American culture, a few paragraphs from any of the magazines or manuals of the 1850s should dispel them. Recipes were chatty little conversation pieces, vague but gently encouraging in tone. Everything was very ladylike, free of the quantitative details which burden the mind and smack of science and the schoolroom. Here are just a few items from the pages of yesteryear:

Muffins. With warm milk, a liberal allowance of yeast, flour, a little salt, and an egg or two, make dough a little softer than for Sally Lunn. After kneading or beating, get it to rise slightly on a hot iron plate—turning them to bake upper side when under side is done. The great object is to keep them light and moist . . . the usual size and thickness you learn from the specimens sold in shops. After toasting, muffins should be crisp, but crumpets soft and woolly. It is like eating a bit of blanket soaked in butter. If you are pining for crumpets and have no iron plate, you may bake them in the frying pan such as used for cake-making.

Rice Dressed in the Turkish Manner. Take eight ounces of rice and wash them many times in water, steep them in some hot water, drain them, and put into a sauce pan. Then swell the rice with some good gravy soup, taking care not to add too much. Divide the rice into two portions, taking one half and

116

beating it with some ground saffron, four pepper-corns in powder, a piece of butter, some beef marrow, and a little jelly prepared from a fowl. Mix them all together, and serve up in a soup tureen or deep dish with the gravy soup by itself.

Cleaning was a grim and hazardous project for the housewife of 1860, but home decoration was a riotous adventure, if the current descriptions can be trusted. For example:

To Clean Black Silk with Very Little Trouble and Expense. Take entirely to pieces the dress, jacket, etc. and well shake each piece. Spread over a deal table a clean sheet of paper, and on it lay a breadth of the silk. Brush it well on both sides with a fine soft brush. To a clean quart pudding basin pour a half pint of cold water, adding half a pint of good sweetened gin, which is better for the purpose than unsweetened, as the sugar stiffens the silk. Thoroughly wash over the best side of the silk. Wash it from edge to edge and wet it well all over. Place it in a clean towel until a large iron is well heated. Iron the wrong side quickly, until dry. This simple process stiffens, cleans, and makes the silk look new.

To Remove Grease Spots from Dresses (woolen), Furniture, Carpets, Tablecloths, etc. Make the poker red hot. Hold it over the grease spot, within an inch of the material. In a second or two the grease will disappear. Be sure not to let the poker touch the material to burn it.

To Destroy Crickets or Beetles: Put some strong snuff in the cracks and holes from whence they come. The parings of cucumbers will, if strewn about near their holes, drive them away.

The Music Corner: An upright piano should be placed with its back to the room. This position is not only good from a decorative standpoint, but a performer likes to be shielded by the instrument.

Hang a square of tapestry over the back from a brass rod. If possible let the painted subject relate to music or sentiment, and have it sufficiently large to cover the surface of the piano. Across the top of the piano lay a scarf of Liberty silk, or another painted panel. The only bric-a-brac that combines with this drapery is a pair of candelabra, the quainter in style the better. With this as a foundation many schemes may be carried out. Bas-relief heads in plaster can be swung from the brass rod without injur-

117

ing the wood of the piano. Medallions of Beethoven, Mozart, or Wagner can be purchased. A long panel of cherubs goes well, or a line of Delft or Japanese plates.

A low settle may be placed beneath this, and a number of cushions placed on the seat and leaning against the piano will add to the coziness and grace of the decoration.

It is the home economics movement, unparalleled in any other country in its totality of government laboratories, graduate research, industrial subsidies, and classroom teaching, which has cleared all such folderol from the home life of the American people. The average woman may still be naïve in politics, romantic in love, and bewitched by cosmetics, but in her household routines she stands for no nonsense.

Since its earliest beginnings in the 1880s, home economics has developed in the schools, in the government laboratories, and in industry as both a science and an art. Practical in every aspect, and always well subsidized, it has grown up close to the American soil, expanding with the growing economy and deepening its roots with every technological advancement.

Modern living would be unthinkable without this accumulated body of knowledge. Educators therefore face several important questions: How much of this knowledge does the twentieth-century woman need in order to fulfill her role as homemaker? How much is available in sources other than formal classroom education? What training is appropriate for the earlier grades? for high school? for college? How can we allow for individual differences in intellectual capacity, background, and social outlook?

An adequate curriculum in homemaking would look at the woman completely impersonally and apply itself to all of her problems. But what is the essence of the modern woman, old or young, married or single, aristocratic or proletarian, urban or rural? And what are her problems, personal or financial or social? Home economics must combine with many other disciplines to furnish the answers.

Compared with earlier times, life for the American woman in

the twentieth century is wider in scope but has less depth, is perhaps no less strenuous but has difficulties of a quite different kind. The modern woman is better informed on such subjects as household matters and principles of diet. Certainly she has better recipes—far different from those for the muffins and Turkish rice of the 1850s. Foods are readily available in infinite variety; and more important, they are available in finished and usable form, so that her former long hours of work in preparing them are largely eliminated.

Clothing, too, for herself, her menfolk, and her children, is available in more attractive and functional style, requiring little exertion on her part. If women sew or knit today, it is for the sheer pleasure of creating, or for added elegance of their wardrobes and household equipment, rather than for the maintenance of the basic essentials of clothing for all the family. Women's clothing not only shows more variety and simplicity than it used to, but it is cosmopolitan in its fashion. No longer is the country cousin conspicuous with her rural style; every newspaper has its fashion column, and the 4-H clubs, the chain stores, and the two-pound, mail-order catalogues have leveled the standards everywhere.

The American woman today is not only more comfortably dressed, but she is far cleaner and better groomed. She has excellent soap, cleaning fluids, bathtubs, and household equipment, as well as cheap and convenient public services for laundry work and cleaning. What a contrast to the lady of the 1850s who cleaned her own black silk dress! The beauty shops can camouflage any substandard features, and the inexpensive, well-designed clothes leave her no excuse for dowdiness. Especially important is the dentist who, even more than the beautician, reaches all ages and classes with his beautifying corrective work.

The modern woman also has fewer children, and the span of years devoted to child care is therefore shortened. Technological advances have eliminated many of the hours spent in incessant routines. The prepared baby foods, the cooperative nursery schools, the simpler styles in clothing, the diaper services, and the baby sitters have greatly changed the work of the young parent. This aggregate of services has not necessarily reduced the actual hours of time which children, especially those of grade school age, require, for the new styles of living bring other time-consuming activities. Shopping and chauffeuring, daily rather than weekly bathing, more frequent travel and cultural excursions, regular visits to clinics, and more cooperative community projects are the newer duties which keep the average parent occupied outside as well as inside the four confining walls.

The aged, the chronically ill, the physically handicapped, and the financially incompetent are also no longer dependent on the housewife's care. Public institutions and social security planning have relieved her of much of the former household drudgery of caring for her less fortunate maiden aunts, choleric uncles, and orphaned cousins.

Since she no longer has to spend so many hours in the kitchen, the modern woman has achieved greater mobility and cultivated more cosmopolitan entertainment activities. She travels by car, bus, or plane, turns on the radio at will, sees as many movies as she cares to, and enjoys the stimulation of books and magazines. She has plenty of company, through school or community activities; her church, her clubs, and her fraternal organizations can offer her as much education, entertainment, or community service as her own fancy and her pocketbook dictate.

The fortunes and misfortunes of the homemaker are the stock in trade of the comic-strip artist and the cartoonist. They have set up all the necessary stereotypes and provided a sharp and fluent vocabulary. Together with the radio and the movies, the cartoons and comics constitute for the layman the major sources of information and directives in family living. And both the popular and the smarter magazines often match these caricatures in pace and style in their excursions into this field. For example, Edith Stern's hypothetical but much-quoted advertisement gives a sardonic twist to the joys of family responsibilities:

Help wanted: Domestic: Female. All cooking, cleaning, laundering, sewing, shopping, weekday chauffeuring, social secretarial service and complete care of three children. Salary at employer's option. Time off if possible.[1]

Agnes Rogers draws a more serious picture of the American woman:

> As a wife, she is expected to be the shrewd dispenser and possible contributor to the family purse; the comforter when her husband is depressed; the wise counselor in his business problems; the enchantress who holds him by her radiant youthful loveliness; the gay companion with whom he likes to rough it in the woods. Moreover she's a member of the community, a citizen of the world and as such must take an active part in local affairs and be thoroughly familiar with the latest developments between Stalin and Tito. That isn't all. She is still the guardian of finer things in life. The church is her special province. Not as vestryman—she must not aspire to matters of broad policy—but in a more humble capacity, she must work faithfully and devotedly. She must keep up with the new trends in the arts, read new books, listen to new music and in general contribute to the support of matters cultural. This impossible array of standards gives the woman the idea that she has failed.[2]

This sort of thing makes excellent reading and it is all too true. We lay it aside with both a smile and a sigh. It can be equally well translated into more academic language, and after a stimulating evening of discussing the complications of family life, the needs of the different classes, the psychological and social needs of wife and mother, the relationship of the youth culture to the adult culture, and the hazards of transition from one consensus to another, we have some sympathy for the cloistered professor who waved it all aside with a despairing gesture: "I do think it is all very interesting, but I don't see what *Education* can do about it." He, par excellence, is the man women must educate.

In more practical vein, one recent study of more than a hundred college-bred mothers and homemakers has analyzed the basic frustrations of the household in the order of their frequency (not necessarily the order of importance) as follows:[3]

1. *Broken time spans.* Household tasks are constantly being

shifted and interrupted. There is no opportunity for concentrated effort in one field, and especially no continuous blocks of leisure for writing, reading, or pursuit of a hobby. Too many different and unspecialized types of tasks are required, with no logical sequences and with little possibility of better organization for efficiency. These shifts and jumps and frustrations in employment are psychologically intolerable and physically enervating. The pressure for hurrying and worrying at one time and the temptation to dawdle at another make housework seem formless and endless and make genuine leisure an impossibility.

2. *Unused abilities.* Homemaking must be classified as an unspecialized occupation, the kind of situation where the highly trained manager must also serve as the unskilled janitor and sweep out the factory. Most of the work of managing and caring for a home and family does not demand the use of high intelligence and skill, and therefore women worry about two things: whether their intellectual ambitions and habits can be resumed after the few years of child care are over, and (especially true of the women who have relinquished responsible earning positions) whether they are justified in spending so much of their time and talents on the mere physical labor of washing, cooking and running the electrical equipment.

3. *Unrelated tasks, and disorganization.* This difficulty is in special contrast to the repetitive processes of the factory or office that enable the worker to perfect her routines and at the same time carry them out with the minimum of mental effort. Too many household tasks have a makeshift quality and involve a compromise with time and money which is renewed every day.

4. *Social isolation.* There is very little social interaction in housework. The worker has to be, for the most part, self-motivated; she cannot enjoy the stimulus from fellow workers or the exchange of ideas with differing and changing groups of workers. The contacts which she has with others are discursive rather than fixed and stabilizing. Even her relationship with her children is not continuous and satisfying; in the modern family the children are oriented toward a number of different focuses in

school and community, and their position and attitudes in the household are not fixed and dependent as they were in the nineteenth century when the family was a more self-sufficient institution. Her isolation is often aggravated by the more anonymous neighborhoods of today in contrast to the gregarious living of former village life.

5. *Discrepancy between effort or achievement and reward.* There is a much larger variation in the time given by women to their household tasks than in the working hours for men of all occupations and classes. The woman may run her home on from two to sixteen hours a day, from $2,000 to $20,000 a year. The amount of her leisure as well as her rewards in terms of social approbation varies widely with the economic factors. The psychological rewards vary no less but are more closely related to the husband's status and gratitude than to the wife's efforts and abilities. College alumnae ask almost pathetically for assurance of their value as housewives and mothers.

These are obvious and convincing discords, but educators—especially college educators—must not be deafened by them to some of the more inconspicuous harmonies of family life. There are literally thousands of competent homemakers who don't experience these dilemmas. They seem to be placid in temperament and to find intellectual stimulation in their families and friends. They respond to a creative challenge in the domestic workshop, display a sense of humor, and enjoy sound health in mind and body. They are apparently very seldom polled and never analyzed. Perhaps these are "the forgotten women," too normal to be newsworthy.

The less privileged socioeconomic family would show somewhat different patterns, less intense in some categories and weighted more heavily in others. Both the personal inadequacies and the societal resistances vary with the individual and with the circumstances of her life and education. Mrs. A. compassionately assumes the hospital bills of the 25-year-old daughter who has allowed her insurance to lapse because she spends her thirty dollars a week on clothes and gay living. Her son's teeth are defective because she can't get him to drink milk or visit the dentist. Mrs. B. loves her fine husband and her three-year-old daughter and her sparkling little four-room house, but she is depressed and discontented because she is embarrassed by her father's shiftless habits and oppressed by the constant bickerings of her in-laws. Mrs. C. has just succeeded in finding and furnishing a little one-room apartment for herself and her child but lives in fear that her husband will discover her new address and come to beat her up and wreck her furniture again.

Gilbert Seldes sharpens the contrasts between these diversified types of women in our society, especially between the more aggressive, sophisticated, and thoughtful woman and the one who is ignorant, dependent, and unimaginative.[4] His contrast is drawn very simply between those who do and those who do not listen to the daytime radio serials.

Seldes finds that the listeners reveal reduced imagination and scant personal resources, a dulled use of intellectual power as though they were rooted only in the past. Their ideas are routine, they struggle for personal control of themselves and their families, and they fear that they will not succeed because the environment is entirely against them. They can hope for solution only by some lucky accident. Interpersonal relations are stereotyped and strained; there seems to be constantly some block between man and woman—a fear of sex, of domination or separation. The world is monotonous, repetitive, filled with petty detail; the unknown holds no challenge, only apprehension.

Says Seldes, "They have been trained . . . to be wives and mothers and unconsciously to carry out and maintain the rules, moral beliefs and values of their social level. This they do effectively . . . Yet they see life as monotonous drudgery, personal relations as troubled; they hope to escape by some stroke of magic (for example, by magically achieving education); they do not look forward to the future; their hopes are dim."

The nonlisteners to the daytime serials were not given to stereotyped thinking; they exhibited imagination and had developed resources within themselves for solving their problems.

They saw people not as troubling one another, but cooperating to solve difficulties. These women were not hampered by the terror of losing a husband or by the irrational fear of infidelity. They did not feel the need to dominate men, although many of them as professional women were in continuous competition with men.

These nonlisteners did not feel that their lives were tragic. They did see some disappointment, frustration, and bad fortune in the life about them, but they did not assume, as did the listener group, that nothing could be done about these ills. The future looked pleasant and challenging because they did not look for a magical solution to human problems. They believed in personal effort and they used their imagination to cope with the unfamiliar.

Surely few who read these comments can doubt the grave maladjustments in family relationships and personal development which characterize large segments of our population. Following this sharpened awareness of the needs come the usual uncertainties of all education: How can it provide appropriate information and promote the desired intellectual habits? Can the basic ideas reach youth's unfolding imaginations equally well through any discipline, scientific or humanistic? In theory or with practice? For the dull as well as the bright? Is German or Latin the better route? Or history, economics, psychology, or mathematics? How much training in which subjects, and in what years?

The extent of work in homemaking indicated for any given student would obviously be determined by her individual needs. Not all students, for example, are required to take courses in English composition if their proficiency can be demonstrated in the entrance examinations.

Let us look for a moment at Patricia, who entered college as a freshman with a major interest in economics and history. Patricia lives in a suburban city of 10,000 where her father is a physician. She and her older brother and her younger sister enjoy an eleven-room house, surrounded by plenty of playing space which has served as social center for the neighborhood. Patricia's mother has shared the household duties and management with her children, and they have learned to cook and to plan meals, parties, and picnics.

The three children have watched their parents buy food and household equipment and have participated in planning and buying their own clothing. They have listened to family discussions about nutrition, infection, and excessive fatigue. They know that too much candy is bad for the teeth, that most men dislike most vegetables, and that you drop bread but not milk from your diet when you want to keep your slim figure. They have thumbed the etiquette books on formal table setting and the government bulletins on moth control and the removal of stains. They know what it takes to make the cook an efficient worker and how to organize the young folks to clear away the picnic debris and wash the dishes.

Does Patricia need a college course in food preparation and meal service? in problems of adjustment in the family? or half a semester in the home management house? Or does she need a course in the chemistry of foods, or child psychology, or genetics, or euthenics, or the family in modern society? Can we count on her, after she graduates, to read the current magazines, listen to the conversation of her friends and parents, patronize interesting restaurants, indulge in window shopping, and learn from the widening circle of her own social activities?

Will Patricia, or even some of her more inept friends, live up to our expectations and rise to any occasion, buy some cookbooks, and read up on nutrition and child welfare when the need arises? Is it unrealistic to assume that the information gained from the advertisers, the fashion magazines, the household equipment demonstrations, and the parent-teacher meetings can be successfully combined with knowledge gained from basic courses in chemistry, botany, sociology, and psychology, if the home environment has provided during the growing years a rich experience and a permissive and affectionate family environment?

College planning is more uncertain in the field of home economics than in many another field because of the greater importance of the home background and also because of the vastly unequal precollege experience among entering freshmen. Not only must the social derivation of the students be taken into account, but also their vocational interests and future status. What can be recommended for Mary, who enters high school from a broken home, who plans to help support her mother by secretarial work, and who will probably practice the combined roles of earner and homemaker most of her life? Shall we advise her to study nutrition and general household efficiency, or adjustment in the family, or interior decoration? How much general cultural ("good citizenship") training can she sacrifice for vocational and homemaking requirements?

Whether today's student is groomed for home and family life in courses precisely labeled "home economics" or in the offerings of some other departments is immaterial. Many of the things she should know may be found between the covers of the textbooks in economics, history, and psychology, in world literature and philosophy, as well as in family and marriage courses.

No one could describe in a few pages all the facts and ideologies which must be included, nor could anyone cover in one short summary or any one course the many volumes of stimulating and pertinent discussion which have appeared even within the last decade. In all these pages there has been much that is sound, much that is merely startling. One such book, one summary, one formal course, is, after all, only the road map to guide the explorer in his own traveling, to anticipate for him some of the possible destinations, and to alert him to the experiences he may encounter along the way.

In the woman's world there are three divisions to be mapped out for youthful study and education, corresponding to the three spheres of her future activity. For the purposes of orientation and survey, these large and irregular areas might be designated as (1) her inner life and states of mind, (2) her day-to-day round of operation, which would include her physical routines as well as her relations and interactions with other human beings, and (3) the circumstances and realities of the larger social world outside the home.

These organized segments of her life are, of course, interrelated. Every function in the second area—for example, her care of her children—has its counterpart in the first, the area of her own internal feelings and purposes; and it is likewise molded by the third, by the events and pressures in the outside world. If she loves her children excessively in order to fill the emptiness of her life, she must be prepared for the school years which will wean them away from her and bring her conflict and disruption. These interlockings are inescapable, and much wisdom is needed to discern and manage them.

To adjust the activities of the second, the intermediate, area to both her personal identity and to the world of affairs is the never-ending dilemma of her life. She must learn to live with the past of her own experience, the present of her daily routines, and the hovering uncertainties of the future. It is education's job to prepare her for these overlapping areas of homemaking. But formal education is no panacea, and other agencies also carry many of the responsibilities; church and community also share either purposefully or inadvertently in the learning process. Education cannot assume the full responsibility for the ultimate adjustments, the final reconciliation of self and life. The schools can be held accountable for only their fair share of these burdens. Many of the solutions rightfully belong to other institutions in society—to government, church, clubs, and sports.

In the daily round of home activities in this intermediate operational area lying between the subjective zone of attitude and feeling and the outer zone of the total society, the simplest are the physical activities of keeping house, cooking, cleaning, gardening, building, and decorating, and, perhaps, more important than all others, budgeting and buying. In the outside world the fluctuations in styles, the constant technological advances, and the enticements of advertising are the pressures which bring distress as well as satisfaction.

Technical knowledge is needed about standards and quality in food and home furnishings, especially about the manner in which these commodities are affected by the processes of manufacture and merchandising, by political and economic factors. How else can the housewife make the best choices among the cans on the supermarket shelf or coordinate her activities with those of other housewives to influence prices and qualities? Some knowledge is also needed about the efficiency of her bodily movement in household tasks and even more about the management of other human beings—husband and children—in order that work loads may be streamlined and distributed effectively.

The new fashions in architecture and building could do much to help the housewife in gaining efficiency and the inner poise which goes with it, if only the American family could throw overboard the outworn model of gracious living borrowed from European aristocracy and evolve a more realistic pattern based on their own new materials, different climate, changed living habits, and more relaxed social relationships. This is the era of plastic floors and upholstery, bamboo curtains, foam rubber mattresses, simplicity rather than baroque elegance in furniture, informal dining, ease in cooking and cleaning. The new fabrics and modes can promote a higher standard of living with an original, "built-in" kind of graciousness which would permit the generous and ingenious American spirit its proper range.

In these housekeeping roles, the inner attitudes and feelings play their accompanying part. Physical fatigue is not so devastating as mental fatigue—the boredom which is first irksome, then smothering. Housewifery can produce an artificial dependence on the family if too many of the direct contacts with the outside world are cut off. Integration with the passing scene may be lost simply through time-consuming drudgery, or because the dominating husband or family obscures too much of the view, or because nothing in previous education or experience has opened the windows to the more enticing vistas of art and literature or to the stimulation of civic action and service. The independent spirit must be cradled tenderly in the schools, must be sturdy and well nourished at the outset, if it is to survive these early years of husband and children and household cares.

Another function of a woman in this second area of household routine and interpersonal relationships concerns the companionship and care of her husband. She must learn to know him as the head of her home and household, as an earner, and as her sex mate; and later she has to study him anew in his role as father. She must accept his individual attitudes toward home and wife and children just as she must in general accept the attitude of the world toward them. He may regard all women (except his own wife, of course) as inferior, or at least as inhabiting a sphere far removed from his own world of men and ideas and action.

"We will build a new and different life together," he will promise her. "You will never become soured and bitter like your mother, or dull and dumpy like the boss's wife," he will say with cheerful confidence, but his mere determination is not enough to forestall the apprehended eventualities; that would call for information and insights which he is counting on from *her* dowry. *His* contribution to the marriage contract is in more material form.

A large part of the relations between husband and wife takes the form of attitudes and feelings, about themselves and about other people, which they may take pleasure in sharing. The basic personality may reveal itself not in consciously accepted attitudes, but in the less calculated words and deeds which grow out of the inner convictions. In spite of himself, the young husband feels his superiority. Not that he was born so; but as our society is organized, it is the man who has been allotted most of the advantages along with his greater share of legal and financial responsibilities.

The woman, on the other hand, tends to accept the attitudes and opinions of most men about most women. This occurs principally because she has been overwhelmed by these views in her formative years. She accepts the fact that she is expected always to compete for men's favor, that men's jobs and opportunities are the ones most glamorized, that women's primary jobs—the jobs with which they contribute a full fourth of the nation's wealth—are without prestige and often without dignity.

In this respect, any young wife should be prepared to quote Kimball Young to her husband, unless, of course, he too has already read the following statement:

The real variable is the individual, independent of sex or race. The traditional position of women results from lack of opportunity, failure of men to permit them to take part wholeheartedly in the culture, that is, from normal capacities. In this regard women are in a position analogous to that of children, non-literate peoples and those in the lower economic strata of society. They are not what we call intellectual because they have not been taught to handle the materials of knowledge.[5]

But it is one thing for one scholar to concede this verbally, and quite another for all men to behave as if it were true; and in the meantime, full knowledge of her individual situation projected against the long history and the complicated present status of her sex is surely woman's most useful weapon. With this she can protect herself against both the inner resentments and their outer manifestations in aggressive behavior. Long ago, George Eliot recognized that "a man's mind has always the advantage of being masculine. Even his ignorance is of sounder quality," which is merely a better way of stating that up to the present generation man has the more powerful social sanctions on his side.

For both men and women there are long steps yet to be taken in achieving a full personal and social maturity in our culture. It is doubtful whether women, either individually or as a group, have developed emotional stability in keeping with their rapid strides in the economic and social spheres. Societal pressures are too unrelenting; taboo and conflict have confused them. Women's education, both from mother to daughter and from teacher to pupil, has not dealt frankly with the affective side of life.

Men, as a rule, are not sufficiently mature in their own feelings to accept maturity in women. Mass media of communication have intensified their time-worn desire for the more superficial qualities—the youth and beauty and sex of Hollywood, over-dramatized and intellectually undemanding. They expect to pay for these with only material goods, not with the spontaneous exchange of thought and feeling between mature personalities. One of the most revealing examples of wishful thinking came from husbands and wives in the *same group* of respondents to a questionnaire. "Do you ever talk over politics and current affairs together?" asked the questionnaire. "No," said the husbands; "Yes," said the wives. To the wives such conversations were important and memorable; to the husbands they were negligible and forgotten.

Many are the social scientists who warn us that what we need is not equality and uniformity but more variability in both sexes, more stimulation for social innovations, more freedom for devising new roles for women and for men also. It is neither dependence nor independence for the woman or for the man that is wanted, but interdependence for each upon the other. Everything that emphasizes the separation in interests, outlook, and attitudes of men and women is a deterrent to social progress.

Both men and women are too close to this revolution in attitudes and values to understand all its complications. Joyce Cary goes so far as to call it the greatest social revolution in the true sense that the world has ever seen. If the understanding of these social forces and their implications is so troublesome yet so vital, we could scarcely expect that the needed concepts would find their way into the consciousness and thinking of men or women without explicit indoctrination in the schools.

Without this understanding, how can women speed their own progress and keep their poise and inner calm, to say nothing of their sense of humor? It is easy enough to predict that the long-term results of this inevitable movement toward sex equality will be beneficial; it is obvious, too, that its ideologies are compatible with the broader ideals of both Christianity and democracy. But it is hard to focus on long-term benefits and philosophical implications when the immediate effects on all the participants are both unpalatable and disorganizing.

Often the entering wedge of friction between husband and wife is the wife's employment, and many a man feels that career activities are justifiable for his wife only if they can be fitted successfully around a happy home life. In other words, the burden of home responsibility in the present stage of our evolution is on the wife, and this predication is her starting point. It is up to her to explore the circumstances thoroughly and plot her strategy ingeniously. Fortunately the research shows that there is no superiority in the quality of the marriage adjustment for either the working or the nonworking wife. In spite of what the movies, soap operas, and popular magazine fiction indicate, the two-income family can be a very happy one. Continuous, full-time employment for the mother may not always be possible, but successful homemaking is well within the reach of all the working wives who have been educated to attack the problem with conviction and imagination.

Those who oppose woman's drive toward gainful employment feel that it is only a symptom of a maladjustment, not a solution. They see the malaise as based on neurotic, competitive jealousy between men and women. Actually the resentment of the husbands can be traced to three rather special circumstances: (1) when their own sense of insecurity in their job oppresses them, (2) when their wives neglect them and their home life, and (3) when the woman has the better job or earns the larger salary. Of course, he is irritated when she is not available for his social responsibilities and their congenial life together. And it is not unlikely that the attitudes he encounters among his colleagues and his friends will be damaging not only to his self-regarding feelings, but even to his business prestige, his outward behavior, and ultimately to his income.

Fortunately the records show a variety of good results from outside employment which both spouses may discover and cultivate. The higher income does much to enhance the home life, ease financial strain, and allow luxuries; the wife's personal growth makes her a more healthy-minded person and increases her husband's interest and respect; the necessity for close family cooperation may generate a better psychology of man-to-wife relationship and more efficiency and independence in the children. In another generation those dramatic successes of adventurous cooperation may be too commonplace to reach the best-seller lists in current reading.

Cogent arguments are still to be found in these modern decades for a clear division of labor, following the familiar old patterns, between the man and woman, with the wife relieving the husband quite completely of all home responsibilities. For some careers and with some temperaments, the man cannot rise to the achievements expected of him or reach the full development of his capacities without freedom from the distracting routines of daily life.

Relaxation in the nonoffice hours is the antidote for the pressures and strains of ruthless business competition. Creative work has its own special methods; the long, quiet, sometimes tedious hours of cultivation are not to be washed away by daily flash floods of household crises. Weary hours in the laboratory, in the practice room, in the library stacks, can never strike a balance with equally long hours with the lawnmower or the children's picnics. Especially in the early years of development and competition, the rising young professional man does need that "body servant," that insulation for his productive life which later successes will bring him in the form of his aides or his secretaries, his laboratory assistants, his disciples, his office nurse, his cook, his gardener. Here indeed are some of the truly continuing and insoluble problems of married life.

The inherited traditional patterns served such contingencies very well, which is one of the reasons why they are so long in dying. As Milton expressed it:

> For contemplation he and valour form'd,
> For softness she, and sweet attractive grace;
> He for God only, she for God in him.[6]

Long-range educational perspectives, however, must include not only the nature of the current marriage relationships but also the frequency with which each pattern is found, and this old-fashioned pattern so poetically described by Milton for his generation can scarcely be expected to return to its earlier popularity. College women would most certainly find themselves allergic to it.

It is largely in the higher socioeconomic strata, in the managerial and professional classes, in the college-educated groups, that the newer patterns will seem so appealing, so necessary. It is only in these less populous classes, the typical college strata in contrast to the larger numbers of blue-collar and white-collar workers, that self-fulfillment may be accomplished through work, where the individual does rise above the machine that employs and supports him, where the supplementary satisfactions of home life are less enveloping for both partners.

Society cannot afford to lose the contributions of its most fertile minds and creative artists, and the business world will not run smoothly without its own special breed of managerial talent and competency. Nevertheless the question of whether the husband's contribution is worthy of the "sacrifice" of the wife can be answered only in relative terms. Perhaps his contribution is so obvious that he can sustain his justifiable domination, affording her rich satisfactions in her supporting role—especially if she is the kind of wife who finds her fulfillment through the successive stages in the chronology of homemaking. Perhaps he may be touched with the faint suspicion of Dorothea's husband in *Middlemarch,* that he is not unmixedly adorable, "and like the rest of us, felt how soothing it would have been to have had a companion who would never find it out."

At the beginning of his career, he is grateful for the comforts of his home and for the luxury of having children without assuming the responsibilities for them; they give him the very drive, the inspiration, that he needs. But as he grows in professional stature, he needs a different kind of stimulation, more worldly, more intellectual. What then sustains the wife if her simpler habits can no longer provide for her husband's needs? Does the thoroughly domesticated species of wife continue to meet his demands? How can we be sure that a truly satisfying marriage partnership will endure?

Too often, perhaps, the older marriage formula is built on values so false and shoddy that eventually neither of its participants finds enduring satisfactions, and the husband's larger demands rob everyone and pay no dividends. The business code "demands" expensive lunches, clothes, and cocktail parties, which in turn require such financial sacrifices in home life that nothing can be bought to fill the leisure hours but the weekly routines of movies, radio, and television.[7]

Only in the utopias have some of these deeper lying problems of modern marriage been "solved." Two psychological truths, however, cannot be overlooked: (1) Creative talent makes heavy and incessant demands on the total personality; it begins its development early and cannot afford to wait for middle age. Marriage and children drain off energy and earnings, both of which may be vital for either partner in the early years. (2) The submerging of one personality within another is a recognized barrier to lasting mental health and emotional maturity. Activities and interests may be shared, but not spiritual resources; each must develop his own. Early sacrifices, however generously made, may lead to later resentment if individual growth has been stunted.

It is clearly evident that most of the current economic and social forces are strengthening the trend toward equality for women. This does not mean that any one of such forces calls for either radical acceleration or aggressive resistance. Education takes cognizance of all the forces and may play a part in modifying their directions. If it does not at least anticipate them correctly, how can it deal adequately with its more important function of forearming for future encounters all the young personalities entrusted to its care?

Finally, in the exploration of the operational area of the average homemaker and its relation to her inner feelings and outside forces, consideration must be given to her complicated relationships with her children. We dismiss at once the "service station" concept of the family, with the mother as manager, cashier, and window-washer, motivated and directed by owners and managers beyond her control and offering the interchange of only material goods and services. Today's mother does not truly serve her children by endlessly doing what children could do as well for themselves as they practice their daily lessons in self-reliance and cooperation.

The essential role of the family is to provide emotional security for its members. It doesn't matter how much time the mother spends with her children if love and faith are given in generous proportions. It doesn't matter whether the discipline is loose or tight if it is constant and motivated by mature affection and understanding. Society will discipline the child and give him its own terrific drive toward achievement, but his family, says Margaret Mead, "his slender little family, just a couple of parents alone in the world are the narrow platform on which he stands." [8] Too many words in too many college courses have recently been showered upon students, teachers, and parents to demand any further paragraphs on all of these very important ideas. The modern picture includes the father as well as the mother, and the children most of all, in planning, building, using, and enjoying the American home.

The feelings and attitudes of the mother, her inner life, probably achieve their greatest importance in her relations with her children, because the innermost thoughts and tensions of the children are an outgrowth, a reflection, of her own. The mother-engrossed child does not readily throw off his maternal domination. All too easily, if the father is passive or indifferent, the mother becomes too exclusively the object of his love and identification, the principal agent in his socialization. As his conscience develops through this loving discipline, duty and right become for him feminine figures. Niceties of behavior and thought are concessions to feminine demands; he may later resent them as such and doubt that they are good in themselves. With too little time spent in the companionship of the father and in family activities, he may derive his standards of behavior and thought too much from his contemporaries in school and playground. The father and the family unit are the steadying and balancing forces most needed in building a stronger social ethic in our culture today.

In view of all these factors, drawn from the three spheres of family life, the goals for our teaching seem to emerge more clearly. We may announce them as follows: to foster in each student—woman, man, or child—that combination of intellectual and emotional growth which will free him to work out independently a life that satisfies both his needs and his capacities. But at the same time his education must enable him to make his maximum contribution to other members of society; and for women at the present stage of their evolution, that contribution would include not only her service within the family but also the organized endeavor to further progress of all women within their own group. Education for homemaking cannot be conceived in any other terms.

This wider perspective must serve as the key to the problem of home economics curriculums in the field of higher education, where the development of a fair and unemotional appraisal has proved especially difficult for both men and women. The subject does not seem to invite the neutral and objective point of view. It is usually considered as being either the most recent and brazen of the threats to sound scholarship or the welcome inspiration which will solve all women's educational problems.

Frequently the subject matter of home economics is inaccurately labeled, sometimes for purposes of good strategy and often from just plain carelessness and inertia. Chemistry of foods, economics of the consumer, or genetic psychology sound better to some ears than the science of cookery, household administration, or child care and training. A general term such as "nutrition" may indicate an emphasis on chemistry, on physiology, or even on economics and psychology; a course in "the family" may be purely social science complete with history, philosophy, research, and statistics, or it may be quite humanistic, personal, discursive, or practical.

Some see in home economics the mecca for the lazy or under-nourished mind, whereby techniques are emphasized rather than ideas, and a limited segment of the subject matter is stretched over one or two so-called college years. Others offer its cultiva-tion as the current remedy for all women's troubles, a revival of the slogans and sentiments which have made our social system work in the past: It is an "honor" and a "privilege" to work in the kitchen, make beds, and watch children, and women should guard these areas carefully and exclusively as their own.

According to one psychologist, large doses of home economics, intellectualized as much as you please, constitute the shock treat-ment for the restless housewife: reconcile her to her lot. Some educational planners have come to believe that the younger gen-eration will actually prefer homemaking curriculums, although more realistic merchandisers will take no chances. In a contest sponsored by a New York department store featuring the typical college girl, the privilege of advertising her as putting marriage before a career was carefully written into the contract and signed by all contestants before the final judging.

Home economics has sound subject matter of its own, which may be no more and no less scholarly and substantial than any of the sciences or humanities, even though it cannot be classified categorically as either the one or the other. It has something to offer the dilettante as well as the scholar, the freshman as well as the senior, and a man as well as a woman.

It can serve as a major field and reach into related fields of learning as profitably as any other subject. From its own well-established pivot it can orient a student to a full circle of present-day scholarship. The best teacher of Latin literature can, through the medium of his subject, teach his students much about people and personalities, philosophies, logic, poetry, drama, geography, economics, and life in general. Home economics can do the same, and can sometimes do it even better. It all depends on the per-sonality of the teacher and the versatility of his training; and as often as not students feel that much that is taught is of doubtful value, whether in home economics or Latin or any other field.

For an intelligent appraisal of home economics, the professional aspect must be differentiated from domestic or homemaking aspects. It has become a well-paid and satisfying professional field for women, partly because of its own richness and variety and partly because it suffers least from competition with men. It includes the dietitians in hotels, hospitals, and industrial and educational institutions, the whole army of workers in the clothing industry—designers, manufacturers, buyers, sellers, and demonstrators—and the interior decorators. It has opportunities in teaching, merchandising, personnel work, research, and art in the professional and business world. And it has always had that double attraction for the lucky student in being at the same time personal and professional. It can hardly fail to make her at least a more efficient, if not a more ardent, homemaker and often endows her with a more attractive appearance and personality as well.

Professional training in home economics is not as clearly separated from the humanistic aspects of education as are, for example, engineering or pharmacy and not as closely interwoven with the liberal subject matter as is, let us say, the curriculum for clinical psychologists or teachers of literature. It is this professional training which many of the liberal arts colleges do not offer per se, even as they do not offer the technical courses in secretarial work, music, physical therapy, medicine, or law.

The other broad aspect of home economics—the training it offers in homemaking—is more central to the problem of education for women. This aspect is more difficult to evaluate, however, because it is less amenable to precise definition. In its more shallow ranges, the homemaking curriculum includes merely the household skills and arts: cooking, sewing, home nursing, home management, and child care. These courses are often extended to include nutrition, textiles, fashion, economics, design, child psychology, and personal relationships. The curriculum may also include courses in citizenship, social work, and social problems, or in chemistry, physiology, psychology, and fine arts. If these subjects are incorporated into any liberal arts curriculum, then ample time must be allowed for the courses in the humanities and the sciences that are typically required for the bachelor of arts degree.

Obviously much of the controversy over home economics can be traced to misunderstandings about what it comprises. If by a homemaking curriculum we mean an aggregate of courses such as nutrition, the family, child psychology, economics of the consumer, and home architecture and decoration, together with all their proper prerequisites in psychology, sociology, chemistry, economics, and the fine arts, few educators would deny its "liberal" qualities.

On the other hand, it may be argued that a more truly liberal and at the same time more appropriate curriculum for woman could be built around her development as a *person,* not as a *woman,* even as the liberal arts curriculum for man would be dictated by his human, not his masculine, characteristics and needs. This would mean that the woman would study the humanities and the basic natural and social sciences according to her intellectual interest and talent for them and because of their importance in our current culture. The mastery of these courses would make it easy for her to acquire later, when she had greater maturity and motivation, the more specific information, attitudes, and techniques needed in homemaking.

This must be the current assumption in the case of men, since there is no curriculum calling for physics followed by household mechanics and electronics, and none (except perhaps for professional architects) beginning with fine art and architecture and continuing with domestic planning and building.

An actual listing of the nonprofessional courses in home economics would perhaps be the most precise method for defining the subject matter available for the college woman who is to make it her major interest. The following list has been taken from the departmental schedule in one midwestern university, and it is therefore a fair approximation of what is meant by homemaking courses. Psychology and chemistry were listed as prerequisites.

Textiles and Clothing (Lecture and Laboratory)	Nutrition
Clothing for the Family	Food Preparation and Meal Service
Clothing Construction and Selection (with Laboratory)	Economics of the Family
Art in Everyday Life	Home Management and Administration (with Laboratory)
Home Furnishing and Decoration	Modern Problems of the Family
Weaving and Handcrafts	Personal Adjustment and Family Living
Child Care and Development	
Home Nursing	

It is immediately obvious that there is no curriculum comparable for men, although men are beginning to show interest in courses on personal adjustment or mental hygiene of the family. It is assumed that men do not take the primary responsibility for homemaking, not even for plumbing, landscaping, building repair, or buying and investing. It is also clear that the courses which are listed above would be extremely practical, pleasant, and useful.

In evaluating the worth of homemaking courses to the college woman, several questions are pertinent. How difficult is it for the housewife to obtain the information through current books and magazines, demonstrations, advertising, and informal club discussions? Does knowledge gained from homemaking courses match the intellectual level of other courses in the liberal arts curriculum, or would the courses be more appropriate at a lower age or for the less able student? What other subject matter would be crowded out of the college woman's schedule in the time devoted to them?

The answers must take account of the fact that for the serious and able college woman, as for her counterpart among college men, the campus years are the most significant in her intellectual development. She wants them to be devoted to subjects in which she needs the help and stimulation of her teachers and classmates and to those which will challenge her mental powers to the full. She wants formal training in subject matter which has the richest values and the greatest usefulness.

The homemaking curriculum as defined above scarcely meets these criteria. This holds true, however, only when we are discussing the best possible curriculum for the college woman of superior background and intellect. Not to be overlooked are the vast majority of students who are not so generously endowed. For them particularly—and to a lesser extent as occasional elective subjects for the more able—these courses, taught by wise leaders, can have great significance and are essential to progress in our society. Even at the college level this subject matter will prove more profitable and stimulating than many of the traditional college courses, for it is better suited to the needs and the abilities of many of the freshmen who are attracted to the contemporary campus.

... 7

Education for Citizenship

I<small>F IT</small> is to flourish, a democracy must have an informed citizenry and able leaders. In theory, therefore, the schools would be expected to provide every student with a knowledge of his duties and privileges as a citizen and to induce the more able to carry the larger responsibilities of political leadership.

But there is a wide chasm between educational theory and actual accomplishment in this field of citizenship. The momentum and high purpose generated by the deep convictions of educational leaders often seem to be dissipated long before they reach the student in the classroom. On the campus the student learns to emotionalize his convictions, and gains some firsthand experience with certain techniques of democracy. He becomes highly jealous and sensitive in regard to his individual rights, but never really comes to grips with his responsibilities so that he can knit these two into a social whole. The conversion of an unthinking liberty into a socially responsible freedom seems to be the never-solved dilemma of the campus citizen.

As we consider the various aspects of this problem, ought we to look for any differences in the citizenship responsibilities of men and women? Both are living together in a government of their own creation. In the United States they are, for the most part, living under the same laws. They vote for the same candidates, suffer from the same wars, and enjoy together the benefits

144

of peace. Both need to learn the same history—political, economic, and social, and to practice, in the very same classrooms, identical methods of democratic interaction. Each in his own right must earn the faith and insight which are the common coin of exchange in daily living, the capital which each community, state, and nation eventually demands from every citizen for its own survival.

Although young men still risk more in war than women, modern warfare demands increasingly more physical suffering and anxiety from women. Women's orbit is a little farther from the center of action and experience and it is correspondingly harder for them to warm up for effective participation. They therefore need more realistic experience in practical politics, while men need special preparation for their military service. In all other respects, the education of men and women for citizenship can be counted as the same.

Training for citizenship falls in the general field of the social sciences—economics, sociology, government, history, and the newest branch of social psychology, group dynamics. These are difficult fields for both teacher and student. Laymen, and more especially the professionals in the natural sciences and humanities, can hardly realize the handicaps which beset the social scientist in dealing with his logic, methods, discipline, and interpretations. The elements he works with are inconstant and fluctuating. The individuals he studies differ from one another, groups differ from other groups, society differs in every geographical region and from one era to the next. Nor do these differences, laboriously discovered, remain consistent. History does not possess the uniformity of the elements in the chemistry laboratory; it must be re-explained and reinterpreted every half century. The basic ideologies of nations, of classes within nations, and of individuals within classes are extremely divergent.

On the other hand, persons outside the circle of social scientists seem to assume that these elements are constant. They speak of a human trait such as "integrity" as though it were unitary and consistent, and plan courses and curriculums to teach "it" to youth. But integrity is not an entity; it is action-linked and has no existence except in action.

One may have high integrity about his religion, his business behavior, and his patriotism but very little in his sex relations; a child may have the highest integrity toward his family and yet be quite nonchalant about cheating in examinations. Such concepts as "the upper middle classes" or "the family" or "democracy" or "race prejudice" do not carry the same meaning in Texas and Vermont, in 1925 and 1950, in the proletarian's modest house and the aristocrat's mansion. And if the social scientist does try to be more precise in delimiting these abstractions or redefining them, as often as not he is denounced for speaking a jargon.

The biologist or physicist in his laboratory is seeking a fact or a theory which will be useful today or tomorrow, and under circumstances which will vary but little if at all. In fact, if the physical circumstances get beyond his control, he is very quick to hedge or withdraw; the meteorologist, for example, dares not predict the weather for more than a day or a week in advance. The humanist composing his sonnet or compiling his criticism is writing for an immediate audience; the delay may be for a month or a year, but hardly more. But the social scientist, including especially the educator, works only for the future. The plans he draws must be long-term—the bonds to mature in twenty years, the ninety-nine-year lease, World War III (in five years, twenty-five years, or perhaps never), the education of the younger generation for a life which will reach its peak twenty years hence and probably continue for two more twenty-year periods.

He works not only *for* the future but *against* a cultural lag, which means that he projects his plans twenty years in advance for a society that won't even catch up to his present thought for at least another decade. In the meantime the social scientist is dealing with individuals who are spontaneous and self-active, each with an independent repertory of thoughts and actions that he is bent on pursuing. When a person is eighteen or twenty, his high spirits and temporary advantage cannot be distinguished from valid freedom, the God-given and American-guaranteed brand of freedom which is his natural right. It is in this lagging society that the student is asked to acquire ideologies whose value it is hoped will be useful to him in a distant future.

In spite of so many handicaps, educators, philosophers, social scientists, and clergymen are committed to certain kinds of stability and conscientiously look forward to progress, make prophecies, plan curriculums, draw lessons from history, and revise their principles with unbounded hope and justifiable confidence. They continuously refine their techniques, find more inclusive generalizations, and search out more reliable trends.

All the members of a heterogeneous and competitive society could not subscribe to the same definition of citizenship, but they look forward to results that are remarkably uniform: a society of informed individuals assuming responsibility for a peaceful world in which each may develop his capacities as fully as possible.

Good citizenship would recognize no sex differences. Every individual has at least the voter's responsibility, and to this extent the education of men and women would be the same. Democratic interaction between individuals in both smaller and larger groups is a never-ending process. It begins in the family, gathers force in the schools, and permeates adult society. It is the process by which the individual absorbs or learns his culture, adapts himself to it, and reaches maturity within its framework.

What a crucial role the mother plays in this process! How will she acquire the wisdom and diplomacy to do her part successfully?

History reveals two basic approaches to education for a democratic society. In one the attention is centered on the individual; in the other, on society. A good example of individual emphasis is Christianity, which asks that a person have a change of heart, that he be "born again," that he receive the "inner light." Here a reorientation of the whole personality is called for, which would then express itself in right action and ultimately in better society.

Norman Foerster expresses the importance of good citizens: given good citizens, they will inevitably produce a good society. The quality of government will depend on the kind of people who make up the nation, their intelligence, their character, their philosophy of life, their dominant interests and motives. If they are naïve or corrupt, no mechanism of government will work well; if they are good, almost any mechanism will work well.[1]

In the other ideology, the good will of the individual is assumed, and the reform must be made in the social institutions. The adherents to this theory analyze the evils of society and concentrate on their correction—by peaceful methods if possible, and by revolution if necessary in a "righteous cause."

John Dewey clarified these two focuses in social thinking and led the way to the new emphasis on the interrelation of the two. In this same vein, Lewis Mumford warns: "We must resume the search for unity, and we must begin with the personality and the community in all their richness, variety, complication, and historic depth, as both the means and the end of our effort."[2] The educator John B. Johnston had earlier charged the college to serve the institutions of our society through proper service to the individuals within those institutions.[3]

The human individual is a sensitive, malleable entity, constantly changing as the physical and social environment affect his thinking. Therefore, the university and all other instruments of education must train students to direct these social changes in an open and orderly fashion rather than by subversion or costly and painful upheaval. From its study of the past the college must seek to interpret the present. The important decision before the student is not change versus the status quo, but ill-considered and impulsive changes induced by the actions of the acquisitive versus changes continuously directed by intelligence toward the good of all. Revolution and force are the evidences of failure of the educational process, for it is the task of education to condition us to peaceful change.

Harry Elmer Barnes agrees that education is the only means at our command for bringing about social change in an orderly fashion without running the risk of violence and revolution, but he is more pessimistic about the outcome: "Education is not yet ready to assume this responsibility. We have made education available to the masses but we have not adapted it to present day life. . . . Education cannot guide social change until we give far more attention to the social studies and teach them more realistically." [4]

In discussing the good citizen, the Harvard Committee emphasizes the individualistic approach. The good man possesses an integration, poise, and firmness which come from an adequate philosophy of life, and the goal of education is to appeal to the intelligence of the whole man in action. Almost with reluctance, it might seem, the committee eventually turns to the society in which this intelligent action will be centered: "Yet we are not arguing for an education that is student-centered. . . . Like an ellipse, an educational institution has two centers not one. . . . And truth compels us to add a third, society." [5]

Cultural literacy must necessarily be found in the study of history, and the anthropologists argue that it can best be achieved from the study of widely differing civilizations, especially from familiarity with the more primitive tribes. The need, however, according to the Harvard Committee in 1945, is for a history not of alien cultures but of modern civilization. The focus in general history should be on Europe, in which Western civilization is grounded. The method of instruction should not be a factual "survey," but a teaching process which includes an appreciation of the gathering and weighing of historical evidence. But the schools cannot do everything: "Other social institutions are concerned with helping the individual develop personal competence, while the schools have the special and major responsibility of furthering the growth of intellectual abilities." [6]

This is one of the rare endorsements by the Harvard Committee of Robert M. Hutchins who, with "no friendly voice," had earlier set forth his own theory that a university education should inculcate exclusively the intellectual virtues, which are the product of rigorous intellectual effort. "We are beginning to behave as though the home, the church, the state, the newspapers, the radio, the neighborhood club, and the boy next door did not exist. A college should do nothing that another agency can do as well." [7] Hutchins would insist, however, that every student study, along with metaphysics and the natural sciences, the social sciences—the practical sciences dealing with the relations of man and man, including ethics, politics, and economics, together with such historical and empirical methods as may be needed to supplement them for the guidance of human actions.

Harold Taylor, president of Sarah Lawrence College, deplores not only the colleges' failure to create the right patterns for individuals, but the deliberate cultivation of the wrong. He claims that the campus ideal is a fraternity man with a declared lack of interest in political affairs, a member of the football team, a student with a good record in each course, a man who is popular with everyone, well known on the campus, and a member of many social clubs. Says Taylor, "The large successful universities have confirmed this stereotype by the plans they make for the campus social life of the students and by the value system implicit in its organization . . . Even the liberal arts colleges seem bent upon becoming training schools for conservative industrial executives." [8]

James B. Conant has made the strongest case for social sciences in the curriculum and for their support in further research. He announces that research in sociology, anthropology, and social psychology must be supported as adequately as in physics and chemistry. He calls for a study of the total social situation in a community, so that education may be grounded in the diverse motivations of different kinds of people. In other words, his idealism is distinctly of the practical variety, and there must be more of this tough-minded American idealism to insure against any disguised toryism gaining the upper hand. Constant self-criticism must prevent the planning of utopias from usurping all the energies of practicing educators.

Conant stresses these three postulates: (1) the individual is sacrosanct, (2) he has obligations to other individuals, and (3) our type of society requires a high degree of personal liberty and at the same time active and sympathetic cooperation toward certain ends. These postulates must be placed in their historic settings, and it is the pedagogue's task to present attractive and convincing reasons—logical, religious, and philosophical—for accepting them. American history would be central to this training in civic competence, although Conant does not underestimate the importance of campus life in this training: "A loyalty to the type of society we are slowly endeavoring to shape on this continent can be evoked to the extent that the school itself is a society exemplifying the ideals we extol." [9]

The constant plea for a wider diffusion of education also runs through the pages of the report of the President's Commission on Higher Education, which recommends that every citizen, youth or adult, be encouraged to carry his education as far as his native capacities permit, and that all education be adapted to contemporary needs. It devolves upon the state, therefore, to supply education, to the end that "at all its levels and in all its fields of specialization it shall be the carrier of democratic values, ideals, and processes." [10]

The Jeffersonian and the Jacksonian theories of democracy are reconciled in the Harvard Committee's ultimate declaration of educational policy: we must "raise the average and speed the able while holding common goals before each." Shall the educational content be exactly the same for both the average and the able? The able student must be made into that good man and leader which the average student must learn to know and appreciate. Is the difference in the learning process quantitative only, or qualitative as well?

The role of the university in answering these questions for a democratic society is a challenging one:

Where can important problems be discussed more thoughtfully than in a university? Where are conditions more suited to a sound appraisal of urgent issues than in university classrooms? Laboratories, libraries, and the source materials are readily available. There, too, are competent faculties devoting their lives to

151

scholarly study and investigation . . . the situation is conducive
to impartial, dispassionate, critical, and informed analysis. . . .
The students have the *right* to expect a thorough, competent
presentation of important problems, and any interference with
the university which renders this task more difficult is a dis-
service to them and to the communities from which they come
and to which they return.[11]

These are strong pronouncements in view of all the other important disciplines which must be crammed into the curriculums
of our schools. The concepts of citizenship are not readily absorbed by the immature mind. Growth in personal and social
values is slow and requires time for seasoning and maturing. One
may question whether the formal schooling in either secondary
or college programs can even lay the foundation for so broad and
complex a structure.

Perhaps citizenship training, however defined, should be the
primary concern of the many adult education programs. In this
respect, the adult education movements in Great Britain and in
the United States present a notable contrast: ours is largely
professional and vocational, while theirs is concerned rather with
citizenship and political philosophy. Our adults use these opportunities for advancement in their earning power, but even during
the war years the British Workingmen's Educational Alliance
found relaxation and enlightenment in Plato and politics. Groups
of incendiary watchers would arrange for speakers with whom
they could argue on government and economics.[12]

But for Americans, those subjects and skills which were not
begun in school seem somehow closed for a later and more leisurely pursuit. College alumnae will acknowledge the loss: "I've
always regretted that I didn't take (or wasn't made to take)
more history and sociology," or "Nobody took economics when
I was in college"; but the regret doesn't go deeply enough to
make them organize their efforts for a correspondence course or
extension class. They resort to such means only when they must
fulfill the certification requirements of their professions, or when
they need refresher courses in their business enterprises.

Adult women, especially in such organizations as the League of Women Voters and the American Association of University Women, have shown some interest in promoting study groups for practical politics, citizenship, and current affairs. Parent-teacher associations have perforce given much informal discussion to local problems of government, but the more prolific social clubs of all kinds rarely venture even casually into these citizenship fields, and their community effort usually takes the direction of charitable and social work. For citizenship training, in spite of all argument and effort to the contrary, the school years are still of maximum importance.

Some kind of education for citizenship is present in any curriculum. The high school and college girl, along with her brothers, will find herself obliged to choose a minimum of work in the social sciences—in civics, economics, history, labor relations, government, and the like. Gleanings from many writers have yielded the following stated objectives of education in this field of citizenship:

Knowledge of human society and man's interrelated social, political, and economic institutions—their historical development, underlying principles, and respective values for human life.

Knowledge of American civilization and its European origins, its own distinctive character and contemporary tendencies. Knowledge of other cultures, primitive and advanced, oriental and occidental, their significance and their interrelation with American culture.

Knowledge of current world affairs and pressing problems, such as the conflict between dictators and democracy, strikes, taxes, and world trade and its relationship to world peace.

The habit of attempting to understand particular events in relation to a larger frame of reference.

The ability to read intelligently and critically newspapers, books, magazines, and any other writings on matters of public opinion.

The ability to appraise critically popular beliefs and generalizations.

Progressive development of the balanced and mature personality required for constructive participation in a democracy, and clear appreciation of the role of leadership.

Differentiation of democratic from other forms of government and knowledge of its characteristic varieties, techniques, assumptions, and hazards. Allegiance to this democratic way of life.

Competence in understanding those personal, social, and economic adjustments which are more practical and successful, less theoretical and ideal.

Knowledge, of course, is only one aspect of good citizenship. Many other mental faculties must be cultivated: conviction, attitudes, appreciation, values, faith, habits of action, cooperativeness, practical skills, self-discipline. Knowledge, the intellectual aspect, is the most easily managed in the classroom and on the campus. Transforming the textbook arguments into workaday attitudes and behavior, into the character aspect of citizenship, is a much more elusive process. And the third aspect, skill in the practice of democratic activities, may appear to be easy to cultivate, but it is actually the most uncertain of all.

Knowledge is the basic prerequisite for both conviction and right action, but the desired *values* for the individual do not inevitably flow from the pertinent information; nor does *effective behavior* follow from proper values. The student may acquire the facts of our national life from his social science courses. He may enjoy the depth of perspective gained from history and the breadth added by economics and sociology and still not build them into his faith or his philosophy of life. Scholarship in the social sciences is no guarantee against bigotry or acquisitiveness or any of the other obstacles to good citizenship. And likewise, one may have a value system which includes all the most desirable virtues—faith in the mission of his country, faith in the moral law, faith in the team method for solving problems—and still not possess the skill in his dealings with other human beings to make himself an effective or even an acceptable citizen.

The education of our daughters as citizens, then, is made up of three different phases: (1) providing information and understanding in the social sciences, (2) encouraging the acquisition of certain values or attitudes or faiths, and (3) helping to develop

154

skills in interpersonal relationships. In other words, they need to know thoroughly and to judge intelligently the society and the country in which they live. The rights and privileges of others must be built into their inmost consciousness, with the acceptance of compromise and faith in reason as their most spontaneous motivations. And they must have practice in all kinds of group action and interaction, must exercise their personal qualities in every kind of role, must experience at first hand leadership, cooperation, and passive acquiescence until they can employ them in real life as easily as the skilled stage actor plays his various roles.

Can our daughters, while they are gradually acquiring the knowledge as it has been prescribed above, also receive instruction in democratic attitudes or values and in democratic skills and actions? Current religious values, which often coincide with many of the current democratic values (brotherly love, tolerance, conscience, personal integrity), are sometimes definitely embraced in the college curriculum—in the church-affiliated colleges, for example—but denominational doctrine as such is necessarily excluded from the formal curriculum in schools that receive public moneys and support. Even in these, however, religious values are not dismissed, and the campus welcomes and encourages the off-campus churches and private foundations which provide the services demanded by the students. Because of the overlapping of religious and democratic values, the state has always counted on the churches for the propagation of the virtues of the Greek-Hebraic ethic. To that extent it has neglected to develop its own mechanisms in the public schools for teaching such values. "Love thy neighbor as thyself" is not exclusively a religious value; it is also fundamental for democracy.

The old-fashioned college professor, steeped in religion as well as scholarship, has largely disappeared. The new species of academic man has been trained, and now practices, on a much larger campus, with greater specialization and in a more vocational atmosphere. He no longer identifies himself with all the larger ethical and social values, but only with those directly associated with his own highly specialized subject matter. Inculcating democratic habits does not always come within the province of the general teaching staff: time is too short, or the classes too large, or the subject matter inappropriate.

It is the extracurricular activities which provide the most appropriate milieu for the student's practice of his democratic skills. He need not, of course, rely on his school or campus training for this experience; he may acquire it in the family, the church, the club, or the community. The President's Commission, however, charges that higher education should be the carrier not only of democratic values and ideals but also of its processes.

The Harvard Report, commenting on the value of student government and debating societies in promoting active, responsible, and intelligent citizenship, points out one of their weaknesses: "It is rare that such organizations or activities can develop materially that sense of perspective which ordinarily follows only upon the study of instances of ideas removed in space and usually in time from immediate experience." Others hold a more optimistic view of the campus as a place to meet the student's deep need for learning to be the "good citizen of a democratic state" and to furnish that kind of undergraduate experience which alone makes real the search for truth, the promotion of good will, and the issuance of these two in responsible behavior.

Perhaps only on the campus with an able and earnest student body, a dedicated faculty, and a high *esprit de corps* may one hope to find the circumstances most favorable to an outcome of this kind. On such a campus, democracy may become not an abstract political theory but truly a way of life, as President Havens of Wilson College maintains: "I do not mean by 'experience' merely a mock election or an exhortation to register and vote when you come of age; nor yet visits to court houses and electoral stations and prisons and county homes. All of these are valuable. We need more of that kind of experience than we have. What I mean is that the college or university must so shape itself that its students live democracy in their daily life, fulfilling its laws of consideration, honor, decency, and assumption of duty." [13]

Not every parent and not every college president would subscribe to the theory that the campus is primarily the place for the young woman to acquire the knowledge, the values, and the practice of good citizenship. Many of the church-affiliated colleges would emphasize Christian principles rather than democratic values as the more inclusive and the more important for women, feeling that the woman who maintains a Christian home and rears her children in that faith is discharging her first responsibility in a democracy. Others would be of the opinion that both democratic values and processes are better acquired in the family and in social and club relationships, and that time should not be stolen from academic pursuits for extracurricular work of doubtful value on the campus.

But if the campus *is* endorsed as the center for acquiring the democratic way of life, what kind of program or curriculum is feasible, and how can its success in producing good citizens be evaluated? Parents have been ill informed and colleges too complacent in these matters. They need to take a searching glance at the typical campus population and the characteristics which make its government problems different from those of the adult world, to grasp the assumptions on which successful campus government must rest, and to make a realistic appraisal of its problems and functions.

First, the campus population, whether large or small, provides a laboratory very different from that real world in which the young woman will later practice citizenship; in fact, it provides a misleading and artificial milieu. Because the campus group is made up primarily of young people, it drives forward with tremendous energy, showing none of the checks and balances which come with a mingling of persons of greater age and experience. The ratio of power to responsibilities is highest in this age group. Childhood frustrations have been accumulating, but there is no balancing accumulation of regret. There is a strong thrust for independence and a staggering emotional resistance when this thrust meets the rigid institutions of our culture. There are tidal waves of interest in sports and elections and a touching devotion to romance, but otherwise the students exist in a kind of sociopolitical vacuum.

The turnover in a college population is exceedingly rapid, and association is fleeting, allowing the group neither the benefits of long-term planning, nor experience in building stable institutions, nor continuing familiarity with their functioning. Only a small margin of time and energy is available for governmental activities, in view of each individual's preoccupation with his studies and of the absence of paid or professional officers.

The class structure is unbalanced because of the disproportionate concentration of the higher socioeconomic classes. Every campus group represents a high selection in terms of intellectual capacity, although this will vary from one campus to another, depending on the admission practices. No campus constitutes a replica of normal adult society—truly it is quite abnormal—and this is the one most important fact in planning student governing activities, a fact which parents and teachers alike have too often failed to reckon with.

The classroom teacher takes it for granted that some of his students are highly intelligent and will learn easily and pleasantly, whereas others will acquire a minimum of learning with a maximum of effort. But it is not so easy to apprehend the range of such traits as honesty, open-mindedness, trustworthiness, and cooperativeness, or to plan campus governments to deal differentially with students of varying capacities.

We accept readily the fact that some students are highly intelligent and learn easily and pleasantly, whereas others acquire only a minimum of learning with a maximum of effort. But the fact that all the character traits—honesty, openmindedness, trustworthiness, and good will—are also found in very unequal quantities among the students is not so well known.

Whenever we measure ethical standards of students we find

that they follow the proportions of the normal frequency curve. On a typical large campus, for example, with its heterogeneous group, about 7 per cent of the students will never cheat in examinations; at the other end of the scale, another 7 per cent will always try cheating unless they are prevented from doing so. And of course there is a large middle group, the majority of the students, that will drift in either direction according to the climate of public opinion.

The answer to the much-debated question of whether or not student self-government and an honor system will work lies in facts such as these. The relative proportions under the normal curve, with 2000 or 20,000 unselected students, will not change. The only feasible objective for an honor system, with its parallel lesson in citizenship training, is to move the whole curve a few notches toward the approved end of the scale.

If students are to share in campus responsibilities, what are the minimum assumptions, in view of all these considerations, that would insure the success of campus government? First, it must be assumed that the majority of the students have a general good will—a desire to live up to the best in themselves and to cooperate with others in achieving desirable goals. Such good will may be partially guaranteed in the case of the private college, with its privilege of limiting and selecting its students. It may be further assured through carefully planned attention to religious and spiritual life, and it will gain additional strength from ceremonials and from the emphasis given by strong traditions.

Usually, however, in the heterogeneous and unselected student groups impelled by a miscellaneous assortment of motivations to pursue a college career, the general "good will" is latent rather than active and needs carefully organized effort to bring it out. In fact, the promotion of the necessary good will and favorable attitudes, the building up of the right values, becomes a job for professional personnel workers, since it is obviously beyond the capacity of the untrained and transient student leaders.

Another assumption that must be made is not only that a

159

majority of the students are in sympathy with the objectives of the college but also that they are emotionally and intellectually capable of achieving these objectives. Consider, then, the dilemma of any one of the larger state universities peopled with a substantial number of freshmen whose diminutive learning capacity excludes success in the classrooms, with students motivated toward athletic competition or convivial social life, and with any number of emotionally immature or unstable personalities. Can such students be identified immediately and selected for differential treatment? The campus regime which is suitable for the student of average motivation and capacity presents insurmountable difficulties to the substandard student.

It is easy to see that trained counselors are needed to identify and to deal with the student who is emotionally immature or disturbed; it is not readily apparent that the presence of large numbers of students who are intellectually unable or unwilling to compete creates a problem which cannot be met by students without professional leadership and cooperation.

A third assumption for an effective student government is that the factors originating in the outside world and beyond the control of the college are not contrary to, and more powerful than, the factors within the institution which are brought to bear on the campus citizens. In fact, when it is estimated that the deleterious factors are becoming too strong, it must be assumed that there will be counteracting movements on the campus. The pressure to win games, the ultraromantic and unrealistic ideology of the cinema, the hysteria and unrest of impending war, and the urge toward high grades at any cost require a counterbalancing thrust of vigorous moral and spiritual leadership. On what kind of a campus are the leaders united for these needed efforts? In the woman's college? The large state university? The church-related school?

An additional assumption must be that the learning process whereby the student evolves appropriate standards for himself and his group is rapid enough to offset his immaturity and inexperience. The current mores and codes of conduct are no longer authoritative and fixed, but relative, flexible, and self-determined. These facts cannot be concealed from students, and consequently there is danger when the standards of behavior are to be evolved from the group out of its own traditions and needs that a youth's lack of perspective will make him endorse experimental standards unacceptable to society. The student is after all still legally a minor, still a learner; he does not feel the restraints imposed by responsibilities of family, occupation, financial investments, or business pressures. In contrast to the adult, he is still subject to much authority and protection on both home and campus.

Paradoxically, therefore, the campus must provide the forces which make him choose the right actions "of his own free will!" Ideally these forces should emanate from those students who have gained the maturity and the right to speak for the student group, but unfortunately these students graduate all too quickly, and the campus loses their natural leadership. Their power must then be vested in those persons who remain on the campus— students, faculty, and staff. On which campus can be found this most necessary infiltration of mature thinking and leadership?

On the smaller campuses, or in the church-related schools or women's colleges, the policies of selection of both students and faculty, the chapel or church services, the courses in religion or ethics, and the campus traditions and ceremonies inculcate and emphasize such virtues as tolerance and integrity. From such sources as these, both student and staff leaders derive conviction and courage and the student bodies develop a valid and pragmatic faith.

Ideally, then, good campus government must promote effective group dynamics and interpersonal relationships through a system of planned and shared experiences in which desirable changes take place within the individual personalities as well as in the group. More realistically, it must furnish a working model of good government, able to deal fairly and quickly with all problems which concern students and to propagandize its actions adequately for its own prestige. The governing body must have a self-conscious awareness of the specific functions assigned to it in the total ongoing process of the institution and must take care that it speaks for the entire student body, not for just a handful of aggressive journalists or for some disgruntled and vocal minority.

The superior success of governing groups in the women's colleges is readily acknowledged, and one of the underlying reasons is the clear definition of the administrative areas of student and of faculty. Supreme in the significant issues and problems assigned to them, the students discharge their responsibilities fully. Too often the student senates on the largest campuses have very few real issues to deal with and therefore play an exciting but empty political game. The outstanding goal of their "campus politics" is to learn how to achieve a winning majority, not how to adjust the majority and minority groups to each other or how to achieve a continuing balancing process which will reconcile the self-interested demands of all conflicting pressure groups.

Campus governing groups work too exclusively on the primary level of democracy, the immediate, face-to-face level. Student leaders, each loyal to his own party group, easily become proprietary rather than community minded and confuse leadership with personal popularity. To remedy this situation, professionally trained leaders, not faculty volunteers, are needed who can teach the students to perceive clearly and accept emotionally the interlinking of themselves and all their organizations with the higher and broader campus authority and problems.

Preoccupation of the student with his own free and independent status has blinded him to the framework of authority and the responsibility which society has placed over a university itself. High administrative leaders too often hesitate to play their necessary roles in helping the student to set up his goals and his programs within this comprehensive social framework. Their reluctance to interfere with the student's intellectual self-determination has been carried over to his citizenship development, where it is less appropriate. In neither field can any individual remain truly free, and counselors and administrators have the same responsibility as the classroom teacher to give the student both truth and realism.

Especially in the social sciences, the lessons of experience for the student are much too slow and uncertain, since they cannot be as artificially arranged and controlled as the experiments in the chemistry laboratory. But in campus government as in chemistry, the student functions primarily as a learner and must accept principles and pressure on the same terms of authority that adults accept them. To be less authoritative, to make guidance gentle and lenient, is to admit that there is nothing at stake. This is essentially what the administrators of huge, unselected student groups find it expedient to do. Good individual and group counseling are luxuries in their budgets, and many of them must be satisfied to contain where they cannot control. Meantime the student does not learn how to select effective leaders, how to choose wisely among civic and charitable projects, how to temper his self-expression to his own status, or how to embrace the ideologies appropriate for his protected position in his alma mater.

It seems obvious that we must rid ourselves of the notion of the sanctity of students' complete and autonomous control of their own affairs while at the same time substituting the good group-work techniques of professional leaders for both the authoritarianism of the older colleges and the *laissez faire* of the overgrown new campuses. "The major problem of our time is to produce socially minded, cooperative adults without sacrificing individuality," declares Franz Alexander.[14] Parents, counselors, and most especially the students themselves have much to lose in turning their backs on any of these problems.

The democracy of today is different from the democracy of Athens, of the nineteenth century, or even of the 1920s and 1930s. Only a democracy flexible enough to change when its economic bases change can be of any value to students who will live to practice it in the twenty-first century; for them there may be more changes in ten years than their teachers saw in fifty. Foreign policy must be changed as it encounters shifts in economics, politics, and philosophies of other nations, and the changes may be radical when different concepts of human nature, of basic science and truth, are faced.

True, there may be discrepancies between the democratic processes practiced at home and abroad, as the circumstances vary, but all such discrepancies need not be the cause of unrest and uneasiness if education has provided the necessary understandings. The development of new attitudes and values for self-confidence and stability is always difficult. The new and dynamic bases will never be as comfortable as the old. Science and world events constantly create new needs. To meet them society evolves methods and theories faster than scholars can codify them. Men cannot live by the precepts found in ancient books. Students must learn—that is, they must be *taught*—an awareness of these truths.

How much of the compromised ideology of this "democracy in practice" should be revealed to the youthful idealist in the classroom? How much of it needs to be withheld from those of more limited intelligence, to avoid confusing them unnecessarily? What is the minimum that should be taught the preoccupied artist or scientist, to free him of too distracting involvements? Each citizen has many objectives—vocational, esthetic, and economic. He must learn to support himself, to take care of his health, to enjoy his own life, and to maintain a happy home life for others to enjoy. An arbitrary division of the curriculum into elements suitable or necessary for certain groups and the possibility of segregating the future leaders in economics and politics may seem in themselves to be undemocratic concepts, but educators must face them, must learn to deal with them, as they pertain to both men and women.

... 8

Education for Politics

WOMEN are in politics whether they know it or not, for there is no way to escape participation if only on the voting level. Work at the next higher level—the small volunteer jobs in the parties or in the women's groups—is often peculiarly appropriate for the young married woman. The limited responsibilities and the flexible working hours may come just at the time when she is much preoccupied with her children and not able to undertake any full-time activities that would take her out of the home regularly.

There are also many women who are fitted by temperament and training for successful careers in the world of politics and government, for both government and politics have special needs for women. Democracy is new, as history goes, and today it is being sorely pressed everywhere. It cannot dispense with the support of any citizen, much less an informed and thoughtful one. Women, and that means the individual woman as well as elected women leaders and women in groups, are desperately needed for thought and action.

It was the hope of many women, and the fear of many men, that the success of the suffrage movement might sweep women into public office and disrupt the existing political organizations and programs. It had seemed possible to the early enthusiasts that, from small beginnings and in increasing numbers, they could accomplish on a community-wide scale the good work they had always done in the home. In fact, such were their announced objectives and their "threat."

Among the women's organizations the story is current that when some of the early leaders of the suffrage movement returned to their home states from Washington in 1920, they met at once with local political leaders to work out the details of their future plans. These seasoned politicians expected demands that a full quota of women receive the usual political spoils, appointments to state and local offices. But the women, naïvely interested in results rather than political machinery, formulated their demands in terms of better health programs, pure food laws, better marriage and divorce laws, child labor legislation, mothers' pensions, and other needed social reforms. It is interesting to imagine the feelings of their male "colleagues" as the full significance of the selfless devotion of the women leaders unfolded before them. Whether or not demands for political spoils would have been heeded and whether or not the women would have been able to deliver the expected votes are matters of speculation. In any event, it is the conviction of the women leaders that they chose the wiser course.

With the passing of time, the men relaxed their fears, and the consideration given to the demands of the women waned appreciably. The vote for women had been dreaded by the men and had been delayed as long as possible. In England it had been given first only to the women above thirty, in the fear that the excess of two million female voters might prove disastrous for national stability. In the United States, also, men were apprehensive about the unknown, and so for a brief time

. . . they were willing to make concessions, to tease with promises, to placate with welfare legislation. The sorry sequel to this theory is that with acquaintance the threat of the woman vote diminished. The party bosses found that things were much the same after all. They grew thrifty with gifts, took courage to deny, and about 1925 the downhill road for women's bills began in Washington, and in the states.[1]

On the other hand, one who searches the records from 1920 to 1950 will find many gains to be credited to the efforts of the women since they have participated in government, most of them exactly along the lines foreseen by the women in the suffrage movement. In examining the list of achievements, however, it is obvious that the intelligently planned and carefully timed campaigns of such well-organized and democratic groups as the *League of Women Voters* account for much of the success. Permanent registration, extension of civil service, revision of state constitutions, Pure Food and Drug laws and other health and sanitation provisions, better working conditions for women, jury service for women, school attendance laws, and smoke abatement are on the list. Administrative reforms of corrupt government have frequently been effected.

Women's interest in peace has been one of the most powerful motives for working in politics and government. They began in 1922, and for over a decade representatives of twelve of the nationally organized women's groups worked together in their annual Conference for the Cause and Cure of War. After World War II they likewise combined their efforts in postwar planning and in study and support of the United Nations. From the market basket and inflation it is not too long a step to reciprocal trade and to consideration of planned international economy and higher standards of living as means of war prevention. No student of political affairs can possibly challenge the fact of women's actively working to solve our governmental problems. If there is any failure, it is only in publicity.

There are several good reasons why the mature and educated housewife might be expected to hold public office with singular success. In the first place, she is better able to devote the necessary time to the work. She has no law practice or business which will suffer while she is attending legislative sessions. It can be the major project in her life, and she can organize her household duties to allow for it. Her absence from home will not jeopardize the family income or business or profession. Likewise, since she is not directly involved in any other business or profession, her opinions and her vote may perhaps be freer of occupational prejudice.

Then, too, because her legislative seat is her one major project, she will have much more time to devote to careful study of the issues and their effect upon the geographical area and the people she represents. These advantages would be especially enjoyed by the women who sit on the local governing groups, such as the town council or the park board, for it is the women rather than the men who have the leisure and freedom from business and professional obligations for the necessary study, for personal investigations, for the time-consuming committee and subcommittee meetings.

One might protest that women do not have adequate preparation for political functions. However, they have a traditionally keen interest in community welfare and much firsthand experience in dealing with community problems. It is the woman who does the budgeting and spending and knows the importance of proper consumer legislation. She cares for the sick and is, therefore, the first to be involved if preventive measures and sanitation are not adequate to maintain good health.

Youth problems and delinquency problems are also hers because they involve her children. Their interests have educated her in the functioning of all the various community organizations. She has been the indispensable worker in the church, the parent-teacher association, the scouts, and the hundreds of social and charitable clubs. Records show that many women have already chosen the social sciences as their major interest in high school or college, and often experience in teaching or social work or volunteer community service has given them training and insight which would prove invaluable in local government service.

But there are also impediments to woman's exploiting the opportunities in these fields. Some grow out of the virtues and some out of the shortcomings of women, and still others come from the prejudices of society. Many women are too idealistic in their attitudes and expectations, because of their lesser experience in the grim, realistic details of local government. Their plans call for long and drastic steps rather than the short, com-promising ones which the more sophisticated know to be neces-sary. Their very zeal misleads them. "The Governor appointed a woman to the job of inspecting our canning plants once," reported one business man. "We had had men up to that time, and when they arrived at the plant we showed them around, gave them lunch, and they gave us their suggestions, but hell! when that woman came, *she inspected!*"

In politics there is little courteous camaraderie, but plenty of logrolling and mutual backscratching. It is a cruel and crafty game, which calls for a long and devoted apprenticeship. It will take as strong a political machine to place and keep good women in power as it did to maintain any former generation of party bosses and their retinues. Women leaders and groups of experi-enced women in dozens of small and large communities will need to build these machines, not for the same goals nor on the same principles, but by the use of the same loyalties, the same re-peated emotional and personal appeals, the same methods of propaganda, and the same system of reward, though the latter may provide prestige and opportunity for service rather than financial gain.

Women have much to learn before they work on a par with men in this field, for political action has changed somewhat since the days of Dorothea Dix. She inevitably succeeded in arousing public opinion by direct appeals to the press. But when the legis-latures were in session she concentrated her effort on the task of "leading the leaders." Sophonisba P. Breckinridge writes of her as follows: "Personally she never cared to appear in public. It was thoroughly distasteful to her to do so. To come to close quarters of eye, conscience, and heart with impressionable and influential minds, to deliver her burden as from the Lord to them, and let it work on their sensibility and reason—this was her invariable method." [2]

Political action today does not stop with such limited gestures and sentimental pleas. It goes behind, and is inextricably mingled with, the whole election process. The pressure groups compose actually the "third house" that parallels the bicameral legislatures in the study and preparation of issues. Since these organized lobbies do not possess the constituted authority, their aggressiveness is limited to advocating programs of legislation, addressing questionnaires to candidates before elections, and publishing the voting record of those in office.

Lobbies may be either special interest groups working to promote commercial or profitable ends or public interest groups who promote the views they believe in although they do not stand to make any personal gain. In either case, lobbying is expensive in time, money, and energy. And it certainly provides no means for developing the creative spirit or for building up one's sense of personal worth and individuality. It is a game played strictly according to rule, calling for selfless cooperation with all the other team members.

The college woman need not assimilate the hundreds of pages of details which would have to be "crammed" (and promptly forgotten because not used) for passing a major examination on American government. She does, however, require as a minimum the comprehension of four items: (1) the principal organs of national government, including their defects as well as their virtues; (2) the ideologies underlying the governments of other nations and the economic and social conditions which support them; (3) the problems with which government must cope and the political issues they raise; and (4) the relation of the individual citizen to the voices of democracy—nominations, elections, parties, and pressure groups.

Truly interested students have much to gain from college courses in practical politics if they are taught not by the cloistered academic but by professors actually in touch with leaders in party organizations. Rare is the campus which can provide the proper climate for a rewarding and practical student experience, a climate which fosters an ardent and enthusiastic spirit and, at the same time, a critical and objective judgment. The smaller campus, well integrated with a small community—Vassar, Bowdoin, Pomona, Reed, or Ohio Wesleyan, for example—

can much more easily serve as a laboratory than can a large campus in a big city.

It is obvious that the climate of our own national public opinion does not always encourage participation in, or any association with, either governmental or party functioning. Strong forces will impinge on the graduates, the young men as well as the young women, to keep them out of politics. The greatest restraint is economic: politics doesn't pay as a career—in fact it may not even pay expenses—and it is also something less than profitable as a side line for the business or professional man. There is a diffidence and inertia to be overcome in seeking to penetrate what seems to be someone else's business. In many quarters there is the conviction that politics is a dirty game, with temptations which had better be shunned by the honest citizen. As of January 1945, 68 per cent of the families in the United States had expressed their opposition to politics as a life work for their sons. Politicians themselves are often quite firmly against having young college men and women enter politics. And finally, there is the deep conviction that one person, one individual worker, just doesn't count.

The indictment of all college graduates, men and women, by Havemann and West is a severe one: only 17 per cent had contributed to a political cause or organization, only 3 per cent had done any fund-raising, and only 6 per cent had held an elective office or even tried for one. They are alert, informed, and conscientious about going to the polls, but they do not carry as much weight as their positions in life would justify.[3]

The weight of tradition is amazingly strong against having women in office, although, on the whole, the women in the political arena have made consistently good and even excellent records. This is partly because women must be well above the average available candidate to be considered at all. Men are sometimes glad to admit the superiority of these officeholders and point to them when reassuring their womenfolk that women do have their full share of running the government.

Men have a kind of self-protective pseudo gallantry that prevents women from carrying their full responsibility of citizenship. For example, women are still not permitted to do jury service in some states, partly on the theory that they might be too sentimental and injudicious, but partly also because they must be protected from the harsh realities and sordid features of courtroom experience. "Being protected when you feel yourself strong enough to take care of yourself is another of those limitations on freedom, like being 'kept in your place'," said Mildred McAfee Horton to her Wellesley alumnae group. "Women have not achieved the stature which frees them from this kind of embarrassing gallantry." [4]

Honorary titles and complimentary offices are often given women as gracious substitutes for more important opportunities, Miss Breckinridge reports. "There is no protest from the men when the women softly or vehemently offer resolutions, and second nominations with deferential grace. The decorative aspects of women delegates are appreciated."

Anonymous testimony, quoted by Miss Breckinridge from women who had held party or public office, is colored with sentiments of this same kind:

It is my opinion that they do not want women in office, they only put them in for expediency—to keep women voting and working for them politically. Usually they do not give them offices of leadership but chiefly honorary positions.

We feel that the women have not received as much consideration politically . . . as was given to them when the franchise was first granted. . . . They know that we have done 50 per cent of the work and the voting, too. . . . And we are getting a little bit weary of political speakers coming before us and telling us that all the women have to do is put their shoulder to the wheel and they can put the ticket over.

In my state, many of the men are of the older generation who feel that politics is not a woman's business, and they are far from cooperative. Women are encouraged to run for office only when defeat is certain. If victory seems possible, the nomination is always claimed by men.

Women must stand side by side with their husbands and brothers, pursuing with them an intelligently conceived coordinated plan. It is time for us, men and women, to drop the word "auxiliary" from our vocabulary. There is no more justification for our thinking of women as auxiliary to men in the political world than there would be for thinking of a girl in a family as auxiliary to her brother.[5]

Perhaps what the national organizations for women need in order to be thoroughly successful is a flourishing "men's auxiliary." But the women, too, offer their own peculiar weakness, which stems from their divided allegiance, personal and public. It is the same weakness that is frequently, and justly, laid to their door in the professional and business world. It appeared very early and is described frankly by one who had firsthand and discouraging experience with it:

When it appeared that women might be given the right to vote before the next national election, politicians of both parties rushed to place women on their party committees. In their choice, the men paid women a high compliment. They believed, it was evident, that women would want the highest type of women to represent them. And in their eagerness to capture the women's votes for their party they put this type in their committees. They also believed that women would want women on these committees who could lead women. They, therefore, named women whose leadership had been tried and tested. . . . And then these men listened to these women whom they had chosen; even when they did not have a vote on the committees, their opinion had weight. And why? Because the men saw them as powerful leaders of women.

Since then, women have come officially to have a place on party committees. They are elected to them as are the men. But in too many cases these first women have been succeeded by a different type, who give their proxies at committee meetings to the men by whose influence they have been elected, who do what they are told by these men to do, and who are without achievement or previous leadership of women.

The same thing is true of the women delegates to conventions. There has been a steadily decreasing number of independently-minded women, of eminent women among them. The kind of woman who could or would urge her state's member on a Resolutions Committee to vote for a measure which she thought was based on women's values, who could sway delegates at a convention, has all too often been succeeded by the wife of some officeholder whose aim in politics is to help him to success, or a woman who follows her instructions from some men in order to advance herself to office.

Naturally the same kind of women are elected to the party offices. They become the women vice-chairman of state and county committees. I make no attack on the ability or integrity of these women. Some of them are very fine. Many of them have real political gifts. I have known one or more of them who ran the men on their state committees. For this reason they have sometimes been cited as proof of women's participation in politics. On the contrary, such women are evidence that women do not participate. For they participate in politics by ignoring other women. They have few women followers. For their power and success they depend upon men.

Such women never bother with so-called women's measures or movements. They have no use for feminism. The League of Women Voters, for instance, is anathema to them. And so they do nothing to forward the participation of women in politics. Small wonder that politicians think woman suffrage a success. The bogie of the feminine influence, of the woman-vote has been laid.[6]

Still other difficulties and resistances were recognized by later women workers in the ranks of the national parties. Thirty per cent of them made vigorous protests in 1944 against the secondary positions open to them and the minor influence which they wielded. Marguerite L. Fisher reports their giving the following as some of their reasons for the situation:

There are women on the committee who have nothing but a feminine viewpoint, and those women have influence only when matters concerning women are being considered.

. . . some women feel rather inferior, and reluctant to take their rightful place, or else they are too aggressive.

Only a few women members have real influence, largely because in many instances their selection is dictated by log rolling rather than fitness or ability. Personal wealth gives them influence in some instances, but frequently this merely means that they seek publicity and are not necessarily competent.

From a party vice-chairman in a southern state comes a comment perhaps more typical of that area, but characteristic of many women from all geographical areas:

The men have not changed their attitude much. The customs down here are still very conservative, with the men feeling that the women should not assert themselves too much along political lines. This makes it difficult to get the women aroused because they know the strong opinion the men have on this issue. The women prefer to keep the pedestal the men built for them to stand on.

And still another attitude:

There is often jealousy of women in high public places, especially if they hold a remunerative position. A woman to be followed by women must submerge herself in the cause so that women are all working on an equal footing.[7]

Another weakness which the opponents of the woman suffrage movement exploited was the so-called emotionalized activities. The concrete evidence seemed to them quite patent in the passage of the prohibition amendment. But this is probably unfair, as one writer asserts in the following paragraph:

Without question women in greater proportion than men were responsible for the amendment to the Constitution that later established prohibition. The repeal of this is proof that the majority of American citizens finally decided that this most spectacular evidence of women's political impulse was disappointing and contrary to public policy. . . . The evidence is now clear that if prohibition did not successfully solve the evil of intoxicants, it is just as certain that its repeal has done no better. It is illogical to use the history of the Eighteenth Amendment as proof that the opponents of woman suffrage did correctly forecast the social hazards of the emotionalism which they believed inborn in women.[8]

Nothing could point more clearly to the change which experience brought to women than the paradoxical end of the prohibition drama:

Time marched on and women marched with it. Consider now the more recent and far more successful attack on an intrenched evil, almost diametrically opposed to the philosophy Mrs. Carrie Nation represented. Within late years, no more telling proof of feminine influence could be cited than the legislative somersault resulting in repeal of the Eighteenth Amendment, under the pile-driving impetus generated by the then Mrs. Charles H. Sabin, now Mrs. Dwight W. Davis.

Once the Eighteenth Amendment had been written into the Constitution, the disposition of the American public, in the main, was to observe the statute whether or not it was held to be a bad law. Just at that phase, a score or a hundred Mrs. Sabins might have inveighed against it without success. It was only after the expert manipulation of the greedy breed of rum-runners, who saw their golden opportunity and exploited it to the full, had spawned an almost equally predatory breed of so-called enforcement agents that an aroused press spread the alarm.

Steadily sentiment crystallized which a courageous woman of the caliber of Mrs. Sabin could have focused even earlier had she elected to act. As it was, she emerged at the moment when the average American needed only a banner to rally around. She provided that banner. Advised by men and women keenly aware of every tactic that might be utilized in harnessing the forces that responded to her summons, she spurred the wave of revolt to its crest and, within an incredibly short interval of months, watched it break over Congress with such an impact that the opposition, the "drys," was utterly routed.

That the Women's Organization for National Prohibition Reform won through in less than two years is attributable largely to its coterie of professional advisers, who knew these principles and applied them.[9]

Two important principles have emerged during the short history of women as voting and participating members of our national community: (1) If women are to play more than a passive role, they must be part of the machinery which determines the candidates and the issues, namely the two major political party organizations; and even more important, they must be willing to become candidates and learn to win elections. (2) The leaders cannot advance far as long as the great majority of women remain uninformed on public affairs and politically apathetic.

The "fifty-fifty plan," which calls for equal representation on national and state committees and which has been adopted by both national parties and partially at least by all but eight states, has helped immeasurably so far as the first principle is concerned. Only widespread educational programs can take care of the second. Women who are urged to concentrate on evolving "an authoritative curry," who are taught to cultivate femininity, serenity of spirit (which might be mere complacency), or a clear idealism (the handy package of consecrated platitudes) must also be taught how these "virtues" can be used against them. Men use their elaborate protective courtesies on the personal and social levels to enhance their own and the women's pleasure. But in business and politics the same tactics may be used, and just as courteously, to undermine women's effectiveness. Teachers of the social sciences have an obligation to make these facts clear to both sexes.

Scholars have long since identified sex attitudes and status in meticulous detail. Talcott Parsons asserts that in a situation where competition on equal terms between the sexes is not possible, the feminine glamour pattern has appeared to offset the masculine occupational status and its attendant symbols of prestige. The male is trained in most family, occupational, and political structures for the superordinate roles and the female for subordinate positions.

Training for these sex-differentiated roles and personalities is subtle and informal and it begins early, through the insistence on sex-appropriate language, clothes, hairdress, gait, pitch and intonation of voice, play, recreation, and work. And of course for most of these sex-appropriate behaviors, there is certainly no biological basis of sex-linked traits. But as in other types of inferior social rankings, the female subordination allows, even encourages, a certain degree of chronic aggression and sabotage against the superior rank.

"Feminine wiles," a kind of cleverness compounded of affection, aggression, patience, and fear, have become such a comic-strip stereotype that their effectiveness has been largely reduced.

177

Whether the patronage, protection, and mastery which constitute the socially prescribed behavior for the men tend to be diminished also is not so clear. A more productive equating of roles and privileges will after all depend more on the women themselves than on the comic strip characters which are after all created by men.

Women in the United States lag behind those of some foreign countries in the proportion who gain seats in national parliamentary bodies. The figure is 1.3 per cent for the United States, in contrast to 1.6 per cent for Great Britain, 6.2 per cent for France, and 10.7 per cent for Denmark. In the state legislatures, however, the American records are usually better, and the reasons for this may be the greater homogeneity of population and less complex government of the states, which make them quite comparable to some of the European countries. When there are 160 million people to govern, the legislative functions become enormously complex. The legislature must be in session longer, and the women must be free to leave their families for more extended periods. Geography also plays its part in making things difficult for American women; in smaller Denmark or England, women can serve in parliament and go home for week ends.

It is obvious that women will need some special training to be successful in practical politics, and there may be many ways for acquiring it—for example, by offering college courses in the history and status of women and the principles and techniques of their accomplishment in the world of government; by letting women enter politics and learn about it as men do, on the job; and by giving women the values and motivations which will push them into community activities where they can perceive their proper roles in the functions of government and learn its techniques.

College courses in the history and status of women seem to be unpopular, which is not surprising in view of the strong drive for vocational courses and the lack of zest for courses exclusively for women. It is also conceivable that the courses offered are more erudite than stimulating.

For adult women in the community there can be a truly liberalizing influence from such organizations as the American Association of University Women and, especially, the League of Women Voters. The problems studied and the help given by the League are outstandingly timely and pointed. This group deserves the praise given by the critics who have studied it and discerned a remarkable combination of singleness of purpose to promote political education through active participation in government and a sustained critical objectivity in its dedication to public interest.

From some of its many anonymous workers it gets its best advice: "We made a nice clean campaign and lost the election. The moral is that politics is not a dirty business but it is a profession. Amateurs should beware. One may have principles, friends, money, a party or a cause—but winners heel the wards."

. . . *9*

Education for Leisure

TO BE *educated* for leisure, to be instructed and disciplined for the rapturous and spontaneous play hours—what a paradox that must seem to the school child who forgets that he has ever fretted on a rainy day, "What can I do?" or that he complained to his "progressive" teacher, "Do we have to do what we want to do today?" But pleasurable spontaneity is always the final stage, not the beginning, of the learning process. Only after long study and discipline does the learner achieve the mastery that frees him for improvisation, for impulsive creation.

Everything must be learned, hobbies as well as professions, even baseball, trout fishing, knitting, and bridge. Some of these skills and accomplishments are absorbed unobtrusively by a kind of cultural osmosis, but others require more urging and strategy and deliberate effort. The question is not what shall be taught, but what shall be taught through institutionalized learning.

Perhaps to the retired sixty-year-old, restless in his sudden wealth of enforced leisure, this paradox of a disciplined spontaneity and relaxation does not seem so preposterous. Traces of the Puritan heritage are still lurking in the national consciousness, for the Puritans labeled leisure "the devil's playtime" and consequently did not include it in their virtues. Nor did

180

the era of the pioneers develop the concept of leisure. Subsistence required many hours of labor with hands and body. Fatigue, cold, and dim candlelight filled the closing hours of the day, indeed of life itself. The idea of leisure is new to the modern worker; he does not accept it as casually as he accepts his other rights and privileges, and often he discovers that it is a laborious job to cultivate and enjoy it.

It is modern technology that creates the surpluses of time and energy and worldly goods which Americans spend so ungraciously, and it is the woman especially who has a superabundance of this leisure. Household work, especially for the middle-aged upper-class woman, is not a full-time job, so occupations must be found to complement her daily routines—sports, travel, clubs, fashion, the arts, sometimes politics or volunteer work, and sometimes embroidery, gossip, detective stories, and soap operas. Often she has far more leisure than she wants, so that it is not her pleasure but her problem.

Western society no longer takes it for granted that some men will be supported by inherited wealth without assuming some executive or professional or artistic work to enhance or justify this heritage. Little by little we are also rejecting the concept of the woman in the role of a dependent only. Rare indeed, and perhaps in these days to be found only in our largest metropolitan areas, is the wife who may be classified as one of Veblen's conspicuously consuming dependents, with all of her time devoted to the nonuseful expenditure of energy.

In modern times many so-called leisure activities really contribute to the basic necessities and the amenities of life and are, therefore, purposeful and serious rather than frivolous and expendable. No longer are the small, parasitic groups—the aristocrats of wealth or lineage—the sole patrons of yachting, racing, skiing, book collecting, or orchid growing, or of the famous vacation resorts, or of the opera and the symphony. These pastimes are patronized more often by the movie stars than by the *haut monde*. Sports and gambling are big businesses, selling to the poor as well as to the rich. The arts must be supported by the masses or go out of existence. Baseball, fiction, and especially the movies, radio, and television are tailored to the proletarian taste, molded by the common man, stamped and sealed with the mark of his patronage.

Especially for the middle classes, leisure-time activities have tended to be productive. Sheer "escape" activities have never been in good odor, and for women particularly they carry a derogatory connotation. We prefer to assume that sports are cultivated for health, for character development, for keeping youth out of mischief, and as a preventive against juvenile delinquency, as well as for adult escape and insurance against mental or physical breakdown. A vacation trip is almost universally "justified" in the interests of invigoration for the year's activities.

Club women write and give papers on international politics, child guidance, home decoration, and gardening. Men's luncheon clubs raise money for charity, sponsor legislation, and bolster community spirit and civic conscience. These activities are timely and uplifting, and contribute to the projects of our working hours as well as of our larger existence. Our world has become so complex and competitive that even our spare time must be devoted to the study and improvement of what we do in our serious hours.

Women especially are made to feel this burden of their leisure-time activities, because in our society the woman is still expected to assume the major responsibility in the family and community life for promoting cultural projects. Hers is an informal, however, not a professional responsibility. She is not normally expected, often not even permitted, to preach the sermons, produce the dramas, or conduct the orchestras. She is a more unassuming handmaiden of culture, raising the money for the minister's salary, marching the husband off to the concert, making the costumes for the high school pageant.

"Of course, some middle- and upper-middle-class women do have time to play," says David Riesman in explaining *The Lonely Crowd*. He continues:

Such women can move into the peer-groups of the bridge players, the garden clubbers, any of the other groups of pastimers. The transition sounds easy. The difficulty is that women are being driven out of many of the areas in which they formerly occupied their leisure with amateur competence. For example, they are no longer welcome as ladies bountiful; the social workers have so professionalized the field of helping people that any intrusion by benevolent amateurs is deeply resisted and resented. Likewise amateurs can no longer help sick people, unless they are willing, as nurse's aids, to help registered nurses be professionals by doing all the dirty work for them. They cannot help others enjoy themselves, because settlement work and recreational activities have also been professionalized. While they can discuss politics and race relations in the League of Women Voters and the YWCA, they can do so only under the packaged and, in fact, quite excellent programs provided from central headquarters.

Thus everywhere they turn to put their part time energies to work, they face a veto group and its insistence that, to participate, they must "go through channels" or become slaveys, and money raisers for those who control the channels. And money-raising itself is now increasingly professionalized, with only the money-giving left to the "participants." Reacting to this situation, the women either sink back into indifference or conclude, like their working-class sisters, that only through a job, a culturally defined job, will they be liberated. Instead of moving toward autonomy in play, an autonomy toward which they could also help their men, they simply add to their own domestic problems all the anxieties men endure at work.[1]

But other phases of the leisure hours affect both sexes more equally. Both will experience the increasing amounts of free time as the advancing technology shortens the working day and gives us the forty- or the thirty- or even the twenty-hour week. Both our young women and our young men will need education for new assignments and skills, to say nothing of new attitudes and standards, for the enjoyment of these added hours.

Both sexes will have more hours of leisure and freedom, and fortunately, in our culture, they will be able to spend them together. In other eras and in other countries men and women have tended to separate from each other for their diversions. For the European man, *café* life, clubs, and shooting are much more exclusively his own than for the American man; in American society, the exclusiveness tends to be on an age rather than a sex basis. More and more American marriage partners complement each other and find joint interest in photography or travel or sports.

The college crowd, old or young, pairs off for the football games. Men are drawn into the amateur theatricals when women sponsor them, and the men's fishing expeditions lure the women as well as the fish. Bridge, poker, and canasta are largely, if not altogether, sexless activities. Men and women, however, enjoy leisure activities for quite different reasons. With football, for example, men like to read the sports page of the paper to get a thorough analysis of the sport; women enjoy the gaiety, the sociability, the pageantry, even the prestige of attending the game.

But the shorter working week may prove to be more fictitious than real, since many families are using the "free" hours either to add to the family income by holding part-time jobs or to pursue crafts for enhancing household life. Occasionally a young couple finds it possible to build a modest home for themselves—at least a cabin in the country—during their free hours and vacations. They may undertake redecorating, do large-scale vegetable gardening, or develop woodcrafts. Especially in the two-income family, the wife needs her week ends for household tasks, and the husband (at least the young, modern husband) may also use his free time to help with such tasks.

Some families spend their free week ends in the pleasures of sports and picnicking, while others participate in more constructive efforts such as sewing or gardening or building. The choice depends not so much on the formal teaching of these particular skills and crafts in the schools, but rather on more personal or temperamental traits: whether the members of the family have developed in the early years an interest and talent in handicrafts, whether they are strongly motivated to raise their standard of living by making, with their own hands, what they cannot afford to buy with their earned income.

In any educational program, opportunity to develop the actual skills should most certainly be available to all pupils in their public school years. Sewing, cooking, woodworking, even ceramics, are social as well as manual skills and should be made as attractive as possible to the child. For the adult, including the college student, the basic principles for these activities are so readily available through printed manuals, free demonstrations, community centers, and advertisements that formal instruction (except in the professional teaching curriculums) should be reserved, as it is in sports, for the leisure or extracurricular hours.

American women can probably describe more easily their objectives for their working hours than for their playtime. Their professional goals are vivid and concrete; their family life and their community life are both well defined; their duties and responsibilities as citizens of a world community are lavishly propagandized. But their ambitions for the purely pleasurable, leisure-time activities are very nebulous, casual, or opportunistic. In fact, to many individuals the essence of enjoyment lies in its very looseness and casualness. Almost any woman has a "five-year plan" for her working career, her finances, her wardrobe, her housing, and even for her love life or her family relationships, but this same woman harbors an inescapable presentiment that to commit herself to a planned program of leisure would dull the edge of her enjoyment.

It is difficult for her to realize that she has as little freedom in play as in work, that folkways and stereotypes haunt her recreations as well as her vocations. Canasta sweeps across the country like a hurricane. No one can escape Bob Hope's particular brand of humor or Crosby's or Sinatra's style of singing. The roads to the beaches are clogged with traffic, and woodland acres are dotted with hot dog stands. Only recently has the respectable woman appeared in slacks, smoked a cigarette, or enjoyed a cocktail. The modern woman's dreaming as well as her thinking is bounded by fashion on the one side and by financial, commercial, and traditional restrictions on the other.

185

Nevertheless, the half-glimpsed fantasies into which she escapes from these boundaries could, under discipline, shape themselves into glowing patterns of action and pleasure that would meet the most varied demands of her leisure hours. Without education directed toward these specific goals, her idle dreams can only shut her away from the more attractive vistas which she might so easily enjoy. With an appropriate and effective education, she might expect four different things of her leisure hours:

First, they should serve as a foil for the working hours, should provide contrast, relaxation, refreshment. Second, they should promote the growth of the total personality in all its aspects, that is, the intellectual as well as the physical, and most especially the affectional and emotional aspects. Third, there are social and cultural goals for the leisure hours which cannot be neglected. One's own individual enjoyment can never be complete unless it is shared, and unless it also promotes the enjoyment of others. The profit must not be personal at the expense of others, and it must contribute to the building up of the esthetic elements in our own society and culture. Finally, and this fourth objective which seems so simple and obvious will prove to be the most elusive and difficult, a woman will want and expect her leisure hours to bring her pleasure.

The value of contrast for growth and refreshment is especially vivid to women, who have suffered more than men from monotony and confinement. But more and more men will in the future be stifled by the routinization of their gainful employment. Initiative and originality have no place on the assembly line. The smile of the salesman or the affability of file clerk or executive is not spontaneous, but a purely vocational gesture maintained with continuous vigilance at a considerable cost in mental and physical energy. And the same costs are exacted from the young mother for her ironclad poise in dealing with her children and her never-ending resourcefulness in meeting household needs.

Leisure must offer both mental and physical variety; different sets of muscles, new roles and attitudes, and fresh interests must be brought into play. There is a place for escape into romantic literature and drama through the printed page or the movies or television. There is room for both the seasonal spectator sports and the weekly bowling or golf, for the school and community teams and social functions and for the commercialized ski week ends and summer fishing and bathing. There is much more room for other activities, especially for family puttering and picnicking and gardening.

It is active participation in family recreation, in the music and sports of the schools, and in community-sponsored projects that promotes social and personal growth not only in childhood years but throughout the full length of adult life as well. Relatively few persons can classify their major employment as a truly creative activity that produces the deep satisfactions required by the most fundamental human drives and interests. On the contrary, the modern economist contrasts for us the routinized and alienated worker of today with the craftsman of earlier centuries who could share in the outcome of his employer's undertaking and catch some of the enjoyment that belonged to its consummation. The craftsman felt a true psychological involvement in successful accomplishment; from the people he worked with, the processes he followed, even the implements he used, came a joy and satisfaction of the highest order. But today's alienation in work, says Mills in *White Collar,*

. . . means that the most alert hours of one's life are sacrificed to the making of money with which to live. Alienation means boredom and the frustration of potentially creative effort, of the productive sides of personality. It means that while men must seek all values that matter to them outside of work, they must be serious during work: they may not laugh or sing or even talk, they must follow the rules and not violate the fetish of "the enterprise." In short, they must be serious and steady about something that does not mean anything to them, and moreover during the best hours of their day, the best hours of their life. Leisure time thus comes to mean an unserious freedom from the authoritarian seriousness of the job.[2]

It is, therefore, all the more important that some phase of

women's education should direct leisure time away from the idle escape qualities and toward that highest function in the human hierarchy which we call esthetic. Man learns only slowly to organize the fully creative and intangible aspects of life which afford him satisfactions of this imaginative level. This consummation, the summing up of all human experience, both the intellectual and the affective, must provide for us the moments of insight which sustain us during the longer periods of activities on the more material level.

These insights and experiences are very close to, and for many persons identical with, religious satisfactions, for undoubtedly the practice of religion can be one of the most beautiful and rewarding of all leisure-time activities. Personal growth through this or any other type of esthetic or creative effort is the crown of all human endeavor. In our culture, religion has received the greatest emphasis and is, therefore, the most available and widespread means to this end.

We have long been accustomed to organized leadership in the field of religion, for it is one of our most stable social institutions, a detailed, serviceable, and commanding structure. Its finances are as sound as its doctrines, its authority as acceptable as its services, its educational programs as important—although not as effective—as its charities. But for many mature women the intellectual refreshment has not kept pace with the social and emotional release which religion offers. It directs its major attention, as do the newspapers, movies, and sports, to the interest and intelligence of the average man or woman.

Those who seek inspiration at higher levels of intellect and learning are not so readily accommodated. They must be counted on to enrich their experience for themselves, on their own initiative, in organizations of their own planning. But like so many endeavors made available through volunteer effort, these are not rigorous and demanding, but polite, sporadic, and anemic. Only the techniques and standards of formal education could apparently make them challenging and satisfying. Adult education remains the church's most significant unsolved problem,

188

and by exercising a vital leadership the colleges could do much to help the situation.

Recreation organized on the grand public scale has been a familiar phenomenon since the time of the ancient Greeks and the Roman empires. Large-scale commercialized recreation for profit made its entrance at a somewhat later date, while organized recreational projects were begun well within the memory of the present generation. To the scouts and the Camp Fire Girls have been added the Hi-Y clubs, hosteling groups, and the many juke box clubs and "Teen Canteens." The United Service Organization of World War II and the expanded public welfare programs, with their subsidized arts and crafts, furnished models and incentives for many of the newer movements. Those responsible for supervised playgrounds and other youth projects now accept the fact that they need professionally trained group workers adept in psychological and social skills as well as in crafts and games.

As the organized church with its trained leaders has dominated the religious activities of individuals and families, so these organized recreational projects supported by public or private funds have come to dominate the erstwhile family patterns of recreational life. Often the mother contributes more time and effort and money in giving her child the advantages (and with them the disadvantages) of these channels than would have been required if she had planned his leisure in the old-fashioned ways at her own hearth. But she does not dare to isolate him or make him "different" by depriving him of the opportunities for social expansion which school and community afford. The domestic brand of recreation suffers in competition with the more gregarious public models.

Sports for college women stress this social and physical growth. Individual skills such as swimming, golf, and tennis, as well as team sports and the dance, make invaluable contributions to the wise use of future leisure. Fortunate are the students on the campus where women's activities receive adequate organization and focus in their own right, escaping the overpowering effects of big-time football, acrobatic cheerleaders, and drum majorettes.

189

If parents can provide leadership within the family, with the participation of the child at a maximum, his psychological involvement and his personal satisfactions will be vividly enhanced. How can we match the creative motivation, the breadth of view, which accrues to the child whose leisure hours have been enriched with the pleasant disciplines of Bach and Victor Hugo, of nature study or carpentering? Even the most dedicated recreational leader on the community playground cannot give the child the individual attention or the affectional climate or the constructive criticism that only a pair of intelligently devoted parents can provide. Parents can assist in the finest and broadest development for their children only as they themselves enter into each community project to provide its directives and supplement its limitations with family projects of their own creation.

Embedded in family and community and school facilities, with their standardized and their individual opportunities for youth, are the genuine cultural goals of the nation and the era. It is the recreational and artistic activities of each generation or national group that set the tone of the affective life and personal relationships, release the emotional expression, and shape the creative and spiritual development, thus delineating the peculiar religion, crafts, and art of each decade. Each nation inherits from its ancestors, borrows from other cultures, and essays its own experiments; by these means it evolves its own excellences and enjoys them in its own specific way.

It matters little which parts of this heritage will be squandered or cherished by the new generations. The important thing is that each generation develop and enjoy the artistic products which form the growing edge of its own culture. Contemporary poets should be heard in their own time; contemporary operas or orchestras must be patronized and debated in their own time. Architects, actors, preachers, dancers, novelists, script writers, and pianists are as important as scholars, senators, industrialists, soldiers, and salesmen in carving an eminent place for a people and a country.

190

But these leaders can be no better than the common men who support them. In art as in no other field, widespread participation in appreciation, understanding, and debate are the most important elements in human progress. "Where there is no vision, the people perish." For every professional artist there must be a thousand amateurs, *good* amateurs—cellists who can play in the municipal orchestra, scene painters and actors for the Christmas pageant. The conservatories and universities must people the cities with competent and sensitive and enthusiastic men and women performers, but especially women, because they have more free time and more patience in teaching. The "star system" of entertainment which limits our public performers to the few who can most readily be built up for huge profits is based on an underdeveloped appreciation and a corresponding lack of confidence in individual judgment. In this sense it is one of the more alarming cultural dilemmas. The problem is not simple, and only education can alleviate it.

Americans should be not a little flattered at the possibilities of connoisseurship and patronage which are theirs for the asking. So many of us ordinary citizens could well afford to invest in the products of the contemporary artists. All of us have been a little spoiled because of our too rich diet of only masterpieces. In the museum treasures and in the colored reproductions, only the most highly successful and the authentically venerable are on display for our view. They are a purchasable commodity, presumably conferring on the owner a significant cultural virtue.

But many lesser and unheralded Leonardos and Vermeers and Whistlers contributed to the artistic glories of their times. Many less successful pictures were acquired by the contemporary patrons, displayed in their homes, and thoroughly admired. Must we say that these more obscure artists were enjoyed in error, or less sincerely? Without these pictures the popular taste and the market which produced the more significant works could not possibly have been developed. Education must surely underscore the importance of the contemporary buyer, especially the young and the small buyer, and of the contemporary listener, especially the "peanut gallery" listener, in the ultimate efflorescence of the art of any era.

The American consumer does not refrain from building a house because he cannot afford a ten-room, two-garage stone house with a view. He builds himself a five-room, one-garage house, lays his plans for a future wing or an outdoor fireplace, and makes the whole enterprise as attractive and comfortable as possible, often by his own carpentering and gardening. Likewise his wife can feel happy and look charming in a coat several grades below mink on the economy scale. There is no false modesty about the enjoyment of such purchases; Americans are all openly and frankly unpretentious about their needs and tastes and pocketbooks—until they reach the world of art. In art there is the conviction that only the best is respectable, that to invest in any but the definitely top level product at top prices would promptly classify the purchaser as second (or fifth) rate, not only in his personal esthetic taste but in his social status!

The reasons for this ridiculous situation lie not so much in our pride but in our art education, or lack of it. In houses and coats we are sure of our values, and are thus protected against exploitation by the commercial vendors. It is relatively easy to acquire the facts and the understanding which build up sophistication in these values. Sophistication in art values is a bit more difficult for it requires a longer discipline, and therefore we renounce our individual prerogative in favor of those who supposedly have the discipline.

When the experts disagree among themselves on the merits of a picture, a play, a concert, or a novel, the layman is perhaps confused, but not a little pleased. He has himself perhaps been entertained but not uplifted, emotionally exalted but intellectually unconvinced. He can, therefore, hardly count his esthetic experience complete until he has read the reviews and discovered what he ought to think and whether perhaps he has enjoyed it by mistake. More precisely, he seeks to round out his sensory, and perceptual and affective, experience with an evaluative one —a critical judgment, a summing up which will crystallize the total effect of the art experience. This he cannot achieve of himself.

We fail to make this necessary evaluative judgment for ourselves because we have not been taught in our schools and colleges either the nature of the process of making such judgments or the variety of legitimate standards which may be involved in them. The newspaper critics and the professional reviewers or commentators are on the whole pleasing and popular because in their disagreement with one another, they reconcile us to our own uncertainties. If even the experts disagree, everyone seems to be fully justified in his individual interpretation and judgment.

It is in the arts more than in any other field—politics, sports, economics—that we have the more consciously delegated these affective and judgmental processes to others. To the extent that information must always be incomplete and feelings and prejudices subject to manipulation by the mass media, the thinking of laymen is somewhat less than coldly logical and accurate on any subject. But in art we suffer not only from the incompleteness of the available data and from the propaganda of the entrepreneurs and the critics, but more especially from our own lack of formal instruction in the intellectual and affective qualities of art. This loss is greater because of the very nature of art: its objective is not to meet empirical criteria but to give personal delight. Without these fixed and easily justified standards we must either repudiate standards entirely or accept them completely on faith, which means renouncing the very possibility of an intellectual or rational approach.

On the other hand, in our classrooms we have learned in systematic fashion the principles of politics and economics. We have discussed the concepts with our teachers, noted the illustrations from history, and followed the practical demonstrations in the community. We have read and criticized the newspapers, and above all, we have assimilated daily examples in our earning, voting, shopping, traveling, and dozens of other living routines. Such procedures develop opinions, standards, principles, and values which are very real and concrete. We revise them continually, and sometimes drastically, but we never abandon them entirely. We realize that they are built into our very personalities, and it would be unthinkable to admit that one person's values are as good as another's, or that there is "no accounting for taste." Rarely do we accept another person's political or economic opinions on faith. We warm up for argument, resist vigorously, and assimilate only those aspects which are congenial to our own views. In art we are less adventurous. We are lazy, content, almost smug in our innocence; in short, we are missing all the fun.

Any one of the many fields of art is as useful as any other for the cultivation of appreciation, for it is the general habit of mind rather than any special knowledge or talent which will lead to enjoyment and motivate further study. Sensitivity and interest for any one of the arts will engender sympathy and understanding for the others. It is the esthetic attitude of mind in itself which creates whatever miracle is to be expected in this modern world of art.

The esthetic outlook is as easy or as difficult to acquire as any other intellectual accomplishment. It is no more unusual or esoteric than skill in languages, or in engineering or personnel work. It doesn't "run in families," in the sense that it is inherited in the germ plasm, but it is acquired very naturally and pleasantly by children from their family life in the same way that they learn from their parents to speak English or German, with good or bad accent, with large or small vocabulary.

Children reflect the interests and benefit from the attitudes of their parents in the arts as well as in other areas. Women do have one advantage over men in that circumstances have made it more socially acceptable for them to interest and occupy themselves in artistic endeavors. To say that the appreciation or practice of the arts requires no more special talent than many other vocations or professions does not mean, however, that any neophyte can achieve proficiency by sudden insight, sheer will power, good luck, extra-sensory perception, or some other spontaneous or inspirational method. The laws of human learning apply as inexorably to art as to French or mathematics.

Even more astonishing to the intelligent layman is the fact that appreciation of serious art is as difficult to acquire as creative skill. The enjoyment of pictures, sonatas, cathedrals, or sonnets requires active intellectual effort and continuous and close attention. This is quite a different process from the comfortable alternation of social excitement and daydreaming that many a listener experiences in the concert hall, which evoke such comments as "I just love to watch his hands," "It made me think of our cruise to the Mediterranean last winter," "I planned the way I could make over my red dress," "I wish he had not sung so much of the moderns," or "I like him better on the radio."

It is important that we study carefully that most paradoxical and elusive of educational programs, training for pleasure. For the days of the American college-bred woman are rich in leisure hours. She has health, intelligence, and worldly goods. Her right hand is vigorous and efficient and her left hand solicitous and charitable, but these gifts and talents are not matched by an equal capacity for enjoying them.

She has perhaps discovered the natural beauty of our landscapes, the endless variety profligate in its richness—the creeping quiet of the seasons overlaid with the violence of storms, the vastness of snows, the shriveling heat. She knows the intimate villages, the cold anonymity of cities, the gentle shore lines, the horizons bounded only by the stars.

She understands also the joy of movement in dancing, skating, or swimming, and the social pleasures in sports, in teamwork and competition, and especially in cheering and winning. There is pleasure for her in traveling and entertaining, in club life of many kinds, in the getting and giving of affection, in emotional tensions and release. Having so much, she is nevertheless restless; her satisfactions seem temporary and superficial, provocative but not evocative. Her days have a past (nostalgic) and a

195

future (challenging) but no present. There is plenty of remembering and becoming and achieving, but not enough of being and experiencing.

This kind of outlook and attitude is so typical of our own present-day culture that it will not be easy to circumvent it with any prescribed educational program. The hope is rather that each individual may see his own need to escape our cultural stereotypes, to eschew constant "expectation" and give more emphasis to "satisfactions," and that he may learn to cultivate the inward look rather than the outward, may find that the search for significance can be as exciting as the search for progress.

Women yearn for the kind of total enjoyment which they suspect they might have been capable of. They envy the abandon of artistic enthusiasm without in any way understanding it. The mysteries and the reverence with which the nineteenth century blocked the way to an intelligent understanding of the arts have been replaced by the esoteric cults and the glamour thrown around them in the twentieth century. The road is still barred and appreciation remains capricious, individualistic, and sentimental rather than the forthright intellectual and emotional experience which is so easily within the grasp of any conscientious student.

Our esthetic birthright has indeed been traded for a mess of pottage. "Because when you get people believing that there is an authoritative well of wisdom to which they can turn for absolutes, you have dried up the springs on which they must in the end draw, even for the things of this world." [3]

So strong is the conviction that artistic talent is given rather than earned, that inspiration is the sole method of the artist, and that genius is foreordained and mysterious, that scholars have been at some pains to trace the history and origins of these apprehensions. One reason is that not many artists are good at verbal explanation, and when they fail to explain themselves clearly in our favorite medium, words, we tend to believe that the matter is in itself mysterious and inexplicable. But the artist has simply failed to develop his semantic habits to the extent of other intellectual workers because he is so preoccupied with manipulation of line, color, rhythm, and tone, and with the study of their sensory qualities and their use as symbols.

This block in communication is reinforced by the natural clannishness of artists. They prefer the company of other artists who have developed the same esthetic outlook, the same non-verbal methods of perceiving and thinking and communicating their ideas. They seek one another's company also because of their common belief in the importance of the affective side of life. It is not that they are any more or any less emotional than the layman, but that they specialize professionally in affective values, are more alert to the finer details and more objective in their analyses.

The layman also has little tolerance for the enthusiasms of the artist because he has not understood the almost abnormal degree of self-confidence required for writing a poem or designing a bowl or transposing a ballad into a ballet and then launching the slender craft on the open seas of public approval. For other workers, very little of the ordinary day's work is self-initiated. Everything is usually well prescribed with material and measurable purposes, and our services are *demanded* by the successive routines and problems. The form of our activities, the goal toward which our ideas must flow, and the very pace and pattern of our feelings are largely predetermined. But for the artist no goal is set, no direction is given, and the very act of setting forth on the quest is left to his own initiative.

What shall he write his poem about? What subject is so important that he must give it his time and attention? What meter shall it have? What rhyme? What form and length? Who will read his finished poem? Can he even find a publisher for it? For this kind of creative work, only the deepest conviction of self-worth will suffice, and the artist must refresh and replenish his inner vitality from his own inexhaustible resources. For his best effort—in fact, for any effort—he needs inordinate successes, positive and decisive responses, and a thorough understanding, if not unequivocal approving, of all that he produces.

But for the artist, with this special need for confirmation and conviction, the usual measures of successful consummation are perversely unavailable. Other workers have very obvious and continuous evidences of their successes and failures. The businessman has his profits; the professional man witnesses the benefits to his clients; the executives, the secretaries, and the artisans watch the successful completion of their various projects, while the creative artist waits for the approval, the acceptance, even the mere tolerance, of his work often until long after its completion. Except for his own subjective impression of its value and his own personal satisfaction in an enterprise brought to completion, the artist has little or no reward. In his education, preparation must be given to meet these personal difficulties, and his motivation to create must be fortified to abnormal proportions. Likewise the dearth of satisfactions must in some way be supplemented; the sympathy which he needs, especially in his formative years and in his failures, must somehow be made available. Curriculums which fail to develop youths with these personalities, which neglect the social forces that are needed to support and encourage them, are bound to fall short of their cultural objectives.

In his need, the artist has most frequently turned to another self-consciously introspective and sensitive group, the philosophers. They too have not found incentives in material benefits and rewards, and they, like the artists, have experienced difficulty in making their methods and objectives clear to the common man. Philosophers have similarly felt the need to discard what others take for granted and to search for new justifications, new principles, new truths.

But unlike the inarticulate artists, the philosophers have never lacked for words. Their business is the building of concepts, the inventing, accumulating, defining, and recharacterizing of words. The philosophers have given the artists words, and have been trusted by the artists to speak for them, to interpret their work to the layman, to explain its nature and essence and create understanding and interest. But this promising partnership, so vital

198

in education for esthetic enjoyment, is no longer proving useful. There are a number of reasons:

1. Philosophy is most successful in clarifying and relating the knowledge already available to it, but not in exploring new fields of knowledge, not in discovering new information and facts. The philosophers use only the completed materials, the actual works of art produced and accepted, and with these data they have made salient contributions. But in discovering how the mind of the artist gave birth to the masterpiece and how the beholder apprehended it—both of them *new and unknown areas of knowledge*—the philosopher is more helpless than the artist. From the point of view of education, it is just this very creative process, and the psychological and sociological circumstances involved in it, which both the artist and his audience have most needed to understand.

For this kind of service the psychologists, especially the social psychologists and even the psychiatrists, with their experimental and empirical methods for exploring human activity and for advancing the boundaries of present knowledge, are better prepared. John Dewey, both psychologist and philosopher, viewing "art as experience," finds that the philosophers may even stand in their own way (much more perhaps in the artists' way) when they harden, freeze, reify, their obviously incomplete data into "so many inherent, aboriginal, divisive kinds of Being and Knowledge." [4]

2. Philosophers, in their relations with the artists, have been more preoccupied in fitting "art," that is, the artists' finished creations and the data and theories of the artistic culture, into their own precise systems of knowledge than in helping the artists relate themselves to the society of their time. Santayana has agreed that philosophers have "interpreted aesthetic facts in the light of their metaphysical principles and made their theory of taste a corollary or footnote to their systems." [5] This is, of course, no criticism of the philosophers, insofar as they have many other goals, but merely an explanation of why they are not useful in a realistic program of art education.

199

3. Although philosophy is a very rewarding study, it is in itself a difficult subject, requiring verbal and intellectual skills of a high order—certainly beyond the level of the ten-year-old child. But art is more immediate and appealing, not in itself difficult and esoteric and derivative. The child can understand and be happy in it as spontaneously as in catching fish or baking cakes or singing or sailing or watching the circus. For adults, too, understanding art by way of philosophy is like traveling by only the most roundabout routes. The journey may be very pleasant if one has ample time and if the ultimate objective is not too urgent.

In the development of science our present generation of scholars and students has profited by a phenomenal acceleration. We have created the maximum interest, taught by the most efficient methods, attracted the best minds, and provided the largest subsidies. But education has been handicapped in its propagation of the arts, by a system of esthetics which has been conceptual and philosophical in an era when other values and standards are being subjected to empirical analysis in social and scientific terms. Here is a cultural lag which we are just beginning to identify and understand, one to which scholars should dedicate their earnest inquiries.

What must be included in our art education in order that each individual may have firsthand, intimate experiences which he identifies and enjoys as truly esthetic? Not the purely sensuous enjoyment of eating or swimming, nor the pleasurable sentiments of loving and receiving affection, and certainly not the emotional excitement of the thrill, but rather the particular blend of the sensuous, the emotional, and the intellectual which constitutes the esthetic experience. How shall we further insure that each individual may know how to arouse these experiences in himself, where to seek the stimuli—pictures, music, poetry, drama—which will develop all his esthetic sensitivities and powers to the highest possible degree? And most of all, how can we teach the individual to *want* these esthetic satisfactions, to desire them, to accept them as his major goals, and to discipline his faculties and his behavior to achieve them for himself?

Motivation will be the most difficult problem; we know most of the needed components of esthetic pleasure, but we do not know how to make them popular and desired. The artist must somehow earn a greater stature in community life, must move out of his garret and into some of the better income brackets. He must be recognized for the intellectual character of his contributions and subsidized as frankly as the other intellectual dependents, those who do creative research in pure or applied science. The arts and humanities must get their fair share, along with science and business, of the best young minds and personalities. The rewards must be made effective and obvious.

Nor can we neglect the audiences, the ultimate consumers. We can, with the psychologists, assume a drive in every individual to achieve satisfactions of the emotional type, but can we discipline and direct this natural thrill-seeking into channels of esthetic qualities? The sex drive, for example, we recognize as a specific drive with a discernible history, with waxings and wanings which are amenable to discipline and modification through learning. We speak also of a more general and inclusive drive for the preservation and enhancement of the ego, to which all other drives are merely secondary goals or techniques for achieving the more compulsive ones. Is thrill-seeking a rather specific subdrive or is it merely a more general rhythm of alternating excitability and relaxation?

Or we may trace, with the sociologists, this ego-maximizing drive—this restlessness—through its shifting patterns to some of its origins in the societal pressures. The older goals, David Riesman explains, the fine houses, horses, or *objets d'art*, the desires that drove men to work hard, are now satisfied relatively easily: ". . . they are incorporated into the standard of living taken for granted by millions. But the craving remains. It is a craving for satisfactions others appear to obtain, an objectless craving. . . . The product now in demand is neither a staple nor a machine; it is a personality." [6] It might be epitomized for many in the one word *glamour*. Or it may be defined as Thornton Wilder defined love, namely, the sense of one's identity rebounding from some intelligent and admired being. No one wants to miss, in his own humdrum round, the qualities of experience that he believes others are having.

How can we isolate and define such a drive, cultivate and discipline it? How can thrill-seeking find its satisfactions in activities which are possible and profitable in our culture and which will foster the emotional pleasure? Ought we not to plan for our school children some practice in the building up and releasing of emotion, not of fear or of anger, and not through plots of adventure and danger, but rather in cycles of intellectual aggression and relaxation, of pure delight in achieving and contemplating? Perhaps we should take Lewis Carroll quite literally and give our fourth graders lessons in "reeling and writhing and fainting in coils."

It is true that the participation which is presently offered in the early school years, and throughout all the public school levels, does encourage some of these creative pleasures. Participation is a vital part of art education, but it is only a part, not the whole. Finger painting, singing, beautifying the schoolroom with color, folk dancing on May Day, playing in the band, taking parts in the dramas—all of those activities develop the sensitiveness to rhythms, colors, and tones and enhance their values with perceptual and social pleasures. But to the extent that self-expression and performance exclude the intellectual and formal qualities in the art experience, this emphasis in the precollege years is especially inadequate, even misleading, as the basis for adult satisfactions and for more mature enjoyment.

Soon enough the child's attempt at creation, at performance, is removed from the sheltering classroom and thrown out to the judgment of his peer group, who evaluate it with the connoisseurship typical of the mass media audience, who require a finished piece of work, who see each amateur pianist as a competitor of Horowitz and each youthful artist a rival of Dali. For the peer judges, these highest standards must be achieved with incredible speed and no visible effort, as they are in the comics and radio dramas, and with no reward for any but the top performer. The winner takes everything; nothing can be gained without the prize itself. Unless very early in the schools the intellectual aspects of artistry are emphasized, unless the emotional overtones of satisfaction grow out of the very act of engaging the mind, senses, and skills in a challenging problem, the permanent benefit is lost; the internalized, meaningful experience can never be realized. Small wonder that the approved midcentury esthetic activity in our society has become not creating or performing, but merely an expression of proper preferences, a continuous game, a process of revising one's taste to conform to the current evanescent patterns!

The details of form, affective value, and meaning and their arrangement in the total art form exact their own peculiar intellectual discipline from the reluctant learner. The child must learn the subtleties and gradations possible within one color and the interrelations of all hues, the intricacies of balance and contrast and of brightnesses and saturations, the qualities of dominance and harmony, the affective values and meanings of all the colors and their effects on one another.

The wealth of sensuous detail and intellectual manipulation which underlie true appreciation of painting is almost inconceivable to the amateur. We "see" not with our eyes, but with our past experience; and therefore, to be able to "see"—that is to perceive, to understand—a painting requires a past experience in which conscious attention has been given to visual details, to the patternings of forms and colors and to their intellectual organization into concepts and principles. The ideologies and histories of painting which are taught at the college level too often have no substance on which to rest. One cannot teach dancing before walking or statistics before arithmetic, or begin the study of the French language with Molière.

"Participation" is not good as an end in itself, but only as an incentive to the mastery of subject matter. The child's participation in the arithmetic lesson is not adequate unless the principles are grasped and facility in using them strengthened. There is no more virtue in self-expression through art materials than in self-expression through language if the results are not in conformity with acceptable practice. We do not allow mere babbling or bad grammar in the child's self-expression through speech. Why, then, should there be any special virtue in free daubing with paints? The learner is equally subject to discipline in both if he would keep abreast of his civilization in his art as well as in his language experience and skills.

Forms and patterns in language for use in speaking and writing are taught to the child very efficiently. Comparable forms and patterns in music or painting or the dance are counted as much less important in the routines of adult life for which the schools are preparing the child. Therefore, the methods for teaching them have not matured, and the emphasis given to them is at a minimum. This state of affairs is but the reflection of the small significance given to the inner life, to esthetic values, in our present society. Perhaps in the past century we have been justified in our emphasis on the material aspects, the sound economic development, and the industrial expansion. In the next century a different focus may be called for. Even in the immediate future, in the adulthood of the present generation of students, the emphasis may shift from industry and agriculture to poetry, music, and painting.

For such an era the first educational requirement is an understanding of the formal elements in all the arts, and this intellectual aspect of the arts involves the same kind of learning process as learning to read or to add or to comprehend the concepts of science. The novice is introduced to symbols and must learn to attend to their details and differentiate each from the other. He gains facility with them through rote memory and many hours of drill and practice, which is often very dull work. Sometimes, if he likes them, he voluntarily spends more of his time in "playing" with them and begins to teach himself. Sometimes he is resistant and neglectful and learns only because he cannot escape from the discipline of school life.

History and arithmetic and reading pursue the student faithfully throughout his long struggle with the learning process, but the arts, counted as unnecessary for meeting his economic and citizenship needs, are year by year eliminated. Thus the burden of learning, which both he and the schools share with such difficulty, is perhaps carried for a few more years and with a little greater ease. Sports and social affairs, which do not involve this burden of intellectual discipline, are substituted for the arts in the hope of continuing the personal, affective, and esthetic aspects of his development.

Music, drama, poetry, sculpture, painting, and religion are offered in courses far more limited in number and scope than the standard subjects in the public schools, and therefore none of the pupils—neither the apt nor the reluctant learners—have the opportunity to fulfill their abilities and their tastes in these subjects. But this feeble emphasis and its decline in the later school years are not as serious as the failure to teach the arts as intellectual subject matter, something which requires a response from the mind as well as the body and the emotions. To the growing personality, the arts are much more than entertainment or relaxation; they are vital to its healthy and fully rounded development in our traditions and contemporary society.

When the arts are used to encourage self-expression, but without the intellectual discipline of form, they encourage only a spurious and empty expression of the self: emotion and bodily energy without spirit and intellect. The intellectual aspect of art involves the sensitivity to sensory and perceptual details and to their exquisite nuances and patterns. It means apprehending all these details with ease and agility, recognizing their interplay, imagining new patterns, and anticipating their unfolding. It validates them with meanings, memories, and associations, transforming them into symbols which sometimes achieve a true magnificence of movement and direction. The intellect alone can endow human activity with the most essentially *human* qualities of dignity, detachment, awareness, permanence. Without these, sports become competitions in animal spirits, religion is mystery, art is reduced to glamorized sentiment. All of them may then be safely exploited for commercial purposes; their potential values for the human spirit will be lost.

In the twentieth century the commercialization of the arts has been staggering in growth and significance, thanks to the mass media of newspapers, magazines, comics, movies, radio, television, sound recordings, and color reproductions. It is difficult, perhaps impossible, to separate the gains from the losses, the shining benefits from the cloying grievances. Folk art has been overshadowed and obscured, and the fine arts pinched and sharpened until their moods have become uncomfortable, insupportable for many audiences. The functions of the artist are changing, but the functions of audiences are also shifting and art education is not growing apace.

Twentieth-century technology and industrialization allow no important function to the artist, only to the industrial designer or the advertiser. The artist was not always as today divorced from the current ideology and denied a proper function in society. He was more versatile, as Leonardo, designing engines of war as well as costumes and pageants; or he was indispensable, as Haydn or Raphael, enhancing the prestige of princes and clergy or educating and entertaining the court and preserving its history in buildings and bas-reliefs, in poetry and dramas, in portraits and cantatas. His social status may have been "below the salt," he may not always have collected his fees, and he may have suffered from the whims or the indifference of dictators, but he had that sense of security in being needed. He was employed. His life had direction and purpose which it does not have today.

The artist is affected not only by his ill-defined functions, but by the fading of all the outworn absolutes and the shifting of traditional standards. He feels the unrest and uncertainty in the same way the minister and the social worker and the teacher and the parent feel it. The established standards that sustained the artists of the past and helped to make their work comprehensible to the layman are denied to the present-day artist: religious beliefs, moral codes, aristocratic manners, esthetic dogmas—all the absolutes of other ages. What is left to him is personal integrity, sincerity, genuineness, and sensitivity, all of which are subjective and individual criteria. And this at a time when our assembly-line economy in all other areas of life is denying the importance and the significance of the individual, stressing that of the group.

Every artist is entirely his own master and this requires a constant self-searching, a perpetual self-renewal, and individual resourcefulness, with attentiveness to all that he himself experiences, hears, sees, feels, remembers. It not only allows the artist to be free; it requires, it *insists,* that he be free—that he paint, write, compose, interpret, anything and everything which may have meaning and significance *for him.*

Therefore, present-day art is extremely diversified and often obscure because it is so individualistic. There is such diversity that it is inconceivable that all art could be interesting and clear to all laymen. Each patron must reconcile himself to an insensitiveness for certain subject matter and certain techniques. The field is too big; it progresses only in terms of averages. The more highly individualized artist will inevitably remain obscure to most audiences. He may have a certain influence on the more successful esthetic leaders (as when we designate him "the poets' poet"), or he may remain forever obscure, even to posterity. Perhaps this obscurity is a high price to pay for freedom, culturally speaking. It is an inescapable by-product of our present process and cult of freedom, which it is the artist's duty as well as our own to preserve.

However, the artist, like ourselves, is to be free but not irresponsible. To whom and for what must he be responsible? To the largest number of people for the acceptance of the greatest amount of art, for the deepest satisfactions and the most enjoyment. Divorced from his audiences, from the simple quantitative implications of his efforts, the artist cannot hope to sustain himself. His most important function is obviously educational.

It is a two-fold function, as in all education: an obligation to find and stimulate an aristocracy of talent and at the same time to cultivate and encourage larger and larger circles of proletarian audiences. Eventually the man-made and artificial gap between the two must be firmly and permanently closed. The artist must emerge as any other leader, pushing himself up from the crowd, recognized for the excellence of his work over theirs, born of their understanding, nourished by their enthusiasm.

The methods for developing artists and audiences will be somewhat different, but before either process can be set in motion on the tremendous and routinized scale appropriate to twentieth-century education, both the artistic creation and the human process which receives it must be explored by experiment, by case studies, even by statistical analyses. Only from such data, rather than from armchair speculation, can artists with semantic skills build a truly useful esthetic, purged of obscurities and pretensions and keyed to the honest perceptions and desires of modern audiences.

These artists and estheticians will need interpreters and popularizers with subtle and powerful skills, for we are not asking them to compromise their goals, but only to feel their social obligations toward their great potential audiences. We take it for granted that the artist is dedicated to his own personal artistic ideals, but we ask that he be equally faithful to his audiences, that he give them a parallel devotion in explaining and interpreting. For this he needs not critics but propagandists, not agents and patrons but ghost writers, public relations experts, advertisers, salesmen, and fans.

Economics has dissociated the artist from his rich patron and thrown him upon public support. Not the dilettante and the connoisseur, but public-school music, commercial art, and industrial design will be his mainstays. If he has something important to give to the human spirit, and if he exerts his true leadership, he must learn how to adapt it to the younger and less willing minds and to be as sincere in creating audiences as in creating masterpieces. He must propagate the forms and symbols of his own medium throughout the long school years, and he must translate them into the common words of communication, so that the musician can talk to the painter, to the sculptor, and to the dramatist, and so that all of these may interpret their works to the layman with increasing effectiveness.

In these new educational functions of the artist, there is a more important role for women than past decades have ever assigned to them. Teaching of the arts is even now expanding, and women have always taken the lead in classroom teaching. Crafts and all the minor arts; radio, television, decorating, and housing; and even fashions for both men and women are creating new genres, new audiences, new jobs. Women—in the school, in the home, in the community, and in the market place—are still the leaders in maintaining the prerequisite attitudes, interests, and sensitivities for the total advancement of artistic culture in their times.

. . . *10*

Women's Education and Education in General

THE Report of the President's Commission on Higher Education, the Harvard Report, the Columbia Experiment, the Eight-Year Plan, and countless other studies on who should be educated in this divided world all testify to the magnitude of our present educational problems. The functions of education have changed, and are still changing almost too precipitously for the layman to follow. Education formerly provided the ladder whereby a few privileged or gifted individuals might climb to fame and sometimes fortune; now it serves as the tremendous elevator, expensively and ponderously mechanized, whereby whole classes of people are hoisted to higher standards of living, to economic competence, and to vocational success.

Experimental programs can be put forward only by well-subsidized commissions or teams of experts. No one can write on education in fewer than a dozen chapters, and any one theory or research project can do little more than point the way to further extensive study. To write, to teach, to debate—alas, to act—in this complicated area is increasingly hazardous.

Any individual woman, therefore, must ease herself into the rigorous thinking needed for her own daughter's education by some preliminary practice in thinking also about the education of her sons and of her neighbors' children and about her city's and her nation's problems in education. Many of the facts and arguments are all too well known to her. What she needs is some axis about which she can turn the whole unwieldy mass and swing it around more dexterously for closer inspection. More than one such axis is in current use by the professionals, each designed for the better display of some one special facet of the educational world.

She may borrow, for example, one very ancient and serviceable axis based on the Jeffersonian and Jacksonian interpretations of democracy. Thomas Jefferson, founder of the University of Virginia, called for sufficient educational opportunities and social mobility to insure that all gifted individuals of any social class could develop as far as their capacities allowed and emerge as the leaders of the state. Under this philosophy, college entrance requirements would be made very high, but all students who could qualify would be subsidized during their college years. The curriculums planned for them would be appropriate only for those who had high ability, who would work diligently and utilize their abilities and training exclusively for the social good. Every laggard would be eliminated, and for all those of merely average intellect, no higher education at all would be provided; they would find their niche at some lower level of activity, and more happily, without higher education.

In contrast, the Jacksonian point of view calls for a system of education which will raise the level of the masses. True democracy presupposes that each man is informed, alert, and aware of his privileges and his obligations. Each has benefited from a "general" education, which differs from a "liberal" education only in degree—in depth, not in breadth, of exploration. The Jacksonian college would admit every student who applied and would try to find some program which would develop each student's interests, understandings, abilities, and skills to his fullest, even though meager, capacity. In this ideology each citizen governs himself and shares in the responsibility for the management of the community, and therefore all human beings have need of the ample and rounded education. The good life, and education which trains for the good life, are equally the privilege of all; in fact there can be no good life without the participation of all.

The modern practices which have developed around these two theories, Jeffersonian and Jacksonian, have, of course, attempted to combine eclectically the best features of both. Dean Johnston of Minnesota outlined the following steps: (1) Find the gifted individuals. (2) Classify all students with respect to their probable accomplishments, and reclassify them from time to time as they progress through the public school system. (3) Discover the interests and talents and capacity through which each student can best serve the social order. (4) Maintain intellectual curiosity for each student, encourage self-criticism, strengthen judgment, and appreciate always the mutual character of the rights and duties of the individual and of society. (5) Finally, offer the facilities necessary for all students to reach full physical, emotional, esthetic, and spiritual self-realization.

Dean Johnston regretted that the ruling classes have not always been the intellectual classes and that we still await a society in which leadership and power are exercised by the higher intellects, guided by even-handed justice according to the Socratic ideal. Physical, social, economic, and political changes affect the thinking and living of the people, and the university must train some of its citizens to lead the way in orderly fashion, rather than by subversion and upheaval. "Society is indebted to the individual who has not accepted its tutelage, or who has pushed beyond the bounds of contemporary thought and action." [1] The objectives of education shift as we pass from the lower to the higher intellectual classes, and promotion of the school child should always follow not the years spent, but achievement. The objectives of any one type of school must be fitted to the needs of the type of students to be found within it.

There will be little quarrel with his philosophy except that it is difficult to rescue these "general" or "liberal" educational values in a competitive system where high specialization is also necessary. The general education of the masses is the measure of a democracy, because a broad critical sense is needed for an individual to recognize competence in any field, "to know a good man when he sees one," to elect the right leader, to know which of the experts to trust when there is disagreement.

The theory set forth in the report of the Harvard Committee is a combination of these two points of view. It asks that we "improve the average and speed the able while holding common goals before each"; and while both the "average" and the "able" will present their specific problems, the greatest problem is in "holding common goals before each."

In general the European countries—Germany and England, for example—have not adopted this latter goal, and customarily separate in the very early grades those who shall receive a liberal education from those who will pursue a largely vocational program. The essential difference is that the separation is made not as Dean Johnston recommended, on the basis of finding the able at a very young age by means of tests, counseling programs, and by repeated reclassification, but rather according to the stratifications of society, with the schools offering liberal education open only to the well born. Those in the middle and lower classes who show conspicuous ability at the time of their competitive examinations are always given an opportunity and are sometimes singled out for encouragement and subsidy.

In England especially, the extremely gifted and ambitious enjoy even greater educational opportunities and subsidies than in the United States, but social immobility and isolation in speech, manners, and ideology close the doors to all but a chosen few. In Germany also, tradition and custom are constant and formidable barriers. It is still current opinion even among educational leaders that "it takes three generations to make a scholar," while here in the United States we happily boast of the chemists, philosophers, engineers, statesmen, composers, and poets who come from the steel mills, the haberdasheries, and the chicken farms, or who may be only one generation removed from the steerage passage.

This is the citizen's dilemma, not the educator's. We must ask ourselves, as parents and citizens, whether we could ever be satisfied with a stratification in our society which would extend itself thus to our public schools. Could we be content with high schools which included, as they do in these foreign countries, only 10 or 15 per cent of all our teen-age children, rather than our own 80 per cent and more? Could we accept, as they do, an educational philosophy in which 80 per cent of our youth are in no schools full time after the thirteenth or the fourteenth year?

All colleges and universities may be seen as arranging themselves as a continuum from the most Jeffersonian to the most Jacksonian point of view. Probably no one of them is purely the one or the other, and each includes to some extent the goals endorsed by both philosophies. The European university, on the other hand, was formerly purely Jeffersonian in its philosophy and is still very largely so. Our universities could easily achieve all of the European excellencies, if we could commit ourselves to their philosophy. Actually, our graduate and professional schools parallel the foreign university both in general philosophy and in the age group served.

Parents of those daughters who have superior ability, who have absorbed professional thinking and attitudes in their family and neighborhood contacts, should seek the more Jeffersonian campus. Here the selective process insures that education will proceed more swiftly, more deeply, more broadly. But daughters who have throughout their high school years found themselves to be comfortably average students will find an education more suited to their needs on the campus which frankly displays its Jacksonian point of view. Both kinds of education will be effective, but they will be different. The intelligent parent recognizes alike the differences in the daughters and in the curriculums most suitable for them.

The sophisticate will be eager to protest that not all the problems of our schools can be made to revolve around this Jefferson-Jackson axis. There are other sharply opposing points of view for which parents and educators are seeking a compromise solution. There is, for example, what we may call the individual-societal axis, which highlights the conflicts between education for individual and personal growth and education for the inevitable pressures to be encountered in the rigid social and economic institutions of the present adult world. "One may well wonder," says Allison Davis, "what happens to the individual who passes from the child centered school to the assembly line economy." [2] There is so little opportunity for the exercise of individual initiative except on the part of the few who occupy the apex of authority of the particular enterprise involved.

Twentieth-century American culture is technological through and through, not only in its economic production, but in its leisure, in entertainment and arts, in politics and government, in home life, and in the manipulation of men and power. The child learns, because the parent and teacher are convinced, that his own individuality is important, that he must have personal integrity toward his own chosen ideals. But simultaneously he must also learn the social goals of the total society, learn to cherish them equally with his own, and above all, learn how they can be endured and integrated with his own drives and motives.

Education is broader than the training offered in the schools. It is the total process of socialization whereby the individual assimilates his own culture. Whether or not it seems to him a "good" culture, he feels its pressures and is ambitious to adapt himself to it. Those who share this anxiety to avoid social punishment and achieve social rewards will be those who strive most eagerly and acquire it most successfully. "In our kind of society, if a child wishes to be rewarded, he must learn to mobilize and bear that degree of anxiety which will serve to make him strive more effectively for the goals of his group." [3] Almost all the good things in life, as educators evaluate them, are achievements of upper-middle-status persons—care of and pride in property, careful child training, sacrifice for future gains, long education, development of skills, motivation to work up to the top amidst the complexities of business, industry, government, education, or the church.

The motivation to rise to a higher class status lies in the severe social punishments and physical discomforts of lower class status. American public education may be seen, therefore, as an attempt on a gigantic scale to socialize into the middle class the great masses of low-status children who form the bulk of the school's population. It is not an easy task to motivate our students, to convince them of the reality of the rewards at the end of the anxiety-laden climb, and to make sure that these rewards and values are real and that they are in the end satisfying. There may be some truth in the accusation that we teach not virtues but tactics, not character but personality.

In addition to this individual-societal axis, still others might be discerned—the general-classical, the cultural-vocational, the traditional-progressive. These are but new ways of propounding old problems, new "jargons" which seem more appropriate for describing and evaluating them for modern ears.

Former Chancellor Hutchins and some of his colleagues at the University of Chicago have maintained the most extreme position on the general-classical axis. According to his theories, the college junior would study (1) metaphysics, the science of first principles; (2) the social sciences, which are practical sciences dealing with the relations of man to man; and (3) the natural sciences, the sciences of man and nature. The departmental system would disappear and would be replaced by the three faculties: metaphysics, social science, and natural science.

Metaphysics would include not only first principles but all that follows from it, such as principles of change and the analysis of man and his productions in the fine arts and literature. Future clergymen and philosophers would be enrolled under this faculty.

The social sciences would embrace ethics, politics, and economics, and such historical and empirical materials as might be needed to supplement them for the guidance of human actions. Administrators, judges, legislators, statesmen, and men of affairs would be trained under this faculty.

The natural sciences, the study of nature, would train future physicians, who would devote further study to physical and biological sciences and secure the necessary experience for serving the patient in an institute attached to a university and to a hospital. In such institutes all the present-day research professors would be found. "The prospective teacher's general education would be identical with that of the lawyer, doctor, and clergyman. With a good education in the liberal arts, which are grammar, rhetoric, logic, and mathematics, he has learned the basic rules of pedagogy. The liberal arts train the teacher in how to teach, that is how to organize, express, and communicate knowledge." [4]

In contrast to this, the Harvard Committee takes a middle position, postulating neither a monopolistic position for books nor an emphasis on the practical which substitutes training for education. It advocates that two thirds of the high school schedule be devoted to general education for all pupils, and the remaining third reserved for training in vocational or business courses, the arts, or any one of the practical fields. The report challenges the elective system at the college level and recommends that six of sixteen courses necessary for the bachelor's degree be taken in general education, including one in the sciences, one in the social sciences, and one in the humanities.

Perhaps of equal importance to these reorganizations of content are the reforms in the teaching of the humanities and the sciences advocated by former President Conant. He decries the fighting of a rear-guard action by the humanists and urges them to alter not only their reasons for teaching the humanities but also their pedagogical approach, so that they may better meet the needs for understanding human nature, for emotional release, and for expanding personal experience not only of the future doctor and lawyer but of the future salesman, truck driver, foreman, astronomer, and protozoologist as well.

The report of the President's Commission advocates at least two years of higher education for approximately all high school seniors graduating with better than the average record, that is, for about half of our college-age youth rather than the one-fourth

217

who are now found in our colleges. This proposal calls for re-thinking, for re-evaluating the goals of all education, and for re-examining the motivations to learning now practiced in our schools. As prescribed in Conant's stimulating essay, both sub-ject matter and method will be in need of reorganization.

Another of these useful educational axes, the traditional-progressive continuum, involves the twin objectives of higher education: (1) the preservation, transmission, and enrichment of our culture, and (2) the development of the individual to the full limit of his potentialities. The very richness of our cultural heritage cannot but lead to difficulties in choosing materials for our college curriculums. Likewise the degree of student self-determination for his own best development is open to debate.

Emphasis on the classic curriculum, together with little self-determination, earns the classification of "traditional," while at the other end of the scale, more student self-activity, with em-phasis on the more recent learning materials, seems to indicate "progress." Obviously in our high civilization, no school can escape societal pressures on subject matter. And as for student self-determination, it has been fluctuating with the current learn-ing theories for at least the three centuries since Shakespeare advised Lucentio on his choice of subjects: "Fall to them as you find your stomach serves you; No profit grows where is no pleasure taken."

The individual woman must identify herself with the ideologies of her time. If the emphasis in our time is on science, she must understand science—both scientific knowledge for practical liv-ing and the concepts of science for their cultural or conversa-tional value. If we believe that her future mental health depends on an understanding of the principles of psychology and soci-ology, then she must be familiar with these principles, and it is far from advisable to postpone training along these lines until the college years.

Early attention must also be given to the encouragement and development of leisure-time activities that are appropriate, inexpensive, and emotion-releasing. And while skills and appreciations are being cultivated, careful planning must be given as well to the value system which gives prestige to them.

If we are committed to a faith in democracy, the necessary sophistication in regard to its problems must be taught, as must a sense of individual responsibility. If the process of interaction between human beings in their business, political, and social relations is to be democratic in form—calling for compromise, for the slower methods of attaining group welfare by cooperation rather than by edict—then the proper techniques for action and for attitudes and habits of mind had better be taught, certainly to women, and with even greater emphasis to the more politically active men. If the economic structure of nations and societies is a basic factor for building world peace, it is essential that our high school and college students be given as much information as they can absorb about natural resources, cartels, one- or two-product economies, labor relationships, business indices, and price controls.

We cannot emphasize too much the necessity for solving our educational problems with constant reference to the other problems and institutions of our society and the rapid changing of our culture. We cannot afford to teach principles of action which flout economic facts and common business practices. Religious faiths, theories, and philosophical and ethical values are not uniform among our 160 millions of people, and flexibility to allow for this heterogeneity must be incorporated into any program which hopes for success. Social changes such as increasing class stratification, the deterioration of the family, the changing mores of courtship, the spectator trend in sports, and the commercialization of entertainment must not be lost sight of. Political theories, parties, pressures, and techniques cannot be idealized, nor the increasing importance of science minimized.

Beyond the social changes with their complicated pressures lies still another area in our perspective—an outer but all-pervasive realm of prevailing values and ideologies, a cultural atmosphere identified by writers of another century as the

Zeitgeist or spirit of the age. More carefully analyzed by the social scientists of the present decades, this atmosphere is not now quite as nebulous, but it is just as unyielding as ever. Well-meaning programs unadapted to it can be swallowed up without trace. The cults of individual enterprise and material success, of sociopolitical irresponsibility, and of romantic and dramatic sentimentality are actually more effective in our everyday behavior than the atom bomb, the TVA dam, and other more tangible factors.

Radio and the movies, newspapers and magazines and comics —all the mass communication media—propagate their own values and images for their own not always admirable ends. To combat them the schools can count as their allies the church, the scouts, the summer camps, the hostels, the recreational programs and clubs, the "Teen Canteens," and many other organizations which are also contributing perhaps more than can ever be precisely defined or imagined to the attitudes and thinking of women, especially of young women.

The sophisticated educator of the present must learn to manipulate her own individual program for the education of women in terms of this vast but understandable frame of reference to which it is firmly anchored. The pressures which push inward and pull outward must be accurately gauged. Fanaticism may be admirable but impracticable; lethargy may be deplorable but sometimes justifiable. Perspective which grows out of continuing study, experiment, and experience is always the most important preliminary to action.

Clear as these abstract issues and objectives may now seem to mother and daughter, teacher and counselor, the worries of the college administrator are only beginning. He must choose among all the methods for curriculum building, maneuver for faculty and alumnae support, and fight for money and students. An understanding of these predicaments must surely be reckoned as a necessary item in the education of any modern woman.

For convenience we may summarize all the intricacies of curriculum building under three methods. These methods are not mutually exclusive but rather are closely interlocked on every campus.

Traditionally scholars reach deep into their own fields and present to the students the essential facts, disciplines, and theories which must be preserved in our culture. We may designate this method as historical or retrospective, in that it keeps its roots in the accumulated scholarship, no matter how far into the future its implications may be projected.

In contrast, a second method, the professional and vocational, is oriented around individual activity and pointed toward the future. It takes note of all the information, skills, and attitudes which will be needed to secure an individual's future and plans his training to meet them.

A third method is centered in the student himself, in his needs as a growing individual to develop and integrate all his qualities —physical, intellectual, and spiritual, and even societal insofar as his needs are also societal and he integrates himself with a society of his own building.

Curriculums set up by the historical or retrospective method represent a long, slow growth—a careful winnowing of the useful from the peripheral and an end result which is rich in substance and meaning. It is an exacting ritual in which the scholars who are themselves the masters and critics of any one field of knowledge organize their subject matter around its own inherent principles and values and agree on an integrated body of knowledge which best represents the field.

This process must be, of course, an essential part of the setting up of curriculums by any method. It is assumed that if any curriculum requires a knowledge of physics or economics or poetics, the familiar, cohesive, and well-rounded aggregate is indicated. Herein lies the danger for the curriculum builder. Scholars in any field of knowledge can hardly participate in the constant re-evaluation of its principles without projecting them into a kind of colossus which has its own life and being, determines its own directions, defies any partition, and refuses to admit any sharing of its own destinies. It becomes internalized

221

and primarily concerned with its self-preservation, often in defiance of other societal needs.

The second method, the future-centered method exemplified in the whole field of vocational and professional education, is more pragmatic. Here the process works from the outside in, rather than from the inside out. The ultimate adult activity is analyzed in terms of the needed knowledge, techniques, attitudes, and habits and these in turn will be embodied in a curriculum to which any individual and groups will do their best to conform. Attempts are made, some of them fairly successfully, to predetermine the minimum (and even the maximum) of intelligence and talent which will insure success, as well as the financial qualifications and sometimes the personality and interest patterns. Present practice in curriculum building by this method presupposes a guidance program as well as a training program, both of them founded on extensive information gathered through experience and research in the field.

Medicine, law, nursing, chemistry, engineering, home economics, accounting, and hosts of other professions operate along these lines. Nursing, for example, has a rather rigidly enforced curriculum based on the skills, information, and personal habits which will be used at the bedside of the sick. This curriculum is prescribed by the national organization of professional nurses and is, of course, periodically studied and revised. The national organization visits and inspects each school of nursing and pronounces it accredited when its teaching and equipment meet all the requirements. It also arranges for the examination which must be taken by all candidates before the practice of the profession is authorized. Like many other professional associations, it provides aptitude tests and counseling services which help the schools in choosing the best candidates from all those applying for admission.

So many of the national professional organizations are prescribing curriculums and accrediting the various departments that their influence on the programs offered by the colleges is very pronounced. They fortify these departments with a most effective argument for more equipment and better teachers, which sometimes works to the disadvantage of other departments.

Although many of these professional accrediting agencies prefer that candidates also obtain a good liberal education, this is not often actually prescribed, and the state and national board examinations cover only the professional studies. Like all vocational training, these professional curriculums represent only the final stage of education immediately prior to entering the actual job; they are not conceived as the whole educational process.

Whether the training comes at the eighth-grade level in the form of apprenticeship and on-the-job training, or at the high school level in more formal classroom learning, or at the college or graduate level, it follows only after the liberal education— education for life, for citizenship—has supposedly been acquired. It is much more limited in its objectives and therefore simpler. The exact knowledge and skills needed by the lawyer, musician, or chemist for his work are not too much debated. Even methods for teaching them are very much standardized.

The liberal curriculum differs significantly from the foregoing curriculums in that there can be no comparable pressures on its content, objectives, and methods. The impact of vocational and professional training is, therefore, all the more pronounced in determining the philosophy and curriculums of any school. Formerly many careers were learned on the job, from shop work and cooking to hotel management and even to nursing, and formal education was almost entirely liberal. Today the training needed for almost any future employment is provided in the schools, and it is the parents who demand that it be so. The most recent surveys show quite clearly that parents are sending their sons and their daughters to college to acquire training for future jobs, in other words, for vocational training. At all stages, therefore, vocational (or professional) is crowding general (or liberal) education into the background. Caught between the accrediting agencies and the parents' ambitions, the college curriculum committees have little leeway for their visions of reform.

This typical vocational pattern of working backward from the adult goals to the classroom training has occasionally been invoked in the planning of curriculums for women. Out of the daily routines, the exasperating problems, and the cultural aspirations of the typical American homemaker have emerged new courses in child care, interior decoration, family relationship, and consumer buying. Even women's larger needs—for communication skills and for spiritual resources and leisure-time activities—have been duly catalogued and have served to reinforce certain curricular items and philosophies.

The expressed convictions that education must be personal, that it must be closely related to one's own life, must give understanding of the world in which one lives, and must increase one's enjoyment of life or one's ability to communicate with and understand others—these are principles worth grave consideration on any campus, in any school. Likewise the reiterated demand for flexibility and for variety to suit all needs not only points to new goals, but implies a universal need for the better counseling and guidance services which can help each generation of students to find the new directions.

Another variation on this same theme, but little different and equally enlightening, has been exploited by women and may lead to even more striking and widespread curricular revisions. Conscientious alumnae have in retrospect evaluated and criticized their college careers and offered their collective suggestions for changes and reforms. It is difficult to apply such criticisms in the most broadly useful way, because each is colored by the present age and economic circumstances of the respondent. Thus the fifty-year-old chemistry major enjoying her leisure hours in a two-car suburban home may feel her lack of training in art or music or drama, and the coed who reveled in philosophy and art may regret her technical incompetence in the unequal struggle between the growing family and the shrinking dollar.

These opinions are suggestive, but they are highly selective and must be constantly tested for hidden flaws. Are the complaints really important, or are the complainers merely eager to make their voices heard? How and why did they choose their college courses? Is it knowledge that they lack, or appropriate attitudes and inner resources? Is the present-day coed's future status any more predictable than that of the older generation now registering the complaints?

A quite different procedure in curriculum building takes its point of departure from the individual student as a developing human being, as the pure essence of manifold potentialities. In this view, the campus must provide all the best possible opportunities for experience, growth, and maturation that will enable the emerging adult to solve the problems and deal with the circumstance which the years may lay before him. This method too has a way of insinuating itself into all other methods, for it contains some of those essentials which teachers must readily learn from their students. Some of its proponents maintain that intellectual potential is the most important element in formal education and that the cultivation of the intellect to the maximum of its power will serve all future needs.

This latter method provides the permissive atmosphere, the opportunity to practice one's attitudes and skills and to develop the habit of organizing one's own courses of action and of evolving and revising one's personal value systems. In fact, the endorsement of these values and methods has now become so emphatic that provision must be made for them, not always in the same terms, but universally in all curriculums and on every campus.

All three of these major methods of planning curriculums—the scholarly, the professional (or vocational in its widest sense), and the student-centered (and by inference society-centered)—are current and quite conventional. At any one college or university one or another may receive greater emphasis in theory or in actual practice, but all of them are always in operation. Each holds sway over different parts or aspects of the curriculum, and all are intricately interrelated and overlapping. They can never be entirely reconciled because they point to different objectives. They are like so many different poles around which the separate particles in the undifferentiated educational mixture tend to cluster. As iron filings form patterns above the magnet, educational bits and pieces can be made to center around various curricular goals so that the general configurations become a little more comprehensible.

Although major ideological considerations might seem to be the prime determinants, actually the many practical problems constitute an equally powerful force in fixing the educational patterns on the campus. Any college president can describe the former with eloquence but the latter with more detail and conviction. Practical problems include accreditation, athletics, academic tenure, public relations, and the student populations as they ebb and flow with the defense programs, the birthrate, and the size of the national dollar.

Financial cost is ultimately the great deterring factor to revisions of educational programs. In view of it, how sublime and how ridiculous becomes the one-to-one relationship of Mark Hopkins, with the teacher at one end of the log and the student at the other! How utopian are even the admirable tailor-made curriculums of some of our best private colleges! As Hutchins has suggested, the function of these private colleges in our society may become that of the pioneer in the experimental programs which give actual substance and therefore greater confidence in our ideals and our directions. Those smaller colleges which provide the welcome spectacle of group endeavor and high purpose toward uncompromised goals may be gradually withdrawing into the utopian distances.

Classes of a half-dozen students provide individual attention, encourage personal growth, engage full participation, create the permissive atmosphere, and include many other virtues as yet uncategorized; they have an incalculable value. But our society obviously cannot support such individualized education for any but a select few. Every parent who sends his daughter to a private rather than a public institution is paying twice for her education—once through the actual college expenses and once through his taxes. In the longest view, the vital question may be three-fold: How can we insure that these patterns will not be lost? How ought we to choose the students who will receive these benefits? (Those especially gifted? The graduate students? Those who can afford to pay? The future leaders of the state?) How can we transform the excellences of these patterns so that they will not be lost to the increasingly larger campus of the future?

It may be argued that the segregation of homogeneous groups of students on the highly selective campus, with the faster pace of learning and a concomitant program of societal and spiritual values, is eventually ineffective because it is unrealistic. Whether the selective factor is religious background, intellectual competence, socioeconomic status, or any combination of these and other factors, the resulting microcosm is defective and cannot prepare the students for satisfactory competition in the heterogeneous world. Many answers may be brought forward to meet this argument, but perhaps the most appropriate may be found in the recent studies which emphasize youth's need for verbalization and practice in developing desirable attitudes and habits.[5]

Translated into action, this concept means that a college student must spend some time in learning a vocabulary to describe and identify ethical problems and moral questions. It means that he must have a chance to deal with actual instances, take action, watch the consequences, and evaluate the results. It is not assumed that he can improvise suitable experiments in the chemistry laboratory, nor even that he can describe or generalize from the classic demonstrations without textbook help and classroom supervision. In the realm of attitudes and values it is not easy to contrive situations and control their implications, and even more help is needed in the devious and elusive process of identifying issues and making right decisions. Inevitably the adolescent molds his own character and builds his personal value system as a synthesis of the models present in his own environment. But that such a synthesis will be a good one is by no means assured.

227

In the unselected and heterogeneous student groups a diversity of models is present, but it is not easy to insure that the socially desirable ones will receive the most prominence and prestige. On the largest campuses, which are also our most realistic, the process of identifying issues and discussing social and ethical values is too often left, for a variety of reasons, to casual student contacts, campus chatter, and "bull sessions." Where evasion of responsibilities becomes the prevailing student pattern, the "realistic" situation and atmosphere may have something less than the desired and positive effect.

When the segregation is further extended by excluding all men from the student body, subtle changes take place in the teaching emphases, the choice of topics to be covered in the various courses, the number and kind of courses offered in the different fields, and the general orientation of the curriculums. These small but significant differences sometimes escape the consciousness even of the teacher and student who work intimately with them.

Not all aspects of a curriculum can be set down in words and paragraphs, and the administrators who argue for precisely similar education for both men and women may be those most unconscious of the subtle but vital differences which a selected student group engenders. In the cold type of the college catalogue the offerings may appear identical; actual practice finds them quite different. Student interests and enthusiasms account for many of the differences, especially in the more personal and practical courses such as psychology, economics, family relationships, journalism, music, and art.

In any case, the solution of the problem of large versus small college, private versus public, or men's versus women's lies not in the further arguing and infinite weighing of the comparative excellences, but rather in devising fresh methods of dealing with students in larger and more heterogeneous groups. We have today in the United States committed ourselves to the largest possible educational program, but other national commitments will not allow us to finance the individualized services which educational leaders are urging. We recognize to the full the students' need for individual attention and guidance, a necessity in terms of both individual differences and the sacredness of the individual personality.

But the most urgent need is, after all, for a creative and penetrating compromise. A philosophy of individual guidance can be only misleading if the number of students who are accommodated is but a small minority of the larger student group. The techniques of large-group discussion, of large-group teaching and learning, constitute the greatest challenge to modern education.

Another phase of this same practical problem in curriculum building lies in the necessity of educating students of all categories on one campus, side by side in the same overgrown classes. In very few courses is provision made for the differences in learning status. Placement and proficiency examinations are frequently given in foreign languages or in English composition. But only rarely are tests given to reveal the equally large differences in other subject-matter courses or in such important realms as interpersonal relations, emotional maturity, social skills, homemaking, budgeting, or the cultural appreciations.

All of these subjects have been advocated as essential parts of the curriculums for women, either in formal classes or informal, extracurricular activities. But we cannot escape the fact that some women students receive prior and adequate training in some of them through family life and general background. Even as college ability tests discriminate between those who can benefit and those who cannot, and proficiency tests select those who need certain further subject-matter courses, some such selective and advisory techniques are needed for all other kinds of competences.

Programs of this sort are not entirely unknown, for they prevail in certain women's colleges in at least some parts of the curriculums. Some junior colleges have done pioneer work in both formal classroom instruction and in supervised campus activities. Schools of nursing give detailed attention to personality inadequacies. In some schools there are no extracurricular activities except as they may be prescribed more formally to meet curricular needs. Such schemes play at least a small part and sometimes a major part in the educational programs of residence halls and sorority houses. Here they may be useful in setting standards for self-evaluation in the same manner that ability and interest tests, in the hands of wise counselors, can be made useful in the self-integration of the student.

Perhaps the most difficult of all the practical problems in curriculum-building is the lag between the student needs and the already entrenched curriculums. It is paradoxical that on the self-same college campus which harbors the boldest thinkers in the academic fields, where pioneer experiments are a matter of course and tolerance of new ideas an accepted pattern, curricular changes meet the most stubborn resistance. In this one respect, the "ivory-tower" reputation of the campus seems most apt.

In the view of the classroom authority, no one but himself can understand the width, depth, and cosmic significance of the subject he teaches, nor is it conceivable to him that the garden of wisdom can be entered by any other gate. In his classroom shrine, conscience forbids him to settle for anything less than the bona fide and exquisitely complete presentation of his material to every available or every qualified student. Dilution, fractionation, adaption, and adulteration are infamous if not entirely inconceivable. Compromise is sheer quackery, and any professor is prepared to fight to the very last student.

Another practical problem in planning curriculums lies in the necessary overlapping of the general and the vocational education. The vocational aspect of modern education for women is much too controversial, and reaches too deeply into the general philosophy of education, to be dismissed merely as a practical problem. Yet in the process of curriculum building it is the demand for both kinds, the conviction that the vocational is necessary and the liberal is good, which creates the greatest havoc and confusion. And how can we draw the line between the purely liberal and the undeniably vocational? Surely not on the basis of whether or not it will help in earning a living.

Until the most recent decades, so large a proportion of the female college population did not look forward to gainful work outside the home that the liberal education was the unquestioned and appropriate pattern for the college years. Today few students accept any college pattern without questioning its bearing on their future jobs, perhaps only those few who plan immediate marriage, who can afford further training in a specialized or graduate school, or who have favorable personal or family circumstances for entering the working field.

It is difficult for the layman to realize how many of the courses organized on the university campus within the faculties of the arts colleges serve only the students registered in the professional schools (medicine, business, music, education) who are seeking "prerequisites." Likewise many students remain technically within the arts college but earn their way into the employment world by using every available credit hour in the technical courses offered by the other schools. Paradoxically, even Latin and Greek may be conceived as vocational courses, since those who elect them plan to teach them.

Although the present decades represent the transitional period, and therefore a restless and difficult period in the employment of women, all women of the present generation will work, and for much longer periods than heretofore. This means that as few women as men, which is very few indeed, will wish for a *purely* liberal education, however it may be defined. The prevailing pattern for the future calls for a mixture of both liberal and vocational training, in varying proportions, with better teaching and good counseling as the catalytic agents by which really significant synthesis may be achieved.

These are the theories, the pressures, the problems, which hold in place the many levels and parts of our total educational structure. Whenever women—either one mother or an alumnae group, or a parent-teacher association or a professional organization—call for a revision in curriculums, these are the diverse factors that will be involved. There is an interlocking of established traditions, economic exigencies, and organized lobbies which makes the huge structure of present educational institutions all but invulnerable.

Every curriculum which needs changing is wedged into its own tight little place along some educational axis. To dislodge it is to start a general upheaval, for it is maintained in its particular position by some accrediting agency or legislation, by some strong economic demand, by some high-prestige group, or even by some key personality who has organized a coterie of sympathizers for that very purpose. When it begins to crumble, to rock a little, its movements inevitably reach out to the American Medical Association, to the AAUW, to the church, to UNESCO, to the law of diminishing returns, to the normal frequency curve, often to the prospective husband, and certainly to the taxpayer.

These agencies and personalities are not working together for the considered good of the greatest number, but they have learned to respect one another's opinions and powers. Many of them, like the individual mothers and daughters, don't relish the position in which they find themselves, but they cannot struggle too much against the vast interlocking directives. Eventually they learn what every individual mother learns—the futility of working without knowledgeable insights and modern methods.

To have a useful insight, a mother must hold in mind the many axes around which educational goals and methods cluster, while perceiving at the same time the problems and procedures of curriculum-building. How these many relationships may be turned to the best advantage of her own daughter will be only the first step in resolving them for the greatest good of all other daughters and their myriad, but often similar, problems.

The merits of any given subject matter, of mathematics or language or fine arts or psychology, cannot be weighed only in terms of its own intrinsic qualities. Each subject earns whatever merit it acquires in education not by looking backward to past glories but forward to future uses and pleasures, not by the part it has played in the developing culture but by its contribution to the developing individual.

... *11*

Planning Curriculums for Women

THE schemes which are now bandied about in educational circles will eventually merge into something which the perceptive observer will recognize as a trend—something half perceived and half created in the observer's own mind. And as time rolls on, the developing trend toward a new status for both men and women will gain such momentum that our present quandaries will seem very quaint and trivial, the evasions and prejudices of our current thinking all the more devious.

In the meantime, many women—students, mothers, teachers, and counselors—are daily forced into action on women's education. The rank and file of thoughtful women, as well as the educational leaders, therefore, need to be alert to the parts they play in perceiving and creating the current trends. But no one aspect of women's life can be reduced to the simple formulas that humanity loves. The more honest the thinker, the more clearly she sees that good solutions require some method for epitomizing and juggling the facts and theories involved in the dilemmas. She literally forces herself to keep on reading paragraphs such as these because she needs to forge beyond them to her own individual decisions and theories.

The preceding chapters have shown some of the factors involved in current educational trends and some of the problems facing both parents and educators in their efforts to appraise

233

realistically the whole broad subject of education for women. It might be well to stop here and summarize briefly some of these important considerations.

We have seen that in general an individual needs, for his own pleasure and stimulation, the wisdom of many different minds and disciplines; as a *practicing citizen,* however, he cannot accept the generalizations made by radio commentators and columnists, or even those of poets and playwrights, however welcome and charming they may seem. "They confuse socialism with communism, race with nationality, psychology with psychoanalysis, old age assistance with old age insurance, span of life with average at death, economics with capitalism, and sociology with everything from social case work to social reform." [1]

Folklore and personal experience, always highly limited, are nowadays reinforced by screen and radio, but they are not thereby rendered more accurate and true. Literature and the arts have their own values, but they are not substitutes for social science, which includes education; more specifically, they do not teach the college woman what can and what cannot be done in her own culture, or how to choose the right techniques for doing it when the proper occasion arises.

Women, it is said, are not interested in abstractions and philosophizing. They are too individualistic and emotional in their attitudes to have produced any philosopher of first rank. If this is true, then it is the clear duty of the women to supply the "superior," "philosophical" minds of the men with the basic and accurate materials for their thinking about women, rather than with any possibly inexact or apocryphal impressions with which they now make shift.

Women can modernize and amend these outworn premises by a combination of charm, logic, and facts from the Women's Bureau. Men, whether eighteen or eighty, will prove formidable opponents in women's battle for their cherished philosophies, but in the popular controversies over men and women, women have nine tenths of the arguments soundly lined up on their side of the barricades. For men, who adore both women and theory, theories about women must constitute the *pièce de re-sistance*. To persuade the men of the world ought to be as easy as it is exciting, to say nothing of the fact that it would transform them into better sweethearts and husbands.

This does not mean committing oneself to a militant cause for women—crude feminism is as Victorian as long underwear. It means rather taking the more practical and workable position which scientists claim the woman prefers. For this kind of skirmish she needs practice in sifting out casual impressions and personal prejudices which the men will pounce on, and in reducing nebulous hunches to concrete realities with manageable dimensions suitable for the more casual club and dinner conversations. Challenges are welcome and exciting; indifference is the unpardonable sin.

The facts we must deal with include, first of all, the wide range among our women students in native endowment—intellectual, physical, and emotional. The radiant health, high spirits, and alert minds of the best of them are startlingly different from the bad teeth, sulky manners, and dreary outlook of the "other half." Participation in a wholesome family life has given some girls at sixteen a better grasp of human relationships or of budgeting and cake-making than others will acquire either in a college course in home economics or in a decade of married life. Some have had mature experience in work or travel; others have had equally significant experience but in frustration, insecurity, uncertainty, and grief. Work and study habits, standards of behavior, spiritual awakenings, control of feeling, and future expectations exhibit an unbelievably wide range in any generation of young adults.

The mere catalogue of these variations, however, is not so revealing as their respective proportions in the general population. Most human traits tend to follow the normal curve of distribution: against the few at the extreme there are always the multitudes in the undistinguished middle. Most people are average people, although of course the average rises or falls with the prevailing standards of living. Even health we have found to be a purchasable commodity, and the more equitable distribution of the good American dollar has been correcting our health averages in an upward direction for many decades.

Inevitably, educational planners, themselves originating for the most part in the upper social levels, have been preoccupied with providing the best available curriculums appropriate to their own superior class. But the new question asks what classroom subjects, and how much of them, the average minds can most profitably assimilate. What will be the best method for helping these average students to help themselves, for pulling up the general average for all our society? These questions are as important for men as for women.

The magnitude of the problem can be glimpsed in the socioeconomic data from one typical university group: one fourth of the three thousand women come from the skilled, semi-skilled, and unskilled workers, another fourth from the farmers, salesmen, clerks, and kindred workers. Only 18 per cent of these women come from professional families, and about 30 per cent from the proprietors, managers, officials, and wholesale and retail dealers. The college teacher needs to know the habits, attitudes, and ambitions of our present-day campus groups in order to be fortified for the difficulties to be encountered. American college students today are not the uniformly highly selected groups of earlier decades.

To be very specific about the most common profession for women, how can we fill the ranks of classroom teachers without training not only our best young women, but also our second best and our average high school seniors for this work? The poor salaries and low status of the teaching profession do not attract at present the best minds available. In 1947, only 4 per cent of all teachers earned as much as $7500, but 57 per cent of physicians, 40 per cent of lawyers, and 37 per cent of dentists earned this amount or more. Our first objective must be to entice the more able college women, including some of the "retired" younger housewives, into the schoolrooms. But even if this venture meets with unusual success, the campus of the future will still be dealing not exclusively with the upper 20 per cent of high school seniors, with the most conscientious workers from the best backgrounds. The volume and rate of potential intellectual intake and output is limited for the less able, and the curriculum for them must be modified accordingly.

Does this mean that we must be committed to only easy subjects, the techniques rather than the ideologies, the practical "how to teach" courses rather than those with the more intellectual challenge and content? Not necessarily; but the ideologies must be those appropriate to this country and this society, not to an alien culture of a bygone century, and they must be taught with more care and imagination than many of the entrenched academicians are prepared to give.

As we noted earlier, psychologists and sociologists are now agreed that there are no significant differences between the sexes in intellectual capacity, in personality traits, in citizenship responsibilities, or in spiritual and personal needs. In all these respects it is obvious that there are larger differences within the sexes than between sex groups. Sex differences are vanishingly small compared to the larger differences between dull children and bright children, or to the differences in personality traits between children who grow up in slum areas of our cities and those who enjoy the advantage of good suburban or small-town life.

In the case of the very obvious difference—the child-bearing function of women—scholars are in general agreement that it is the psychical and especially the social implications, such as enforced absence from the working world, which give it real significance. Consequently, childbearing becomes a social liability, which can, therefore, be shared by men. Modern family and marriage counseling points to the importance of *both* parents in the responsibility for the rearing of children from the very earliest age. Recent data and theories on the emotional development of children lead us to believe that they are better adjusted when they receive attention from both mother and father. Yet in actual practice this goal is still rather distant.

As they grow from adolescence to maturity in our society, men and women differ not at all in their intellectual capacities, very little in their attitudes and personal traits (and these differences may be traced to social factors), very much in the patterns of their life activities, and most of all in public opportunities. The differences in the social pattern of the life of a man and a woman are primarily in the shorter duration and the interruption of the gainful working period for the woman, the limited opportunities which are available to her, and the dual functions in which she becomes involved as a homemaker and a participant in activities outside the home. These dissimilarities, of course, lead to conspicuous differences in achievement, when measured by the standards set by the unencumbered male.

We have discerned another important division of labor between the sexes, a division that is the result of social forces of long standing: women have traditionally inherited more responsibility not only for all phases of domestic life, but also for the varied cultural values in the immediate community. Not so many women are professional creative artists, but women make up a large proportion of the audiences. They appreciate and promote all the arts and stimulate awareness, sympathy, and responsibility in both the spiritual and moral realms. Religious organizations and avenues for social welfare in general owe much to the efforts of women.

The man-made differences weigh heavily on the mental attitudes of woman and create frustrations for her as she encounters societal pressures. As a consequence, too many women feel apologetic, even contemptuous, about their role. In our culture, a woman, thirty-four times out of a hundred, would prefer to be a man—good evidence of her strong feelings of inadequacy and bondage. Society in its technological development has deprived her of her most significant functions and has condemned her, especially in her educational years, to an incessant wavering between traditional sex roles and new, indeterminate, masculinized roles. The consummation of the present trend cannot be easily foreseen, and therefore her choice of either role cannot relieve her conflict, for neither the one nor the other could in itself be completely satisfying.

These three kinds of differences between men and women—in biological function, in the occupational life pattern with its diminished opportunities, and in the traditional, cultural, and social responsibilities and pressures—must all assume their full significance in any plans of educators for new courses and curriculums to meet the individual and changing needs of women students.

Society is never in equilibrium; it is always readjusting. But the rate and direction of the change varies in every century, in every country, in every social class. In our century changes in economics or in ideologies which formerly required a century are now telescoped into a few decades. Changes in one geographical area which formerly were contained within that area are, with today's better communications, felt throughout the world.

We may anticipate, therefore, that the long movement toward a more equable status for men and women, with its obscure roots in past centuries and with its slow creeping successes, might gather surprising speed and force and thrust unbearable stresses on many of our social institutions. We will certainly have the privilege of observing through the successive decades of our own era that there will be different rates of progress in different countries and different classes of society. We may see women in Europe gaining in political prestige and power, in America in living standards and household technologies. Gains by laboring women may be reflected in wage rates, and by the professional classes in wider occupational opportunities.

In the social scene men use their gallantry to heighten women's pleasures, and in business or politics they use it to minimize her effectiveness. The darker side of such progress is revealed in the higher divorce rates, and its brighter side in healthier and happier childhood. In the orthodox church, women may still be held in quaint and worshipful subservience, but in the courts women now share even the privilege of paying alimony. Longer life and better physical health for women are offset by more depressions and frustrations in the field of mental health. All of these movements within the movement are inevitable but unpredictable, confusing but exciting; a lag in any one of them constitutes a danger. The question is whether womenkind in general can ever consolidate their ranks and move forward together on all fronts.

No one in America can have missed the impact of the rapid changes in our economic and political ideas and institutions. We have more prestige and responsibility as a world power, and more responsibilities and burdens as individual citizens in a workable democracy. We have more governmental planning, broader bases for capital resources, shrinking economic and geographic frontiers, fewer large fortunes, and better standards of living for more people. We are at the mercy of the propaganda which pours through our mass media, aimed primarily at a high school culture and new lower-middle classes; in our leisure hours we are spectators rather than participants. Who is so naïve as to expect that educational curriculums could be unaffected by these changes?

In the ethical and religious realm the shift is toward the relative and away from the authoritative. Women have traditionally carried the greater responsibility for the maintenance of standards in morals and manners, and they have also traditionally lived under the "double standard." In esthetics, too, there is a parallel shift away from the individual, the inspirational, and toward the more functional, the more esoteric and self-determined standards in beauty and art. This unequal burden on women has been a powerful force in preserving the moral and ethical equilibrium in our society. Without adequate understanding, without careful indoctrination in our schools, how easily our religious and esthetic values might deteriorate.

It is not so much the institution of the family and its physical habitation but rather the functions of women and our attitudes toward them which are in the noteworthy transition stage. More women are now working, and at a larger variety of jobs, at older ages, for longer periods. Household tasks have been industrialized, have moved from the home to the assembly line.

240

These two circumstances have eliminated the former typical functions of women in society: creating and building a home life, providing food, clothing, and comfort for her large household, and preserving and transmitting her knowledge and skills in the general culture of her times. Bereft to a large extent of these significant duties, modern woman tends to lose her self-regarding values. Her dependence on her husband has become more artificial and his dependence on her has been greatly reduced. Her prestige and even her affective life with her children has been attenuated. Her dignity as a responsible human being and her mental and social health are being compromised.

But the techniques for control and manipulation of the rates and directions of such social changes have now become quite standardized. Advertisers and dictators have made effective use of them. *Laissez faire* has gone out of fashion. Both men and women, but more especially women leaders, should turn to education as the best means of directing their own evolution into channels most profitable for all society.

There are wide varieties of schools and colleges available to women: large and small, private and public, municipal, state, denominational, women's or coeducational, junior colleges, teachers' colleges, professional schools, liberal arts colleges, and universities. Loosely lumped together as institutions of "education," they are by no means equally potent in their social contributions. There are hundreds of small colleges, but they educate only 10 to 20 per cent of the students. The majority of college students today are in the giant state or municipal institutions. Costs vary from $500 to $2500 a year, but at any price, and with very few exceptions, all these colleges are good, because competition and the various state, district, and professional accrediting agents keep them so, and because college teachers have the highest ethical and professional standards.

Colleges, however, are not the only means for acquiring education. The college campus may not even be the best way to become educated, nor the easiest way. Only one thing may be said with certainty: it is the pleasantest way. It is in America that we find by far the highest proportion of the youthful population in the colleges—some 25 per cent against Europe's 2 to 5 per cent and Asia's infinitesimal fraction. In America it is still the theoretical privilege of all classes to reach the campus, and it is only in America that the technical and vocational emphasis is found on the college and university campus. Here the children of both sexes, of all classes, are educated side by side in the same classrooms from kindergarten through all the grades and secondary school. Here the schools can still be the effective devices for social mobility. Although there are colleges of all kinds to fit most tastes and purses, the large majority of our college students live together on the same large campus, with its doors open to all, and with "privilege" accorded only to the able.

And yet the function of education in mobility is by no means simple or clear cut. It must promote economic mobility, but it must do this in a society whose structure is such that movement between the classes is not increasing. Despite extensive scholarship programs, the disparity in educational opportunity between the different social levels is a formidable deterrent to vertical mobility.

Any special curriculums for women will, of course, be projected against the general trends and varieties of educational philosophies. As we have seen, these are both too numerous and too complicated for any but the briefest description, but we cannot fail to note our nation's need, as expressed by the Harvard Committee, to "raise the average and speed the able while holding common goals before each." We know, too, that there is a traditional-progressive continuum, from the most reactionary to the most experimental patterns, and that most of our classrooms carry some of the earmarks of both.

To many of those who read and write about the special problems in women's education, the issues for women are never very exactly differentiated from these more general philosophies. The mother who argues that Latin is more important than home economics for women is not declaring her stand on women's education, but merely her convictions on one of the more general philosophies—the traditional-progressive or the liberal-vocational axis.

From these summaries and arguments, at least three principles seem to emerge and point toward needed changes in the education of women. First, because the life patterns of women will continue to be different from those of men, at least for the next few decades, all women everywhere must be educated to play the dual roles of earner and homemaker and to do both efficiently and with the maximum of enjoyment. Second, because our society is in a stage of transition in roles for women and attitudes toward them, all women must be educated to understand this transition stage, to interpret it to men, and to facilitate its eventual merging into other important societal trends. Third, women's education should be centered, for a wide variety of reasons, around the liberal arts, not only in the colleges, but in the public schools as well. In our society, the general and the vocational education have been offered equally to all children throughout the length of their public school years. The continued significance of the liberal education for the woman student becomes very apparent both in choosing her college and in choosing her curriculum.

Our first principle, the necessity for educating women for the dual roles of earner and homemaker, may seem unsatisfactory to many educators unless we add immediately that homemaking in its broadest sense includes good marriage and family relationships as well as good interrelations with the community, since it has now taken over so many aspects of home life. When we say that a woman must play these roles not only efficiently but with full enjoyment, we recognize the importance of the general as well as the vocational elements in her curriculum, which are needed to make her an individual of culture and charm, a balanced and forceful personality, a good citizen.

The education for the several roles in any woman's future life, for her pluralistic careers, puts three requirements into the educational programs: flexibility, guidance, and the greater use of proficiency testing.

Flexibility in the requirements for any one student in earning any given academic degree would seem to be an inevitable accompaniment to the growing richness and complexity of the academic subjects. Logically we could not expect that the subject-matter fields could expand as they have in the last century while our requirements for the degrees would remain rigid. Not only the expansion of the scholars' fund of knowledge, but also the demand from parents for the vocational training of their children, exerts a strong pressure for flexibility.

Serving primarily as a badge of culture, the liberal curriculum as it has been inherited from the past did not provide for vocational needs. It did offer, however, both breadth and depth in learning: breadth in terms of a few courses in all fields—biological and physical sciences, social sciences, languages and literature —and depth in terms of extensive work in one major department. Gradually this one major field of concentration has been made to carry the burden of the vocational work. It is the one field about which the student is best informed and in which he has taken the largest number of formal courses, although frequently it does not mean that he has penetrated deeply into the subject or that he has explored it exhaustively. It may mean rather that he has spent his time in learning methods and techniques in his field, or that he has covered more of the new developments.

Consider the facts and theories which the student of 1910 and his 1950 counterpart had to cover in history, or in physics. Consider also the knowledge of the present world which is required in order to be a good citizen in a modern democracy. And consider finally the fact that in increasingly larger proportions our present college students come from middle- and lower-status families, with only a meager cultural background available to them either in their homes or in their communities.

Would it not be far better to design new curriculums on new principles and around new objectives than to continue with makeshift repairs and awkward remodeling on the older designs? Every course in the modern curriculum must justify itself in terms of its significance in modern life. This means that every course in the traditional curriculum may be used and even enhanced, but not in the rigid patterns of the past decades, not in the old combinations and sequences, and *not for everyone.* There is no one subject or department that is sacrosanct. Rather, it is the individual and his needs and obligations that are sacrosanct.

If the modern woman needs music and economics and nutrition more than mathematics, Latin, and biology, then it is clearly our duty not to try to sell her on the virtues of mathematics, Latin, and biology, no matter how great our own respect for their virtues. It is, further, our duty to recognize that she can learn many fundamental facts about nutrition without a prerequisite of chemistry, that the best possible course for her in economics might magnify certain topics out of all proportion and omit other topics entirely, and that some students can derive intellectual values from a course in music better than from mathematics. And it is further necessary to recognize that there have always been and there can always be competent, charming, and cultured women who have never studied any physical science or who have never learned any foreign language.

All this does not mean that there are no principles, or that just any haphazard program which the capricious student happens to prefer will qualify him for the bachelor's degree. It does not mean that all counselors or all students must conform to the same new patterns. It means simply that we must keep our curriculums flexible and bend them to the actual and prospective needs of the students instead of fitting the students into the older and the more rigid framework.

Variety in curriculums is already available; the young woman chooses first among the schools—arts, music, education, business—and then selects her major subject from the many departments within the school. But having made these two choices, she typically finds herself in a sequence designed for those wholly

245

committed to specialization, whereas she as a woman is sociologically a "marginal personality" living in a "no-man's land" where the labor force and the homemakers overlap and conflict. This marginal status immediately throws her into conflict with any fixed sequence designed for either one group or the other. Mass education has forced these fixed patterns upon the administrators, who could not handle the hoards of students without them. Their necessity and usefulness have long masked their unsuitability for women, but each year the strain of holding to them becomes more difficult. Resolving the situation will not be easy.

Many of our older and younger reactionaries have learned to talk in the popular verbiage of "compromise" without having an understanding or a grasp of women's real problems. Even the most experienced and sophisticated educator must constantly re-examine his foundations and remodel his convictions. For no teacher can hold his high standards, fail all those who do not meet them, and still count himself an asset in the modern academic world. Those students who failed to meet the admission requirements, or those who returned home after a year in college, have still not been educated. They have not learned how to help themselves to better standards and better lives. Society has been deprived of their best services. They will still be pulling against all the schemes for progress that the statesmen and the educators themselves are hoping for.

Guidance is another of the essentials we have indicated for the new programs, not only more guidance, but better guidance. Most students cannot find their way among all the needed varieties of courses without it, and flexibility can be achieved on no other terms. As the number of students increases, as the present-day large campus becomes even more gigantic, society more complex, and occupations more fluid, students will need more help than ever in finding their way through the academic labyrinth. Standard patterns of courses for one- or two- or four-year students and for certain vocational goals might prove very feasible and would be of great help. Today the two-year program is merely an interrupted four-year design. A thorough reorganization, not a remodeling or a streamlining, of the older liberal patterns, and new ones based on current philosophies, can greatly simplify and clarify the student choices.

Teachers can still do the best counseling. The classroom teacher —sympathetic, adaptable, intelligent, experienced, dedicated—is youth's best friend. But teachers cannot do the best counseling of the new generation of students without special knowledge. Without the current information on women's economic opportunities and the new trends and techniques of modern society, teachers will only perpetuate past mistakes. Traditional philosophies and the old-fashioned liberal arts subjects have carried the greatest of life's values for most of us in the older generation. Some of these subjects can still be rewarding for some members of the younger generation; others can interest very few, if any. Only repeated explorations will determine which of them have significance for the new generation. Without this reappraisal and adaptation there can be no important survival. In the classroom the teacher may be temporarily safe from these revaluations, but as counselor and administrator she cannot escape them.

Is it important for women to do this counseling for women students? What are the advantages and disadvantages of women or of men as counselors for high school and college girls? This reduces itself to a question of whether or not men will take the trouble to inform themselves about problems and prospects of women; it is also a question of whether, without the opportunities and responsibilities of counseling, enough competent women will be sufficiently informed and zealous to promote better understanding.

Are women's needs and problems a field in which men could be expected to take the lead? In this as in other work, the social scientists tell us that every woman faces a double challenge. She must not only prove her capabilities for each step forward, but she must also be ambitious, alert to responsibilities, and determined in her progress toward her goals; she also has a duty to help break down men's current prejudices against the promotion of women and their employment for all possible jobs.

The third essential for educating women to meet their dual role is a fuller development and a much wider use of the whole concept and practice of proficiency testing. It grows out of the need to cover the wider variety of subjects necessary for the dual roles, and the pressures for streamlining wherever possible.

As we saw earlier, most colleges use formal testing to determine the student's proficiency in English composition and in language. On the basis of these placement tests, students are given instruction best suited to their needs and skills, and the whole scheme has worked so well that there is no thought of reverting to our former methods. Music schools also make use of this method of placement, and especially in the more professional schools, mathematics and other sciences are administered on this basis. At some universities a similar system is used both for placing the student and for checking progress toward his degree. Many graduate schools are also admitting, placing, and counseling their students through examination records. "Preliminary" examinations for Ph.D. candidates have become standard practice everywhere.

The best use of all such placement tests requires the full participation of the student in his own appraisal, although our present system of rigid requirements and the naïvete of many faculty advisers in the difficult field of testing tend to discourage this self-examining activity. For maximum benefit, the student needs help from counselors in the process of self-evaluation and in achieving personal and emotional maturity. If citizenship and interpersonal relations are as important a part of the college student's learning experience as personnel officers claim, then these subjects would obviously require as careful a supervision as classroom teaching, as careful a grading of responsibilities and skills as any academic subject.

It is in the case of professional training programs especially that the curriculums could be organized through proficiency testing to the great advantage of women students. Fast learners could run through the required technical training and knowledge with a great saving in time, and students whose previous training or home backgrounds give them advantages could omit or condense some of the formal training steps. Time thus saved could be used for liberal arts or for homemaking courses.

It is questionable whether the bright student who can learn so much from experience on the job has much to gain from the greater concentration on the narrower field during her undergraduate years. How illogical, for example, to formulate our license requirements for teachers or for social workers in terms of semester hours in college courses *for all students*!

Into the very same classes go Mary Smith—whose parents, uncles, aunts, and cousins are all teachers or professional workers, whose I.Q. is 150, who speaks in cultured accents, reads voraciously, and is alert, efficient, and poised—and Jane Jones— who has an I.Q. of 95, poor study habits, limited vocabulary, and careless speech, and who has never associated with professional people or known cultural advantages. We want Jane to have her full and complete opportunity; we are agreed that she will have to sacrifice some of her general or liberal education for acquiring needed professional skills. What we do protest, however, is that Mary Smith must be held to the same slow pace and the weary routines. If Mary, by special reading or tutoring, supported by her family and community background, can demonstrate her proficiency in some of the required hours of work for her professional license, it is surely our duty to speed her along that path.

With proper provision for proficiency testing, much may be said for courses in nutrition, child care, family adjustment, economics, and even citizenship. Students would, of course, have the choice of studying these subjects or qualifying through examinations or perhaps of applying for exemption. At least no college teacher can dismiss the need for formal study in homemaking with the assumption that today's generation of young women learn such things in the home. Such a lofty assumption only exposes the ignorance from which his own "liberal" education is supposed to have liberated him.

College courses in the social sciences now teach us that the function of the family has been changing, that there are large and classifiable differences in individuals, in communities, and in social status. These courses even go so far as to explain how drastic errors in social judgments and action can be made by the well intentioned but uninformed. And again we have not met our problem merely by excluding it from our own classroom or our own campus. The young mother has still not learned how to create a good home life; the community, the church, and the school have lost her best services. We cannot hope for her co-operation in any of the forward-looking projects which our statesmen or our social leaders may plan.

But even testing for proficiencies does not provide all the answers. What can be done for the able and conscientious twenty-year-old, lost in her professional skills and ambitions, who could not pass any kind of test in cooking or buying or child psychology, but who will gobble them all up in six months after she finds the right man? Or who will devise the tests that will properly differentiate Mary Smith from Jane Jones? What tests can predict exactly how many more hours it will take to prepare Jane than Mary?

Even though these may be almost impossible problems, educators had better lose no time in setting to work on them. Because they are difficult does not excuse us, especially women, from making a vigorous attack on them, from taking some bold, even if not clearly justifiable, steps. New mistakes will be no more deplorable than old mistakes, and sincere experiments, including the mistakes that go with them, are more admirable than inaction, in that they provide us with opportunities to learn.

The second general principle in the education of women calls for a penetrating analysis and study of the society in which they live. Society, always more fluid than static, shows today two important trends which are of far more interest to women than to men. The first is the transition in the roles played by women and the attitude of men toward these new roles. Many forces, both material and spiritual, have united to force women from their traditional role of homemaker, and it has now become obvious that no retreat is possible. The younger generations already accept woman in her role of wage earner, but there will be continued resistance from men both to her presence in the higher income brackets and to their own new roles in household management and child rearing.

The second trend, not so well defined and orderly, is the slow but widespread upheaval in our moral and esthetic values. It is of greater significance to women than to men because women have long been the teachers and guardians of these values in the home and in the community.

The uneasiness, the malaise of our time is due to this root fact: in our politics and economy, in family life and religion—in practically every sphere of our existence—the certainties of the eighteenth and nineteenth centuries have disintegrated or been destroyed and at the same time no new sanctions and justifications for the new routines we live and must live have taken hold. So there is no acceptance and there is no rejection, no sweeping rebellion. There is no plan of life. Among white collar people the malaise is deep rooted. . . . Newly created in a harsh time of creation white collar man has no culture to lean upon except the contents of a mass society that has shaped him and seeks to manipulate him to its alien ends.[2]

All future citizens, and most especially the college-bred, white-collar groups, need to develop a historical sense with respect to the status of their own country among the nations of the world. They need a critical familiarity with their society, its general organization, internal stresses, values, and trends. Women need a clear conception of their present place in the history of women, and in the history of society. They need it both for their own mental stability and to interpret themselves to men. The growing emphasis on psychology and sociology in the curriculum are helpful, but they do not reach all women and they do not make applications to women's problems in such a way that the less gifted, practical-minded students can comprehend them. Every

251

alumna of any college, whatever her major interest or intellectual stature, needs an intimate acquaintance with the status and problems of women in the respective geographical areas, in the fluid social strata, under given economic or political conditions.

She must know, for example, that readjustments in women's roles proceed more rapidly in the northern states than in the south, in urban rather than in rural areas, in good times or in war rather than in depression and peace times, and in the upper rather than in the lower classes. The college woman must master the intellectual discipline of the methods and conditions of social change and accept her own possible responsibilities in them either as leader, as interpreter, or as mere follower. This is not to say that the college woman of today should take the lead in any feminist or emancipation movement. The day for that kind of work and leadership is long past. The trend is so well underway that it needs not driving power but a steering wheel.

The crux of the matter lies in the fact that our changing society no longer allows women self-fulfillment within the confines of domestic walls. Many women have already experienced this dilemma, and eventually all women will be affected. The mental health and social adjustment of more than half of the population is at stake, but even more important, our national wealth and economy, the problem of manpower, and many of our community and welfare problems depend on women's as well as men's contributions. Women will adjust much more swiftly and effectively in the coming decades if they are intellectually and emotionally prepared.

In the 1950–1960 decade the married woman who has a business or professional position is working longer hours in her dual role than her husband or her single sister. With the 1980–1990 generation of marriage partners this may not be true, for the household routines will be reorganized. With the passage of time, as women penetrate the men's world in hitherto unsuspected directions, we shall see them performing many functions which the present women leaders hold as unwomanly.

There will be women wrestlers and baseball players, with hard faces and bulging muscles. Successful women political bosses may have to smoke big black cigars, put their feet up on the table, and snarl orders to their henchmen through the corner of the mouth. Pregnant young businesswomen of these modern decades, who in previous generations remained decently concealed, are already taking considerable pride in staying on the job until time to rush off to the hospital. Aggressive and competent working women will more and more frequently be promoted over heads of less able male colleagues. Can we learn to accept all these things? Or at least not to resent them? Are the attitudes of the colleges still a little stuffy?

It is the housewife, unemployed except within the domestic domain, who is becoming the greatest handicap both to herself and to her society. Tradition, or male domination, or whatever it was that restricted her within the home is one of the unstable values in our world today. Her position is already an equivocal one, and with the successive stages toward the full equality of men and women it will become more and more preposterous and intolerable. Education of herself, of her sister in the working world, and eventually of her husband will play a large part in her salvation. It is obvious that the solution of her dilemmas and other concommitant ones will constitute an important and necessary step toward the better mental and social health of all persons in our culture.

There may be a number of different devices to incorporate the requisite subject matter in the curriculums for women. It may be accomplished through informal orientation programs. On the women's college campus there is a subtle awareness and emphasis which is as unconscious as it is effective. Much can be achieved by conscious attention to women's problems in the various social science courses or by a special course in the history and status of women.

It has been reported that women students do not find the more formal courses in their own problems of interest to them, but this should be a challenging rather than a deterring factor. The presence of men students might have a lively influence. Good

materials are lacking. The library shelves yield too many senti-
mentalized details and too many indigestible statistics. There is
much for the scholar but little that is timely and readable for
the amateur. There is not the usual wide variety of basic texts
to choose from, and competent teaching will require more than
the average number of hours of preparation.

Which is the more urgent, the responsibility of women to their
own cause or to that of society? The answer is of no importance
for the two are knit together more firmly than even the marriage
rite itself, with not even the possibility of divorce. If the debt
is discharged in the cause of women, society receives the benefit,
and vice versa. But because society's ills cannot be cured until
women achieve a healthy life of their own, why not enlist women
in the surer, simpler, and shorter campaign? Society cannot
afford to lose the services of any one woman in this double cause,
for those who are not for us are very much against us. Learning,
and especially college learning, can turn the uncertain steps of
youth toward the sure and sunny paths of genuine fulfillment.
But if the turning is lost there will be apathy, cynicism, and frustration, without and within.

There must be none who are lost to reality forever by their
absorption in home and social life, who insulate themselves effectively with a too comfortable income or a superior intelligence,
and who feel cheated because life does not fulfill for them its
earlier promise. Such women are not free in our society today,
however much Americans may boast about their many freedoms.
Women's growth has been stunted by our American traditions.
Women are fettered by prejudice, by their own ignorance; only
a liberal education, a truly liberating experience in their education, can set them free. Choosing a college and a curriculum
within that college through which she can earn her freedom becomes the modern woman's most important task.

. . . *12*

Choosing a College and a Curriculum

THE selection of a college is a critical decision for parents as well as for their daughters. Each daughter must find one specific intellectual workshop where she may pursue with the greatest freedom and confidence the task of educating herself. But the opulent twentieth century spreads before her a bewilderingly rich display of learning materials—its total heritage of science, literature, and history—in maze-like patterns of old and new curricular theories. Her eager glimpses into the future may be more alarming than helpful in choosing the best patterns. She sees the beginnings of many enticing careers, but their endings trail off into dim uncertainties. Only a handful of the opportunities and obstructions can be sighted, and these only with many obscurities and doubts.

There are, of course, some educational certainties, but they are logically obvious rather than practically useful. Certainly the curricular patterns of the present must be unlike those of the past. And certainly no one educational structure, planned by even the most competent architects, can serve the millions of young women in each new decade. Both the apprentices and the master builders must be flexible and imaginative. Daughters must be enthusiastic and adventurous, parents sympathetic but skeptical, if the final decision is to prove a wise and happy one.

One daughter may enter her state university with 2000 other

girls and twice as many men. When she inquired about entrance requirements she was readily promised admission. She may pay $600 for board, room, and tuition, and she may study anything from typing, playground supervision, and clothing construction to Indian languages, orchestra conducting, and psychiatric social work. Thirty per cent of her classmates are earning partial expenses. The social life is full and spirited.

Another daughter, with 400 others very much like her, may choose her mother's college where board, room, and tuition may cost $2000. Only the liberal arts subjects are offered, there is little student employment, and her fellow students do not include men. Regulations are liberal, and there is a well-planned program of social and extracurricular activities. Such a daughter necessarily registered some years earlier and probably worried a good deal about whether her scores on the entrance examinations would be high enough to earn her admission.

Both daughters will work hard for their bachelor's degree, both are taught by conscientious scholars; both are tested and guided and encouraged to think for themselves. Both study literature and history and the sciences and acquire varying amounts of poise, wisdom, and charm. One daughter may find her personality blossoming in her small classes with their intimate faculty contacts, and another may find her self-sufficiency developing from the constant demands and decisions of the larger campus. One loves the simple chapel service that begins her day on the campus. Another finds real inspiration in her sorority rituals. One thrills to her honors courses or her experimental project, another realizes her ambitions in her cooperative work programs, and still another loses all her shyness in a drama workshop.

But other daughters may not be so fortunate. One daughter may never learn to cope with the constant choices offered by the larger campus, while another may feel only frustrated by the simple routines of the smaller one. One may be embittered by her failure to be invited to join a sorority or demoralized by disappointments in dating. Some may never find realistic and useful courses or may go to pieces in examination week. Some may learn to hate the success of the better students or may utterly refuse the challenge of learning or of human contacts.

Every campus attracts a fine group of superior young women —those who are charming and sensitive, those who are militantly ambitious—some of them rich in worldly goods, some rich in talent or culture, most of them seriously intelligent, a few of them brilliant, and a few of them harmlessly dull. There is always a full quota of mousey little homesick freshmen and, of course, the ubiquitous, preoccupied seniors with the worldly manners and the cultivated voices. No one campus has everything, and therefore each candidate must make her own inventory of personal and financial assets and of intellectual needs and social ambitions and then match this inventory with a list of searching questions about the advantages and disadvantages of all the available schools.

Students drift in and out of the various colleges, carried along by current traditions and prejudices and by the great streams of propaganda and rumor which make up the great mass of "information" readily available to them. Seldom does anyone probe through the surface for more information about costs and services. Almost more than financial circumstances, it is largely geographic propinquity, knowledge and influence of school friends, enthusiasm and advice of high school teachers, family traditions, or general attractiveness in terms of athletics and social prestige which determine the college choices.

That the choices have proved generally satisfactory is partly because the colleges themselves are doing a reasonably good job of education and partly perhaps because the general public does not demand any greater satisfaction than it is now getting. We are even more complacent about what we get for our educational dollar than for our automotive dollar. All cars are about equally good for the money invested. We may choose them for some specific, even irrelevant, quality, but their underlying all-round efficiency we have always taken for granted. What we might get if the technological dreamers and the social philosophers and the producers and the advertisers could all get together is something

outside our limited realm of contemplation, in either automo-
biles or education.

The right decisions in education aren't too difficult during the
early school years. Good parents take it for granted that they
will help their children in school projects and experiences. Home
work may no longer involve arithmetic, but it does require not
only endless interpretation and motivation on the part of the
parents, but also a patient enthusiasm that is either genuine
or a reasonable facsimile thereof. Conflict in ideas and methods
is inevitable but not insoluble.

It is with the high school and college years that the problems
suddenly come with a rush, raising clouds of questions for which
there seem to be no answers and scattering traditions and ideas
in all directions. At least we know from the recent studies that
except in unusual periods of natural stress and strain, almost
any young woman can enter the college of her choice. There are
many fancy rumors to the contrary, started, we have reason to
believe, by the few who have been refused admission, and kept
alive by the many who prefer to drift along the path of least
resistance. The lack of general understanding of admission policies and practices leaves the usual parent no arguments to counteract the rumors.

In choosing a college, no mother would wish to place the
daughter who showed little interest or aptitude for high school
subjects on a campus which announces clearly that its courses
are planned for students who stand in the highest fifth of their
high school class. Nor would a father who earns a modest salary
find it advisable to send his daughter to the college with the very
highest fees. She would probably be as unhappy as he with the
disproportionate financial burden.

Geographic location is another important factor. Often it does
not seem feasible for a family to become involved in the incon-
venience and expense of having their daughter travel a thousand
miles two or four times a year to some college which might otherwise prove attractive, although sometimes the strength of tradition or some special educational feature or the desire to know

another part of our country easily counterbalances the draw-backs which travel offers. Some families do not like the long separation which distant colleges entail, and some parents find much enjoyment in frequent visits to the nearby campus and in frequent week ends with the daughter at home. In this respect it is often hard for both parties to be completely objective in making their choices.

Surely the most obvious question about the future campus home for the student involves the curriculums which are offered. If medicine, journalism, acting, drama, merchandising, teaching, or music is the ultimate objective, it is important to know whether the college teaches courses in these fields or whether it offers the groundwork in two or four years which will prepare the student for more professional training. College catalogues will give the answer, or a handful of letters will bring direct answers or visits from field representatives. Comparisons are always in order, and systematic inquiries are usually rewarded with a wealth of information.

There is almost never one *best* place to study social work or drama or creative writing or any other subject, and it cannot be said too often that most colleges are good, though they are very different from one another, each with an abundance of general virtues and some outstanding excellences. They are good because of the many accrediting agencies that never cease to check on them. They are good because after all higher education is one of our biggest American enterprises, with all the aggressive efficiency which grows out of free and healthy competition. They are good also because the field of college teaching continues to attract a high percentage of our most able and conscientious citizens.

Many students, however, have set no educational goal. What is needed may be either a standard liberal arts education as a preparation for further professional study or a year or two of exploratory work in several fields, with college experience and guidance to direct the selecting and maturing processes. The final outcome will depend to some extent on the particular campus chosen, but there is no one campus best equipped to deal with this kind of student.

It would, of course, be ridiculous to contend that there are not tremendous differences in teaching, in attitudes and values, in the intellectual discipline, the vocational counseling, the breadth or depth of the curriculum, and the human experiences to be found on one campus or another. In fact, one of the exciting experiences of the mother and daughter lies in investigating and evaluating these differences. But there is no one best place to study any one subject any more than there is one best place to buy canned peaches. Is Marshall Field's better than Wanamakers? Is a mink coat better than a tweed? The answer depends more on the needs and assets of the individual than on the assets and offerings of the purveyor. There are many places which supply a thoroughly good standard product, there are many factors involved, many interests to be served.

It might seem wise, perhaps, to compare our colleges from the standpoint of their endowment, their facilities, or their scholarly productivity, but factors such as these may have something less than the estimated effect on the seventeen-year-old who sits in the freshman classroom. The impact that any educational institution, great or small, will have on the adolescent mind and spirit is incalculable and unpredictable.

Parents and daughters and college officers frequently talk at cross purposes about such an event as "the campus experience." Mother wants good discipline, father wants vocational training, daughter contemplates the chances of finding a promising husband, and the college officer faces the question of whether the curriculum and atmosphere can meet any of their requirements. Sometimes prestige is the most important factor, and this may simplify the problem for the family but not for the college which receives the student. Sometimes financial considerations narrow the field, and certainly the striking differences in the size and socioeconomic level of the student bodies may constitute formidable barriers for some families.

Neither parents nor college need sidestep the important part that social activities play in the college career. Of course, every student seeks professional, intellectual, and cultural development and every campus can deluge the student with many varieties of culture and learning. But every successful and happy woman needs also to develop her social skills and her security in social relationships. She must be able on the campus and after college to find or create for herself an inner circle of intimate friends and an outer circle of stimulating acquaintances. The college officer may very well ask the prospective freshman: Will you find these circles or be able to create them on this particular campus? And will this college in turn help you to find or create them for yourself as an alumna?

Other questions about these relationships should be asked by the dean: Do you want to go back after college to live in your home town? What college is popular there? Are frequent weekend trips home essential to you? What other girls of your acquaintance have attended this college? Do you like them and does your mother like them? Are any of them similar to you in ability and temperament? Do they like you and would they help you to get acquainted on the campus?

Do you long to escape from all your family and community ties, find entirely new friends, meet unfamiliar ideas? Do you have the precocious self-reliance for this break? Will you seek travel and adventure after graduation and hope to find a fellow alumna in any city or state? Are you happy seeing many new faces, measuring yourself against any competition? Can you choose wisely from a wealth of activities and interests? Will you be discontented with those who spend more money than you on clothes, amusements, or travel?

Are you strictly a one-man girl or equally popular with a half dozen of the boys in your clique? Or are you not dating any man as yet and are perhaps a little fearful of your success in this romantic world? Do you count on finding your future husband on the college campus? Is it your ambition to marry soon or to have a career first?

Are you socially shy but intellectually adventurous? Will you

261

regret that there are more famous scholars teaching on some other campus? Do you demand careful and painstaking teaching? Will you object if your professor talks brilliantly over your head and leaves you to dig out all the information for yourself in the library? Would you rather read than dance? Can you thrill to debates on public questions? Do you enjoy keen intellectual fencing? Do you make your friends and embrace your activities mostly on the intellectual level?

Congenial social development means to some parents, at least while their daughters are at the more sensitive ages, a certain amount of protection from problems which can be more successfully met and even enjoyed by the more mature individual. Experience is the stuff that personalities are made of, and it is the college years which must provide a stimulating variety of experience, an abundance of the most substantial building materials. If a girl has too many of the wrong experiences, some of them may be incorporated permanently into the new personality, may leave a lastingly weakened structure. The atmosphere of the typical college campus is more permissive, more highly charged, and more conducive to romance than any other type of community. There may be more exciting experiences than can be absorbed by the growing personality to its advantage unless some long-range spiritual direction as well as intellectual leadership is provided.

Therefore, the parents at least, if not the daughters, will want to ask the college: Do you maintain a student government structure? If so, is it merely to indulge the students' irresponsible demand for a free voice in campus affairs? Do you dominate this structure or do they? Do you give them and hold them to responsibility for campus standards? Is this a meaningful and vital experience for your students? For 10 per cent? For 50 per cent? For 80 per cent?

What kinds of young men will be coming to your campus and meeting our daughters? How much do you know about the social activities and dating of your students? Who sets the standards

for your dances? Where are they held? Do your officers and
counselors attend them?

By what methods do you build a sense of responsibility in
your students? By the strength of your traditions? By special
ceremonies? By careful selection of students? Is there a strong
esprit de corps? Does your faculty give any attention to the
teaching of spiritual values? Moral values? What steps do you
take to develop good student leaders?

Is cheating accepted on your campus? Is the faculty complacent about it? What steps do you take in preventing dishonest
work? Are the deans and counselors concerned about it? Is anyone charged with this responsibility? Do you rely on an honor
system? Does it work?

Do your students go to the concerts and lectures? Or only to
the athletic games? Do they mingle and converse with the faculty or with any adults? Or only with one another?

Who teaches on this campus? Men and women of energy,
grace of mind, breadth of culture? Or pedants, caught by sheer
inertia in a petty intellectual hierarchy?

Most parents are probably well aware that the Hollywood
version of any college campus is not extremely accurate, but few
of them could perhaps list all the features which do make it
very unlike the typical small town or suburban community
which in size and in other aspects it so much resembles. As we
noted earlier, the campus population differs from the typical
community population in its concentration of age level from
seventeen to twenty-one. Feeling and enthusiasm run high whatever the issue may be. The ratio of power to responsibility is at
its highest, with boundless energy unharnessed and unhampered.
High feeling and pure enthusiasm meet only more feeling and
more enthusiasm, and the absence of resistance may give a
cyclonic whirl to the most trivial or evanescent project.

Romantic feelings and interest in the other sex are dominant
over the intellectual or artistic or professional interests. All is
well lost for love, and the love theme is never too long absent
from current conversation.

Confidence easily swells into overconfidence, for with such a concentration of the intellectually able and healthy and such a great proportion of leisure time, projects are accomplished with much greater ease and efficiency than they could be elsewhere. Never again will these students find such interesting and carefree companions or so many leisure hours at their disposal. On the campus it is the higher socioeconomic levels which are in the majority and life is more felicitous, more urban, less realistic, less grubby.

Never again will the young woman find so many eligible men, and also never again will she find a world of such free and equal competition. Here her classmates accept her as an equal competitor and all her teachers applaud her successes, but after graduation her business colleagues (males) will enjoy privileges which she cannot share, and her employers will not so regularly reward her good efforts with proper commendation.

Because of all these differences in age, spirit, outlook, and activity, the lack of a trained and continuing governing organization becomes one of the most significant aspects of the college campus. Any adult community, no matter how small, has its local officers—the judge, the mayor, the council members, and other duly elected officers. These citizens accumulate experience and wisdom in their years of service. They are compensated for their work and often have made professional preparation for it. More important, they devote a large proportion of their time to the pursuit of their civic duties.

The campus is also a self-sufficient little community with its own well-defined population, its own civic center, its own officers and laws, and its own busily humming industry of teaching and learning. It has problems of health, problems of traffic and safety, and problems of eating, entertainment, building, record keeping, fines, fires, stealing, and sex. As the student moves from home to campus he is not aware of the treacherous differences which lie below the surface likenesses to his environment, or of the inevitable effects they must have on his thinking and his behavior.

But a college group, several hundred or thousand young men and women having their first responsibilities in group living and self-government, must make shift with a new set of inexperienced officers each year. Moreover, these officers, elected in June and perhaps quitting the campus forever the following June, have on their hands their own full-time job of learning, which will not permit them to spend more than one or two hours a week at the job of governing. They revise the old regulations and make new ones, collect, budget, and spend the money, and deal with offenders.

For these functions there are no qualifying examinations, no civil service lists. And on many a large campus they must work in the face of a student code, unwritten but nevertheless recognized and binding, under which no one ever reports another person's wrong-doing, and under which students have a right to their own government, independent of adult administrative controls. It will be obvious, then, that any such controls must take the form of counseling, of creating an *esprit de corps.* In other words, they must be indirect, depending on many complex factors which are obviously hard for the parent of the prospective student to evaluate.

Not only are there many circumstances characteristic of any campus group, but there are also striking differences between one campus and another. Summarizing the various possibilities in higher education for women first calls for classifying the available colleges open to women: women's and coeducation, large and small, municipal or state and private or denominational, junior colleges, four-year colleges, teachers' colleges and graduate or professional schools that are liberal or vocational or both, expensive and inexpensive colleges, east, west, north, or south, in small town or in large city.

Colleges may tend toward the traditional or the progressive; many are fully accredited while some few are not; they will differ in their entrance requirements, variety of curriculums, size of classes, socioeconomic level of their students, and in their scholastic standards. Their histories and traditions will also differ, and the current social and economic forces affect them in different ways. Such mundane things as taxes, inflations, depressions, federal subsidies, wars, philosophies, and attitudes about women are reflected in campus costs, clientele, and curriculums.

Each one of these colleges is so unique that sorting them into appropriate groups and categorizing these groups may not be a legitimate procedure. But it constitutes the first step in any systematic exploration of the total field of women's education, and therefore, in the interests of clarification, necessity dictates that some cursory and unpleasantly statistical summaries be made.

In the United States there are approximately 150 four-year colleges for women; 77 of them are Roman Catholic, 19 Protestant, 38 privately controlled but not church-affiliated, and 11 are state or municipally supported. Fewer than a dozen of these women's colleges have as many as a thousand students, and therefore, when we are thinking of women's colleges we are also in general thinking of the smaller college.

In addition to these 150 women's colleges, there are about 500 coeducational colleges and universities, 400 junior colleges, and 200 teachers' colleges open to women. About 70 of the four-year colleges where women are being educated together with men have five thousand or more students and any one of these would qualify as the typically "large" college. More than 500 of all the four-year colleges have fewer than a thousand students and may be designated as the typically "small" college.

With so many small colleges and so few large ones it might seem that the chances of any one daughter finding herself on the small campus might be about five to one. But of course this is not the case, because, for example, one large state university, with five to eight thousand women, contains the makings of fifteen to twenty of the smaller ones. Actually, and contrary perhaps to the general impression, only about 10 per cent of college-going youth, men or women, are in the "small" colleges with a thousand or fewer students. In 1940 the data showed that almost 20 per cent of our students were on these smaller campuses, but the large college has been growing rapidly, and the smaller ones have suffered losses rather than gains. The college woman of today, then, nine times out of ten will find herself in the large rather than the small college group.

In many respects it is easier to describe and to categorize the large college than the small. Paradoxically the large colleges seem much more like one another and the smaller colleges more unique. The large majority of the giants are state or municipal institutions, and even those under private control are in so many cases located in the large urban centers that they take on many of the qualities of the municipal university. The students are drawn largely from the local population, live in their own homes, and commute to the campus for such schools as Hunter College and Fordham in New York City, Southern California in Los Angeles, Temple in Philadelphia, and Marquette in Milwaukee. Such universities as Boston, Buffalo, Pittsburgh, Detroit, and New York are also privately controlled but largely urban in patronage.

These large universities, whether state or private, seem to be known to the undiscriminating general public for their athletic prowess or possibly for a few of their outstanding scholars or leaders. These features are not by any means their most characteristic qualities; they merely indicate what the noncollege population finds most readable in the daily newspapers. The important qualities, the really significant features, often remain unduly obscure.

By its very largeness, the big campus may seem awkward and sprawling and greedy to the outsider; the small campus, by contrast, seems austere and pretentious. And in every part of the country, for as long as anyone can remember, someone (could it be the small college?) has been giving voice to the sentiment that large colleges are impersonal and indifferent, that the students are caught in the ruthless machinery, that there is no interest in the individual personality, and that the student becomes lost in red tape and regimentation. This is an obviously distorted picture.

Rather, the student may be overwhelmed by the attention he gets and the ease with which he can make warm human contacts. There are excellent and well-run residence halls, with trained counselors available. There is always adequate and well-organized academic counseling, especially for freshmen. There are organizations—church, sports, music, hobbies—scores of them, whose doors are always invitingly open. Moreover, the large campus, even more than the small college, attracts its students from an immediate geographic locale, and any student can meet not only the fellow from down the block, but dozens of others who speak the same thoughts with the same accent, wear the same clothes, and vote the same ticket.

The current emphasis on youth's need to develop independence in thought and personality does not imply that a happy and propitious unfolding must be achieved in a kind of social isolation ward, sterilized against any contaminating ideologies and bare of the enchanting solicitude of anxious mentors. Perhaps the difference between the large and the small campus lies essentially in the greater self-reliance, the more mature aggressiveness, which the larger campus seems to demand. Every student needs at least one wise and warmhearted friend, either teacher or student, if his heart as well as his head is to be in his work. On the smaller campus such a friend is usually waiting; in the large and unselected student group, that one friend, both kind and competent, may be harder to find and easier to lose. The large campus does not dodge its responsibility in this vital matter, but sometimes the student is not equipped to seize the opportunities so richly offered.

On the large campus, the classes will tend to be large. There will always be some small classes, and even a few very small ones—especially for graduate students and for those departments which traditionally attract few students. Language and laboratory classes may have under 50 students, even under 30, but it is quite common for the introductory courses, the typical courses required of freshmen and sophomores, to have 100, 200, or even 500 students. These classes will be excellently organized and well taught.

On the smaller campus, with 500, 1000, or even 2000 students, all the relationships among students and between students and faculty are more intimate. For the smaller campus is not only smaller, it is also a privately controlled or a church-related college. Its student body has been in some way selected and is, therefore, a much more homogeneous group. Inevitably this causes a feeling of solidarity among the students, with a parallel feeling among the faculty, since they also represent a more homogeneous group. Selection operates at the faculty as well as the student level in achieving a campus population at the same time homogeneous and productive.

C. Wright Mills, who has made a thorough study of the white-collar class, reports that men of energy and imagination are not often attracted to college teaching and that the specialization required is often deadening to the mind that would grasp for higher culture in the modern world. On the other hand, psychology insists that the great teacher is the individual with whom the student can identify himself, the individual whose forceful personality and convincing methods draw youth into his own orbit of manners, attitude, and thought. Presidents and deans trying to identify and attract these truly inspiring teachers will meet more difficulties than registrars and counselors who look for the right students. These models necessary for a thriving college community must have intellectual integrity without dominance, learning free from pedantry, social sophistication divorced from social ambition, and imagination that is both fluent and healthy.

That persistent but statistically unsubstantiated criticism of the women's colleges—the dearth of romantic opportunity—may actually turn out to be a rather tidy asset: it does permit a more detached and objective appraisal of the young men. College women learn much from their laborious, self-conscious letter writing, and the intellectual and feministic eternities between

269

week ends are on the whole probably less enervating than the romantic intemperance which the mixed campus allows. Always surrounded by eligible men, the coed may be all the more haunted by her own continuing romantic bankruptcy in these four critical matchmaking years, or she may be frayed by the emotional indulgence of incessant dates; but she can never be free of the constant romantic pressures, no matter how casual the attitude she learns to affect. In any case, intellectual discipline, as much needed as romantic sophistication and much more difficult to come by, is not encouraged. Men are necessary but distracting, and the retreats into intellectual pursuits which the one-sex campus allows can be invigorating. One forthright high school senior put it more tersely: "First you have to decide whether you want to go to a coeducational school or an educational one."

The recent study of the college origins of the young American scholars, based on the proportion of students in each thousand undergraduates who received the current subsidies for graduate work, reveals that the women's colleges averaged 5.6 scholars, the liberal arts coeducational colleges 4.0, and the universities 3.3. Such a study emphasizes only one aspect of the total problem of higher education; nevertheless the final selection of the six colleges which provide the atmosphere most favorable to this kind of learning is especially significant for parents of talented and ambitious daughters: Swarthmore, Reed, Chicago, Carleton, Oberlin, and Antioch. In all of these, the authors point out, football is nonexistent or minor; there are no national sororities; all are privately controlled, nonsectarian, interracial, and nonsegregated; and all choose students who can contribute to their fellow students as well as those who have intellectual capacity and aptitude.

There have been other attempts to evaluate the colleges and universities on scholarly achievements, but such studies quickly get out of date and out of hand. Records have been available at times, for example, on the average scores of students on assorted entrance tests and on the number of professors in *Who's*

Who or in the lists of starred scientists. Systematic ratings by scholars have revealed that certain centers have the lion's share of the available funds and therefore of the distinguished departments but that outstanding departments in any field of learning, like the professors who contribute to them, migrate from one university to another and sometimes turn up in quite unexpected places.

Most of the large colleges have fraternities and sororities, and most of the smaller colleges do not. These organizations, especially in the middle western areas, exert a powerful influence over the thinking of a large segment of the youthful population; in fact, over some adolescent girls they exert a paralyzing, almost hypnotic, effect. For those whose thinking is thus channelized, most questions on the choice of a college will have very simple answers, for they will seek the campus where their entree into the group of their choosing is most assured. The more indifferent or the uninitiated will find the whole system of fraternity and sorority life so well managed and coordinated with campus social administration that they can "take it or leave it," as the students say, with perfect ease. On the other hand, if there is something about sororities which makes it impossible in certain states or communities to assume this nonchalant attitude, then no mother or daughter can discount the possibility of being hurt by them on the larger campus where their traditions are strong.

Essentially these organizations are campus housing units with invitational membership, high *esprit de corps,* and a richer social program than is provided by university residences. Their intrinsic worth to the student may be much or little, depending on many factors, but especially on the exclusiveness and social prestige which they afford. The inherent selective process of the private college has already provided some social prestige with its larger proportions of students drawn from the upper and upper middle classes. The strong traditions and cherished amenities of the campus itself minimize the added gains to be secured from fraternity membership. Free of these prestige urgencies, convinced of its values, and assured of its clientele, the private col-

271

leges can exert a more effective control over the fraternity groups. The local chapters where they do exist may be manipulated, metamorphosed, or even eliminated.

On the large unselected campus, the added social prestige obtained from the intimacy and exclusiveness of the chapter house is far more significant. To the extent that the student expects these heightened social relationships and sanctions or needs the security for her future social life, the pressures may become ruthless and uncompromising. The privileges of membership are much too precious and far-reaching to be consigned to youthful judgment; alumnae and national officers inevitably become involved. University counselors, no matter how excellent, cannot be entrusted to advise on the responsibilities of fraternity selection and management, for they may be expected to take a dim view of the unearned social prestige in relation to other personal and academic values.

In these problems, the university merely reflects society as a whole, both in its values and its methods of obtaining them. Insensate attacks and the unctious defenses are alike unwelcome and unhealthy for the campus, but the official campus attitude and action must reflect the strength and temper of public thinking. Neither the campus nor the chapter house can be any more forthright or courageous in handling its problems than the climate of our society allows.

The sorority has its legitimate function on the campus. It protects its members from indiscriminate contacts, especially in the way of romantic partners with too divergent backgrounds. It usually provides a standard of living a little higher than that of the average housing unit, although modern residence halls are rapidly reducing the margin of advantage on this score. It has freedom to practice its religious convictions without reference to the taxpayer and to embrace political or economic or societal principles according to its own taste and pocketbook. Youth finds peculiar satisfactions in its insignia and rituals and loyalties, although these are now encouraged in dozens of other Greek-letter groups with religious, professional, sports, or service connotations. No student can hope to dodge all of these special affiliations and privileges, and the aspiring student can enjoy as many as she chooses.

Within the chapter house there is sometimes a warmth and solicitude, sometimes a frankly old-fashioned authority. There is also sometimes a spirit of camaraderie, an affectionate sharing of life's pleasures and vicissitudes, possible only for sheltered and well-bred youth. These advantages often add relatively little to the costs of campus life. Their worth after the college years fluctuates so enormously with geography and with professional growth and personal circumstance that no estimate of the dividends on the youthful investment can be made in advance.

One of the many ways in which the large colleges seem alike is in their development of standard administrative procedures for handling large numbers of students efficiently and intelligently. This administrative framework, with all its vice-presidents and assistant deans, is much the same for any large campus, and it is all too easily mistaken for the real heart of the institution. Actually it is merely the vestibule through which the daughter must pass in order to find her more intimate contacts.

In some respects the larger institutions, slow moving and unwieldy as they are, have become the victims of their public relations experts, who in turn are bound by the demands which the public makes on them. Those officers who meet the public, whose signatures are affixed to the outgoing letters, whose faces appear at the ubiquitous speakers' tables, must be built up to meet the public's estimate of a proper college officer. Their names and their functions become a kind of slogan for each college, serving the same purpose as any advertising slogan in giving the public the pleasantly standardized product to which it is accustomed. Behind the newspaper version of the institution is a highly diversified program of personalities and curriculums which makes an entirely different impression on the enrolled freshman, depending on his own capacity to comprehend and absorb it.

The youthful verve of the college population makes each campus a pleasant and stimulating place to live, but there is little doubt that the larger, coeducational campus is the more exciting. The range of activities and personalities is more extensive. More time and energy are required for movement and transitions. The pace is never leisurely; the pressures are more obtrusive. The techniques cannot be subtle, and the standards of behavior and the intellectual atmosphere are naturally somewhat closer to the levels of the world at large than is the case with the larger college.

One of the virtues of most of the larger and public universities is that they cannot make any rigid selection of the students who present themselves. To be sure, there is an automatic and natural selective process continually in operation which, for example, gives a very disproportionate representation of the professional and the higher socioeconomic classes to any college campus. As was indicated earlier, the blue-collar workers, with about 60 per cent of the population at large, will constitute at most only some 30 per cent of even the most unselected campus population. Especially with rising taxes, the student in the more sequestered small college who associates primarily with other students paying $1500 or more for education each year is insulating herself from many of the more realistic experiences of daily living. When entrance requirements eliminate the lowest three fourths of the high school graduating class, the quality of classroom discussion takes an upward leap. Intellectual interests go deeper, standards of behavior are higher, and the pleasurable side of learning is greatly enhanced.

Admission policies for all colleges are especially important, because no college campus in this democratic American society can commit itself to undemocratic practices; and once the student is on the campus and in the classroom, the college teacher must frequently face some troublesome and searching questions. Is the slow learner, the intellectually underprivileged, welcome in his classroom? Does the teacher study the assets of these slow learners? Are necessary adjustments made to the individual differences among the students? Does the leading part in the play always go to the best actor, or does it go to the student who

274

needs the learning or the socializing experience that goes with the role? Is the classroom teacher responsible only for his own subject matter or for the general all-round development of the student? Who is supervising the student's growth in social skills? In thinking about current issues? In moral attitudes and conscience? In general maturity?

When the group is carefully selected and includes only the intellectually able students, those with good cultural backgrounds, those from families who will share responsibility for the students' growth in personality and character, then the learning can proceed at a faster pace. Training in some of the fundamentals can be taken for granted, the teacher can devote himself more exclusively to his specialty, and the whole learning process becomes a forthright, honest, and successful joint endeavor, with both teacher and student finding genuine pleasure in the day's work. When, in addition, classroom hours can be spent on the humanities, history, philosophy, literature, and the basic sciences rather than on the more purely vocational subjects, the more able students and their parents may feel that the campus experience better meets educational needs.

When there is too wide a range in the learning ability between the student of the lowest and highest endowment, the time of the better student is to some extent wasted. If there are large differences in the cultural backgrounds, social skills, language and speech facility, and artistic and religious interests of the students, it is easy for the general level of the activities and mores to drop to the needs of the less privileged. To bring this general level of thought and action up to meet the demands of the most able would require a great deal of time and attention from a staff of skilled counselors. The teaching faculty usually has little taste and less time for these "extracurricular" duties.

On the other hand, it cannot be assumed that the mere selection of able students through admission policies automatically guarantees a high efficiency in learning and in pursuing activities at the more mature and stimulating levels. It merely makes these highly desirable qualities more possible to obtain, if such assets as good teachers, fine traditions, and satisfactory financing are also present.

The otherwise favorable environment of the smaller colleges may be dissipated when teachers have crowded schedules and a wide variety of courses, which may mean either long hours of routine preparation or carelessness and rigidity in intellectual work. Time for research and motivation for scholarly growth may be lacking. The leisurely pace may become so slow that all vitality is lost. Without the impetus of graduate students it is difficult for even the most ardent scholar to push out to the frontiers of knowledge in his field. The more productive and aggressive workers may be lured away by the larger laboratories and libraries of the giant university centers.

Parents and prospective students will need to develop an alertness and sensitivity to such subsurface qualities and to follow the school of their choice over some years and through the daily lives of some of its students and alumni before they can make a thoroughly adequate appraisal of its values and virtues, to say nothing of how these qualities will meet the needs of any given daughter.

The variety of educational opportunities available in America was well expressed by Katherine Gillette Blyley:

I am grateful that higher education has many fronts on which to work in these days of rethinking and reshaping knowledge— the front of the state supported college and university, the front of the private college and university, the large college, the small college, the men's colleges, and the women's colleges.

Variety in education as well as in other things is American. It is American because it tends to preserve independence and individuality. The public supported institutions insure the principle of democratic opportunity for all; the private college preserves education from a prevailing pattern of state control; the small college stands as a bulwark against the academic goosestep of mass education. We put each other in balance, as it were, lest one good educational custom should corrupt the nation.[1]

But the freshman's choice of her college is only the beginning. She faces still further alternatives on her arrival at the campus, continuous decisions about curriculums and courses—social work or teaching, typing or philosophy, music or physiology, basketball or mathematics. The question of which of the professions or vocations she shall embrace leads only to an even more momentous question: What proportion of her college time will it demand?

Perhaps it would be better to phrase this question in a different manner: What proportion of her college time can she afford to give to her vocational rather than to her general education? The answer, although somewhat different for each freshman, comes with amazing force and consensus from every chapter of her future life. For homemaking, citizenship, leisure, and earning, her success—that is, her substantial, three-dimensional success, with depth of understanding, breadth of perspective, and height of satisfaction—demands a truly liberal emphasis in her education.

Statistically, woman is a homemaker. Undoubtedly the majority of women, whether or not they are college graduates, spend the largest number of hours in this role; it is even more certain that most men find the most convincing arguments for continuing the present statistic. Changes in averages are inevitable but slow, and although the historical roles of men and women—the man as a fighter, earner, adventurer, director in the world of affairs, and the woman as mother and homemaker protected within the family circle—have been drastically modified and are constantly becoming more similar, the rate of these changes is difficult to predict.

Certainly in the next few decades there will still be substantial differences in the general life patterns of men and women. Men will still dominate the world of business, professions, and politics, although the margin of their lead will be cut down with every succeeding generation. The inevitable gains which women will make in these areas will have to be made while they are still responding to the greater share of responsibility for child rearing and for cultural activities and the management of the home. So long as this is true, women will need as much liberal education as they can get; in fact, the level of our society in general depends directly on how much liberal education can be absorbed by how many. A woman's functions as mother and homemaker, at least in the present era, take priority over her functions as earner, and the exclusively vocational emphasis perforce yields some ground.

For in the fine art of homemaking, it is the understandings rather than the techniques that are difficult to acquire. Information about foods, clothing, even about child rearing and huband-holding, is readily available for all those women who can perceive their own needs. Household efficiency results from practice, and this is available in the laboratory of life as well as in the campus workshops. It is the outer and material benefits that flow from the inner and spiritual perceptions, not the other way around. Cooking and buying, building and decorating, health and home nursing, finance and management, may be acquired with skill and dispatch if the underlying concepts in the arts and sciences have already been learned. It is the social and economic insights, the ethical and esthetic values, which transform the humdrum household into an imaginative enterprise and build a half-dozen prosaic personalities into a singing experience of family life.

The crucial function for women in homemaking, even more than in the employment field, will be their task of maintaining good relationships while educating the men in the newer aspects of their own roles as fathers and earners. Such a task demands patience and insight and as many other feminine virtues and strategies as women can muster. Their resources for this counter-plotting must go far beyond the repertory provided in the usual vocational curriculums.

For women to achieve success even in the role of earner, it is surprising to find the many reasons which marshal themselves for the emphasis on the liberal arts.

First, there are many employers who argue that the well-rounded, versatile, adaptable worker is more satisfactory in the labor market than is the specialist who has sacrificed more basic training for a narrow proficiency which after all could have been cultivated on the job.

It may be maintained, for example, that extensive training in speech, literature, drama, and writing might be of more importance for women's ascent in the business world than college training in the technical knowledge of corporation finance and business machines. It may be that those who are overmotivated and ambitious beyond their opportunities do not make as satisfactory workers as those individuals with inner resources, a stable philosophy of life, and other qualities which accrue to the student in the liberal arts program at its best. Competition for women is still cruel; for workers of both sexes, the steep road to the top will become increasingly difficult. The native intelligence proclaimed in one's social demeanor is obviously an important ingredient in his success, and although many employers do not clearly differentiate this from training, counselors and teachers must learn to appraise it accurately and provide that breadth which the environment may have lacked.

Second, emphasis is more safely placed on the liberal arts because the economic opportunities for any one woman are very capricious. Only in the largest urban centers does the married woman have free choice to follow her own best career interests. In most cases the woman follows where the husband's work leads him, and she must adapt herself to whatever openings this locale affords her. Futhermore, the nature of her work and her working hours usually yield to his advantage. Nepotism rules and other personal factors may exclude her from pursuing a too specialized career. It is not prudent, therefore, to aim for the narrow end of the funnel. From the purely practical point of view, it is disappointing to engage in a long, esoteric, vocational or professional training schedule only to find later that the only available openings are in fields requiring less depth.

This is not a plea to discourage women from such arduous training programs as those required for medicine and law. Either profession may be practiced in the smallest village, in the most rural areas. In fact, these professions make the woman singularly independent of family or geographic limitations. On the other hand, the woman whose natural talents push her toward classical languages or geology or music criticism needs a special milieu for her work. If she wants to pursue such subjects for the pure joy of working in them, we would heartily approve. The girl who earns a degree in folklore or economics may be very well equipped to enjoy life with volunteer work to satisfy her intellectual interests. Teaching or nursing or secretarial work is, of course, much safer for those who want to be sure of having a good earning capacity.

Third, one of the phenomena of modern times is the evolution of the adult education programs. Professional and business training through evening and extension classes, correspondence courses, and in-service training cover almost all fields. They constitute accessible and inexpensive opportunities to cultivate one's talent by useful and timely training. For any woman these programs are a godsend in the solution of her current vocational maladjustments. If she has been foresighted enough to lay the foundations of her education during her college years, thereby cultivating the alert and adventurous attitudes which will make life more satisfying while she is closely confined within the home, she will easily push out toward whatever further training she may require for her subsequent re-entry into the world of affairs.

Fourth, a more potent reason develops from the more careful scrutiny of the rewards to be gleaned from the actual hours spent on the job. Most important, of course, is the buying power of the earnings needed both to raise her standards of living and to give her psychological independence and health. But beyond this, the white-collar worker—and this includes all college women—has little satisfaction.

In the large-scale capitalism of our society, security has become the most valued goal for all workers, blue-collar and white-collar, men as well as women. Only a few at the top levels get the needed psychic rewards through expressing themselves creatively in their work. Self-fulfillment in employment is denied to most present-day workers, even to many of the college-trained professional classes. This denial throws a long backward shadow over all the vocational or professional training which leads the future worker up to the ultimate human emptiness of his job. The training is required, just as the job is required, for the material needs to sustain life. But for life itself, however we may define its essence, education must be something more than job training, must be indeed liberal, enabling the worker to free himself from that peculiar bondage of the modern job.

Fifth, there are, of course, many professions which still require very highly specialized professional or vocational training. We will rejoice for every young woman who has the interest and ability to pursue them. Professional women workers, organized in all their appropriate national groups, must continue to motivate able young women and to assure them financial aids comparable to those enjoyed by young men.

We need as many of those admirably single-minded and ambitious young women as we can get who will by necessity or choice sacrifice or postpone or delimit romance and family life in order to promote their own professional or business careers. Their successes are an essential step in the transition to the future more equable status for all women. We must applaud them, reward them beyond their just desserts, and push them even further than their abilities seem to warrant. Their opportunities in this man's world will never be commensurate with their powers, and at its best our enthusiastic support can never be inflated to the point of overcoming the resistances they will encounter. But the important thing for educators to remember is that such women *will be a small minority*. In the long run, the large majority of women students will fit best into the more general rather than the specialized patterns.

For citizenship—in the family, in the community, or on an international scale—ideologies and perspectives built on knowledge take precedence over the routine community skills or the casual espousal of good causes. Good judgment and critical appraisal are built up slowly, and they need the help and discipline of the classroom. Enthusiasm rides on the surface of pomp and circumstance, rises and falls with the televised propaganda. But lasting interest, civic conscience, and the inconspicuous effectiveness of informed leadership are not for sale on the easy terms of the market place. Only the trained, inquiring, sensitive mind can function in truly democratic fashion.

For the leisure hours, for spiritual satisfactions, both the impetus and the proper nourishment obviously come from the liberal arts rather than from professional or vocational education. What do we mean by the inner life, meditation, contemplation, esthetics, spirituality—concepts as old as civilization, which the twentieth century seems to have newly discovered? Not the ascetics, but the practicing social scientists are now insisting that educators identify and cultivate the inner life, the peculiar human ingredient which is necessary to both individual and national and human welfare.

The church calls it the religious life and presents one of the most vital programs for its cultivation, but the church does not hold the whole of the secret. The philosophers have identified it and found their own formulas for developing the ethical and moral values. The sociologists and psychologists speak of attitudes and emotions, of ego, motivations, selfhood, personality, even of love. When all of these disciplines have pooled their resources, they may not find their differences easily resolved, but at least each may now rejoice that the cultivation of the inner life has been so emphatically justified. It has achieved not only spiritual significance, but intellectual and scientific and, more especially, economic and political status. It has become the legitimate concern of everybody—of college presidents, the clergy, the White House, the joint chiefs of staff, the NAM, the CIO, and the GOP.

For present-day educational blue prints, the church's program will be parallel and sustaining. Our national constitution guarantees freedom for each to worship in his own way, which is interpreted to exclude any formal teaching of religious precepts in the public schools. To escape any possible accusation of prejudice, we must sacrifice the opportunity to serve one of the child's and the man's most basic needs. The church still reaches the young learners through the parochial schools, the church-related colleges, and the religious foundations on the state or municipal college campus. Often, however, the work is both too little and too late.

Nevertheless, the basic essentials of integration of education and religion are very apparent. The church knows that "the kingdom of heaven is within you" and that it may even develop without benefit of clergy. Whether man can achieve his own serene fulfillment without the consciousness of deity outside himself will remain an unsolved transcendental problem to challenge the church and the philosophers, but education need not wait for the solution. Why? Because no matter what answer lies in the future, education would prepare the youthful ground for the adult's later decision in much the same way, by sound knowledge of self and of current values. Because wherever the answer lies— in the Christian tradition or in some other discipline—it is always a matter in which the individual, not the classroom, makes the final, the significant, decision. Meanwhile, in its practical aspects the Christian tradition is today identical with the democratic philosophy of individual worth and of shared rights and powers. It is thus in a position to strengthen a philosophy which is truly a national issue and rapidly becoming an international one, a problem of our economic, social, and political survival.

In brief then, liberal arts courses—general education at its very best—cannot be too much stressed for every woman of the younger generation. For a woman needs an independent spirit much more than an independent income. To offset the economic handicap and to cope with her changing roles, she needs an inner stability and poise which come not from skills but from knowledge and understanding. Since she is still expected to take the lead in cultural activities and in developing the happiness and welfare of her children, she must know the fine as well as the culinary arts.

Versatility, which springs only from a broad foundation, will prove more useful for combating her peculiar economic disadvantage than a more narrow specialization for which there may never be an outlet. The quoted salary levels of the alumnae of liberal arts colleges in relation to graduates from more specialized curriculums are proud evidences of this statement. If a woman can make herself valuable to her employer for superior qualities of mind and personality, subsequent in-service training and adult education opportunities can provide the specialization which she will need for advancement. And finally, the arts and the sciences and the humanities have in themselves pleasures and satisfactions in never-ending variety to accommodate the widest possible range of student interests and capacities.

Self-evident or convincing as all these arguments may be in theory, in practice liberal education will be resisted by students, by their parents, and by many of the educators themselves. The students will resist it because they have too short a view and are rightly concerned primarily with their imminent earning power to which the cultural subjects do not so obviously contribute. Many of the parents will have a longer view; some at least will endorse a liberal education, partly from deep conviction and partly through sheer snobbery.

One of the strangest arguments (we may not say reasons) for the emphasis on the liberal curriculum is the very high prestige which it enjoys, the inherent value of the degree as a "badge of culture." In part, the value may be a spurious one, or at least a little understood value. Youth has its own ideas about what it takes to win the larger cash prizes in today's competition, "perhaps the degree, but not devotion to the process of acquiring it."

This is a knotty problem, for the prestige value of the degree inheres in its representing some familiarity with the classical-cultural curriculum; at the same time, its prestige aids in securing a job, even though it will not help in performing the tasks demanded by the job. The parent pays with his money, the student with his time, and while both want tangible and immediate returns, they also want to secure that admission card to the company of the elect, the degree. Probably most college teachers have listened to student complaints about having to take courses that "won't do me any good" in terms of job future. Probably many college teachers have replied that the student might transfer to a vocational school which would train him better, and for less time and money. Then comes the rebuttal: "But you *have* to be a college graduate to get anywhere or be anybody!" [2]

Even though most of the daughters and many of the mothers may be convinced by these arguments for the liberal arts emphasis, their hopes may be disappointed on many a modern campus. The educators themselves have set up the resistances, some of them a little time-worn and shabby but still lively, some of them new and bristling. There will be the argument that other institutions—the church, the family, the Girl Scouts, even extracurricular groups—have responsibility for personal development, whereas both time and money are lacking for mass education in these qualities. It will be held that professional accrediting and licensing requirements leave no time for liberal courses. It will also be pointed out that the traditional liberal arts curriculum has become too rigid, too effete and hoary to make good its claim of cultivating values and virtues needed in current culture.

Liberal education is an attitude of mind and spirit; it is knowledge that is touched with beauty, not the easy reverence which is devoid of understanding. It is also knowledge fused with emotion, changing mere tolerance and openmindedness into conviction and confidence, and sometimes into action. It eschews an insipid peace of mind, looks for the challenge, welcomes the crisis. It pursues the meanings behind the appearances, and invokes the dynamics of the thinking process rather than the static properties of truth.

It is slower than vocational education because it pauses in its accumulations for constant syntheses and integration, processes which burn up more mental energy than the simpler process of acquisition. It is slower also because it requires more scope and greater range and because at the same time it enmeshes itself even more securely in subjective experience. Its greatest insights, the flashes of esthetic summation, come not in the classroom but only when the thinking engendered in the classroom goes out to meet actual experience. For this reason, irrelevancy to life is never the mark of a liberal or a masculine education, but only of an inferior one.

Nevertheless, we do the liberal arts curriculum a great injustice when we view it as a magic cure-all to be applied universally to all Americans at age eighteen. It cannot of itself correct all of the follies which may have been inculcated in previous school years, nor can it compensate for shortcomings in native endowment or opportunity. It is not a substitute for religion in promoting the good life. Even as we complete our delineation of its advantages, we glimpse the overwhelming difficulties, the baleful compromises which will be inevitable in its propagation. We have too few scholars who can teach such a curriculum, too few students who have the time and motivation to absorb it, too harsh an intellectual climate for its encouragement, too slender a budget to finance it. But these difficulties only enhance its ultimate values; they do not diminish our conviction of its worth or our determination to achieve it.

What *can* discourage us is the failure of its most sincere advocates to modernize their thinking and their teaching practices, to free themselves of the outworn, and to embrace the new aspects of liberal education which are sound and necessary for its survival. It is as if they repudiate the very truths which their own scholarship has developed and their own education should enable them to accept. Their preoccupation with their own learning has made them victims of the very specialization which they so heartily deplore.

The scholarly philosophers and essayists of earlier centuries evolved concepts and theories on the basis of current information and out of the "research" methods available in their time. They were the psychologists of the classical era, the chemists and biologists of the Middle Ages, even the economists and sociologists of the eighteenth century. Theirs was a "free aristocracy" in the classical or feudalistic sense, a society very different from the Western society of today.

But more important, it is their concept of society, their view of man as a social being, and likewise their means of exploring both man and society which constitute the greatest difference between ancient and present knowledge. The subjective and rationalistic are no longer the only methods of understanding man. Though still vitally important, poetry, art, religion, folklore, and the method of applying logic and reason to dispel ignorance do not stand alone. The philosopher-scholars, the poets, and the humanists have been joined by a host of new scholars and disciplines that are altering the older concepts and analyzing by new methods the ideologies under which the earth's billions of inhabitants are living and thinking in the present era.

The "free" man of the ancient world spent his time in politics, war, and the arts. He was not confined to the "vocations," cultivating the soil, making the shoes and the cloth, turning the wheels of transportation. Today however, making the shoes is a complex end product of many sciences—physical, natural, and social. Today every citizen must have some such vocation, which requires a long apprenticeship or careful education. But in a democracy he is also concerned with every other aspect of social life: health, politics, industrial management, war, crime, divorce, transportation, the arts. That person, either man or woman, has a truly liberal education who can move freely among these complexities, assume his responsibilities with sympathetic understanding, and contribute according to his opportunities to their solution.

Contrary to Plato who proclaimed that "all useful arts are degrading" and to Aristotle who assumed that "no free man should be paid for his service to the state," everyone is now involved in the total mechanism of life and no longer aloof from its mercenary relations. That man is truly "free" who comprehends the intricate labyrinth of social relations; that man is truly *not* free who through ignorance or maladjustment constantly endeavors to do the impossible, makes wrong predictions, works from false premises, or sponsors impractical solutions for social ills. Freedom consists in being able to do what one is capable of doing, what one wants to do, without frustration.

Thus we make a complete circle for our return to the original concept of liberal (from the Latin *liber* or "free") education which allows the individual to practice his freedom, rather than to be merely thwarted and bewildered by unknown forces. If women are to occupy a place in this "free" world, they too must know the nature of that world, and of themselves and their brothers, in order to be free in it. In such a concept there is no room to despise vocational training as it takes its appropriate place in the educational hierarchy. Its integration with all other kinds of life work and with citizenship and the leisure aspects of life is the responsibility of the truly liberal educator.

But resistances can be met. For the student of high intelligence and personal maturity, the answer lies in proficiency testing and the streamlining of professional requirements. The feminine orientation of courses in the women's college solves the problem for many students and could be practiced more widely. The two-year colleges unfettered by standardized degree requirements, the newer experimental colleges, and the private colleges have all made courageous adaptations.

What makes a study liberal is not its uselessness for a vocation, but its perspective and scope, the significance of the values it deals with, the range of the principles which support it, the catholicity of the insights it reveals. These are practical and possible goals, well within the grasp of convinced and sophisticated women if they would organize themselves for effective action.

Compromise is pleasant in prospect, enhanced in retrospect, and disagreeable only in its ruthless immediacy. The practical goal is a maximum of liberal arts and a minimum of vocational training. College presidents must override their many departments to revise curriculum patterns. Parents must soften their strident demands for "education for earning," and students must learn to lengthen their perspectives. But more than anything else, teachers must learn to enrich vocational subjects with cultural elements and to modify purely cultural subjects to make them vocationally useful.

Such processes merely turn the creeping inevitability of compromise into swifter and more constructive channels. The liberal arts colleges and curriculums have already embraced many of the tool courses, the highly esoteric, and the technical: quantitative chemistry, French phonetics, food preparation and meal service, stage lighting and make-up. The professional curriculums, on the other hand—in business, home economics, education, music, nursing—have incorporated many of the purely liberal or cultural courses within their own areas. There is no longer a clear-cut demarcation between the "vocational" and the "liberal" as they are now constituted on many a campus. It may be, for example, that the only difference between the B.A. and the B.S. in education is the substitution of fifteen to eighteen hours of elementary and intermediate Spanish for such courses as Dewey's philosophy of education, the history of American schools, advanced educational psychology, or child study.

What a hodgepodge of sentiment, ideas, traditions, pressures, expurgations, and makeshifts our educational red tape is holding together! Can women muster the courage and organize the forces to cut these Gordian knots?

Notes and Index

Notes

Chapter 1. The Need for Perspective

SUGGESTED READING

Recent good general discussions of the problems or status of women include the following:

[1] *Annals of Political and Social Science,* vol. 251, May 1947. The entire issue is devoted to women's problems.

[2] Simone de Beauvoir, *The Second Sex,* translated by H. M. Parshley. New York: Knopf, 1953.

[3] Elizabeth Bragdon (ed.), *Women Today: Their Conflicts, Their Frustrations and Their Fulfillments.* Indianapolis, Ind.: Bobbs-Merrill, 1953. This is a collection of twenty-six essays from various magazines and authors.

[4] Ernest Groves, *The American Woman: The Feminine Side of a Masculine Civilization.* New York: Greenberg, 1937.

[5] Sidonie M. Gruenberg and Hilda Sidney Krech, *The Many Lives of Modern Women: A Guide to Happiness in Her Complex Role.* Garden City, N.Y.: Doubleday, 1952.

[6] Mirra Komarovsky, *Women in the Modern World: Their Education and Their Dilemmas.* Boston: Little, Brown, 1953.

[7] Ashley Montagu, *The Natural Superiority of Women.* New York: Macmillan, 1953.

[8] Lynn White, Jr., *Educating Our Daughters.* New York: Harper, 1950.

Chapter 2. The Question of Sex Differences

REFERENCES

[1] Jesse B. Rhinehart, "Sex Differences in Dispersion at High School and College Level," *Psychological Monographs,* vol. 61, no. 1 (1947), p. 36.

[2] Simone de Beauvoir, *The Second Sex,* translated by H. M. Parshley (New York: Knopf, 1953), pp. 133, 132.

[3] *Ibid.,* p. 32.

[4] Kimball Young, *Sociology: A Study of Society and Culture* (New York: American Book, 1942), p. 491.

[5] Grace Elliott, *Women after Forty* (New York: Holt, 1936), p. 82.

[6] Beauvoir, *op. cit.*, p. 34.

[7] *Ibid.*, p. 64.

SUGGESTED READING

The following are scholarly discussions of sex differences by social scientists:

[1] Anne Anastasi and John P. Foley, *Differential Psychology*, Chapters 18 and 19. New York: Macmillan, 1949.

[2] Margaret Mead, *Male and Female*. New York: Morrow, 1949.

[3] Amram Scheinfeld, *Women and Men*. New York: Harcourt, Brace, 1944.

[4] L. M. Terman and Catherine Cox Miles, *Sex and Personality: Studies in Masculinity and Femininity*. New York: McGraw-Hill, 1946.

[5] Leona E. Tyler, *The Psychology of Human Differences*, Chapter 4. New York: Appleton-Century, 1947.

[6] Kimball Young, *Sociology: A Study of Society and Culture*, Chapter 26. New York: American Book, 1942.

Chapter 3. Social Change and Sex Conflict

REFERENCES

[1] C. Wright Mills, *White Collar: The American Middle Classes* (New York: Oxford University Press, 1951), p. xx.

[2] Agnes Rogers, "Is It Anyone We Know?" *Harper's*, 192:496–501 (June 1946).

[3] Russell Lynes, "Highbrow, Lowbrow, Middlebrow," *Harper's*, February 1949, pp. 19–28.

[4] Allison Davis, "Socialization and the Adolescent Personality," National Society for the Study of Education, 43rd Yearbook (1944); also, Allison Davis and R. J. Havighurst, "Social Class and Color Differences in Child Rearing," in *Personality in Nature, Society, and Culture*, eds. Clyde Kluckhohn and Henry A. Murray (New York: Knopf, 1949), Chapter 18.

[5] Ordway Tead, Bulletin No. 224, U.S. Department of Labor, Women's Bureau (1949), p. 72.

[6] Simone de Beauvoir, *The Second Sex*, translated by H. M. Parshley (New York: Knopf, 1953), p. xxvi.

[7] *Ibid.*, p. 593.

[8] Donald Adams, *New York Times*, Book Review Section, January 24, 1950.

Chapter 4. Education for Earning

REFERENCES

[1] *Facts on Women Workers*, the four-page mimeographed newsletter summarizing the status of women workers, was published by the Women's Bureau of the Department of Labor. However, the February 28, 1953, issue carried this announcement:

"*Notice*—We announce with regret that this is the last issue of *Facts on Women Workers*. In line with the economy program in government the Bureau of the Budget has not renewed approval for the publication of this newsletter. The Women's Bureau is sorry that it can no longer provide you with this service."

However, on June 29, 1953, a Department of Labor news release carried the note that "because of the continued interest expressed through requests for such information, the Women's Bureau is planning to issue monthly a brief release giving current information on the employment of women. Information on their occupational distribution will be included quarterly."

Most of the data in this chapter have been drawn from the publications of the Women's Bureau, of which Mrs. Alice K. Leopold is the director. Much support for the ideology of the chapter also derives from the Bureau's publications or from the published speeches of its staff members in other journals or books.

The series of pamphlets on employment opportunities in various fields have been indispensable for all vocational counselors. The biennial *Handbook of Facts on Women Workers* (1948, 1950, and 1952) enriches discussions and forums on women's problems throughout the nation. Such bulletins as No. 236, *Women in Higher Level Positions,* and No. 232, *Women's Jobs, Advance and Growth,* have helped women students and leaders to appraise and interpret their position in modern society as well as their employment status.

The Bureau's one- or two-page leaflets with summaries and suggestions about job opportunities and limitations are as helpful to the schoolgirl as to her mother, and sometimes to her grandmother. The low cost of these pamphlets and bulletins, their ready availability, and their infallibility greatly increase their usefulness.

[2] Frieda S. Miller, Bulletin No. 224, U.S. Department of Labor, Women's Bureau (1949), p. 12.

[3] Ordway Tead, Bulletin No. 224, U.S. Department of Labor, Women's Bureau (1949), p. 73.

[4] Ernest Havemann and Patricia Salter West, *They Went to College* (New York: Harcourt, Brace, 1952), p. 149.

[5] Gordon Allport, *Personality: A Psychological Interpretation* (New York: Holt, 1937), p. 517.

[6] Eleanor F. Horsey and Donna Price, "Science out of Petticoats," *Journal of the American Association of University Women,* October 1947, pp. 13–16.

[7] Leaflet No. 14, U.S. Department of Labor, Women's Bureau, 1952.

[8] Havemann and West, *op. cit.,* p. 74.

[9] Semour E. Harris, "Millions of B.A's but No Jobs," *New York Times,* Magazine Section, January 2, 1949.

Chapter 5. Education for Dating and Mating

REFERENCES

[1] Amram Scheinfeld, *Women and Men* (New York: Harcourt, Brace, 1944), pp. 130–150.

[2] Frankwood Williams, "Confronting the World: The Adjustments of Later Adolescence," mimeographed.

[3] Geoffrey Gorer, *The American People: A Study in National Character* (New York: Norton, 1948), p. 122.

[4] Janet Kelly, *College Life and the Mores* (New York: Columbia University Press, 1949), Chapter 3.

[5] Willard Waller, "The Rating and Dating Complex," *American Sociological Review,* 2:727 (October 1937).

[6] Lawrence K. Frank, "Opportunities in a Program of Education for Marriage and Family Life," *Mental Hygiene,* 24:578–594 (October 1940).

Chapter 6. Education for Homemaking

REFERENCES

[1] Edith Stern, "Women as Household Slaves," *American Mercury,* 68:71–76 (January 1949).

[2] Agnes Rogers, "Loss of the Adventurous Spirit," *American Scholar,* vol. 19, no. 1 (January 1950), pp. 89–93.

[3] Marion Bassett, "One Hundred and Twenty-Eight Mothers Consider Our Family Pattern," *Bulletin of Family Research and Education,* vol. 1, no. 5 (November-December 1940).

[4] Gilbert Seldes, *The Great Audience* (New York: Viking Press, 1950); quoted from the studies of radio serials carried on by Wm. E. Henry, Committee on Human Development, University of Chicago.

[5] Kimball Young, *Sociology: A Study of Society and Culture* (New York: American Book, 1942), p. 491.

[6] John Milton, *Paradise Lost,* ll. 297–300.

[7] Seldom has there been such a depressing documentation of the deterioration of social values as in Jay Taylor, "Going Broke on $10,000 a Year," *Harper's,* July 1952, pp. 60–65.

[8] Margaret Mead, *And Keep Your Powder Dry* (New York: Morrow, 1942), p. 91.

SUGGESTED READING

Any good book on the family will contain helpful discussions on this topic.

Chapter 7. Education for Citizenship

REFERENCES

[1] Norman Foerster, *The Future of the Liberal College* (New York: Appleton-Century, 1938), p. 70.

[2] Lewis Mumford, "The Unified Approach to Knowledge and Life," in *The University and the Future of America* (Stanford, Calif.: Stanford University Press, 1941), p. 130.

[3] John B. Johnston, *Education for Democracy* (New York: Appleton-Century, 1930), p. 396.

[4] Harry E. Barnes and O. M. Ruede, *The American Way of Life* (New York: Prentice-Hall, 1942), p. 751.

[5] The Harvard Report, *General Education in a Free Society* (Cambridge, Mass.: Harvard University Press, 1945), p. 76.

[6] *Ibid.,* p. 170.

[7] Robert M. Hutchins, *The Higher Learning in America* (New Haven, Conn.: Yale University Press, 1936), p. 69.

[8] Harold Taylor, quoted by C. Wright Mills in *White Collar* (New York: Oxford University Press, 1951), p. 267.

[9] James B. Conant, *Education in a Divided World* (Cambridge, Mass.: Harvard University Press, 1948), p. 32.

[10] *Higher Education for American Democracy,* Report of the President's Commission on Higher Education (Washington, D.C.: U.S. Government Printing Office, 1947), vol. 1, "Establishing the Goals."

[11] Report of the Indiana University Committee on the role of the university in a democratic society (November 1947), mimeographed.

[12] Lord A. D. Lindsay, Powell Foundation Lecture, Indiana University, October 13, 1946, unpublished.

[13] Paul Swain Havens, "Colleges in a Democracy," convocation address, Wilson College, September 15, 1948.

[14] Franz Alexander, "The Dynamics of Personality," *Social Casework, 1951,* 32:139–143.

SUGGESTED READING

[1] E. G. Williamson, "The Extra Curriculum and General Education," Chapter XI in the 1952 Yearbook of the National Society for the Study of Education.

Chapter 8. Education for Politics

REFERENCES

[1] Sophonisba P. Breckinridge, *Women in the Twentieth Century* (New York: McGraw-Hill, 1933).

[2] *Ibid.*, p. 269.

[3] Ernest Havemann and Patricia Salter West, *They Went to College* (New York: Harcourt, Brace, 1952), p. 125.

[4] Mildred McAfee Horton, "Women's Place Is in the Home: 1949 Edition," *Wellesley Alumnae Magazine*, April 1949, p. 238.

[5] Breckinridge, *op. cit.*, pp. 290, 338, 332, 331, and 294.

[6] Emily Newell Blair, "Why I Am Discouraged about Women in Politics," *Women's Journal*, 16:20–22 (January 1931).

[7] Marguerite L. Fisher, "Women in the Political Parties," *Annals of Political and Social Science*, 251:88 (May 1947).

[8] E. G. Groves, *The American Woman* (New York: Greenberg, 1937), p. 353.

[9] Kathleen McLaughlin, "Women's Impact on Public Opinion," *Annals of Political and Social Science*, 251:105 (May 1947).

Chapter 9. Education for Leisure

REFERENCES

[1] David Riesman, Nathan Glazer, and Reuel Denney, *The Lonely Crowd* (Garden City, N.Y.: Doubleday, 1953), p. 322.

[2] C. Wright Mills, *White Collar* (New York: Oxford University Press, 1951), p. 236.

[3] Irving Dilliard (ed.), *The Spirit of Liberty: Papers and Addresses of Judge Learned Hand* (New York: Knopf, 1952), p. 153.

[4] John Dewey, "Aesthetic Experience as a Primary Phase and as an Artistic Development," *Journal of Aesthetics and Art Criticism*, vol. 9, no. 1 (September 1950), p. 57.

[5] George Santayana, *The Sense of Beauty* (New York: Scribner's, 1908), p. 2.

[6] Riesman, Glazer, and Denney, *op. cit.*, pp. 64 and 100.

Chapter 10. Women's Education and Education in General

REFERENCES

[1] John B. Johnston, *The Liberal College in a Changing Society* (New York: Century, 1930), p. 24.

[2] Allison Davis, *Socialization and Adolescent Personality,* in 43rd Yearbook, National Society for Study of Education (1944), p. 209.

[3] *Ibid.*

[4] Robert M. Hutchins, *The Higher Learning in America* (New Haven, Conn.: Yale University Press, 1936), p. 114.

[5] R. J. Havighurst and Hilda Taba, *Adolescent Character and Personality* (New York: Wiley, 1949), pp. 190–207.

Educating Women for a Changing World

SUGGESTED READING

[1] Dean Chamberlin, Enid Chamberlin, Neal E. Drought, and William E. Scott are responsible for the eight-year study, *Did They Succeed in College?* (New York: Harper, 1942).

[2] The Report of the Harvard Committee, *General Education in a Free Society* (Cambridge, Mass.: Harvard University Press, 1945), is stimulating reading, and James B. Conant's *Education in a Divided World*, published by the same press in 1948, is even more challenging. Robert Hutchins expressed his views about education in several volumes while he was chancellor at the University of Chicago: *No Friendly Voice* (Chicago: University of Chicago Press, 1936), and *The Higher Learning in America* (New Haven, Conn.: Yale University Press, 1936).

[3] John B. Johnston wrote *The Liberal College in a Changing Society* (New York: Century, 1930), while he was dean of the college of Science, Literature and the Arts at the University of Minnesota.

Chapter 11. Planning Curriculums for Women

REFERENCES

[1] Raymond Mulligan, "The American College Girl," *Alpha Kappa Delta Quarterly*, May 1952, p. 17.

[2] C. Wright Mills, *White Collar* (New York: Oxford University Press, 1951), p. xvi.

Chapter 12. Choosing a College and a Curriculum

REFERENCES

[1] Katherine Gillette Blyley, president of Keuka College, inaugural address, 1945.

[2] Arnold W. Green, *Sociology: An Analysis of Life in Modern Society* (New York: McGraw-Hill, 1952), p. 474.

SUGGESTED READING

The one best source of information on size, endowment, libraries, fees, requirements, departments, and curriculums is *American Universities and Colleges*, published by the American Council on Education, C. S. March, editor. It is often to be found in college and high school libraries and is indispensable for inquiring parents.

Education Directory: Higher Education is published annually, by the Office of Education, in pamphlet form and is available from the Superintendent of Documents, U.S. Government Printing Office, Washington, D.C., for a small charge. It is short, complete, and accurate.

All of the annual world almanacs contain much useful information about the schools and colleges of the United States.

The Women's College Board of Chicago supplies at small cost current information and comparative data on many of the women's colleges.

Elizabeth Anne Hadnut's *You Can Always Tell a Freshman* (New York: Dutton, 1948), is especially recommended for both parents and daughters.

Ernest Havemann and Patricia Salter West's *They Went to College* (New York: Harcourt, Brace, 1952), the extension of a study begun by *Time* magazine, points up some of the differences to be found among all kinds of colleges, with perhaps most stress upon their effects on the success or earning power of the graduates. A mimeographed booklet entitled *AAUW Members Look at College Education—An Interim Report,* 1949, contains material of more interest to many mothers and daughters. It is based on the replies of 30,000 women, a much larger sample than was used in *Time's* study.

Index

301

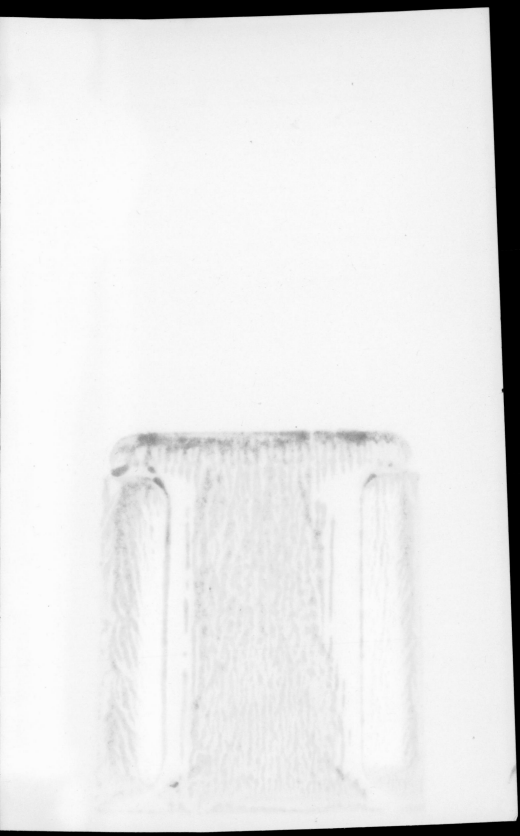